THE BIBLICAL TEXTBOOK OF SALVATION

Compiled

by

Edward T. Pooler

Copyright © 2016. All rights reserved.

No part of this publication may be reproduced, stored in a retrieval system or transmitted in any way by any means, electronic, mechanical, photocopy, recording or otherwise, without the prior permission of the author except as provided by USA copyright law.

The opinions expressed by the author are not necessarily those of Revival Waves of Glory Books & Publishing.

Published by Revival Waves of Glory Books & Publishing

PO Box 596| Litchfield, Illinois 62056 USA

www.revivalwavesofgloryministries.com

Revival Waves of Glory Books & Publishing is committed to excellence in the publishing industry.

Book design Copyright © 2016 by Revival Waves of Glory Books & Publishing. All rights reserved.

ISBN: 978-1-68411-199-2

Published in the United States of America

Dedication

This Book is dedicated to Lord YHWH the Father, Yahshua the Christ, and the Holy Spirit; any or all of whom have made this book possible either directly or indirectly.

And despite their invulnerability, they have voluntarily endured much pain, anger, sorrow, and disgust because they have opened their hearts to us human beings.

They knew what they would endure by opening their hearts to us, but they also knew that confining so much love within closed hearts would have been more painful because they love us more than we can imagine.

The two purposes of this book is: to lead people to salvation, and therefore reduce the amount of pain within those divine hearts.

Contents

Dedication iii
Introduction vii
Divine Names ix
First-Century Christianity xi
The First Book of Moshe (Moses), called Genesis 1
The Second Book of Moshe (Moses), called Exodus 13
The Third Book of Moshe (Moses), called Leviticus 22
The Fifth Book of Moshe (Moses), called Deuteronomy 27
The First Book of The Kings 31
The Book of Psalms 34
Semketh 46
The Proverbs 47
Ecclesiastes 54
The Book of The Prophet Yeshayah (Isaiah) 57
The book of the Prophet Yechezk'el (Ezekiel) 66
The book of Daniel 69
Hosea 76
Joel 78
Amos 81
Mikhah (Micah) 84
Nahum 87
Z'kharyah (Zechariah) 92
Mal'akhi (Malachi) 96
The Gospel Of Mattityahu/Mark/Luke/Yochanan 100
The Acts of The Apostles 127
The Epistle of Sha'ul The Apostle to The Romans 181
The First Epistle of Sha'ul The Apostle To The Corinthians 213

The Second Epistle of Sha'ul The Apostle To The Corinthians	244
The Epistle of Sha'ul The Apostle To The Galatians	264
The Epistle of Sha'ul The Apostle To The Ephesians	276
The Epistle of Sha'ul The Apostle To The Colossians	300
The First Epistle of Sha'ul The Apostle To Timothy	310
The Second Epistle of Sha'ul The Apostle To Timothy	319
The Epistle of Sha'ul to Titus	328
The Epistle of Sha'ul to Philemon	334
The Epistle of Sha'ul the Apostle to the Hebrews	338
The General Epistle of Ya'akov (James)	364
The First Epistle of Kefa (Peter)	375
The Second Epistle of Kefa (Peter)	386
The First Epistle of Yochanan (John)	393
The Second Epistle of Yochanan (John)	404
The Third Epistle of Yochanan (John)	407
The General Epistle of Y'hudah (Jude)	410
The Revelation of Saint Yochanan (John) The Divine	414

Introduction

The book is an attempt to express the oldest, and therefore most accurate, information of the Bible. Most of the complete **1,200**-page Bible includes historical accounts, only the most important historical accounts are included in this book, I have also avoided many repeatings which only need to be written once within a book.

Since this "Biblical Textbook" has only **455** pages, it can be learned more intensely and in much less time. Thus, you can be led toward salvation more efficiently.

Some newer Bibles are less accurate and are therefore less able to lead people toward salvation. I'm sure that this book is not perfect but it is closer.

The purpose of this book is explained on the front cover but an extreme example of condensing without loss is expressed in the next paragraph.

The first four books of the New Testament each tell the same story but each of the four books do have details which the other three do not. By removing ONLY the repeatings, **130** pages have been reduced to only **19** pages which still contain ALL the information of the entire four books.

The foundation of Christianity is Judaism while Christianity is the fulfillment of Judaism. The Jewish Faith and the Christian Faith are two parts of the One True Faith which is the Judeo-Christian Truth.

This Judeo-Christian Truth is the original Christianity as explained in the Bible in: Jude, paragraph #**3**.

Jews need to grow to become Judeo-Christians, while Christians need to accept their Jewishness to become Judeo-Christians.

Divine Names

The oldest known inscription of the tetragrammaton dates to **840** BCE, on the Mesha Stele. It bears the earliest certain extra-biblical reference to the Israelite God: YHWH (Yahweh).

YHWH (Yahweh): is considered in Judaism to be the <u>proper name</u> of the God of Israel. used in the Hebrew Bible. But the mis-pronounced name of "Jehovah" came from early English translators who transposed the vowels from *Adonai* to the Tetragrammaton, and read the word literally so that the *Y* in YHWH, was pronounced as a *J* in English, and the *W* as a *V*.

Taking the spellings at face value may have been as a result of not knowing about the Q're perpetuum, thus resulting in the term "Jehovah" and its spelling variants.

Had they known about the Q're perpetuum, the term "Jehovah" may never have come into being. Emil G. Hirschwas among the modern scholars that recognized "*Jehovah*" *to be* "*grammatically impossible*" (Jewish Encyclopedia (**1901**), Vol VII, p. **87**).

The name Yahshua ("Yah" represents: Yahweh, "shua" represents: saves)

This early Biblical Hebrew name *Yehoshua*` underwent a shortening into later Biblical *Yeshua*`or Yahshua, as found in the Hebrew text.By the time the New Testament was written, the Septuaginthad already transliterated ישוע *Yeshua or Yahshua* into Koine Greek as closely as possible in the **3**rd-century BC, the result being <u>*Iēsous*</u>.

Since Greek had no equivalent to the Semitic letter [sh], it was replaced with an [s], and a masculine singular ending [-s] was added in the nominative case, in order to allow the name to be inflected for case (nominative, accusative, etc.) in the grammar of the Greek language.

<u>Iē</u>*sous* was transliterated to Latin *IESVS*, where it stood for many centuries. The Latin name has an irregular declension, with a genitive, dative, ablative, and vocative of *Jesu*, accusative of *Jesum*, and nominative of *Jesus*.

These are the reasons that the proper name of "Yahweh" and "Yahshua" are used since the names of "Jehovah" and "Jesus" are not used, it is more accurate and more respectable to use Their proper names.

The name of "John" the Baptist is actually: "Yochanan" the Baptist. Bibles written in English have all the words translated into English, even the names. This book shows the oldest known names of Lord Yahweh and Yahshua the Christ along with Jewish names in the proper Hebrew.

I have prayed to JESUS and sometimes The Son of Lord Yahweh responded, I have prayed to YAHSHUA and sometimes The Son of Lord Yahweh responded.

When one calls him "Jesus" he understands that one is simply speaking English, when one calls him "Yahshua" he understands that one is simply trying to pronounce his name the way that he does.

The Jews have accurate historical records but some say his name is Yahshua while others say his name is Yeshua.

I do not know which name is correct but the name "Yahshua" more accurately expresses the deity that he shares with the Father while the name "Yeshua" more accurately expresses that the Christ himself is the Savior.

Whichever name you call him in a sincere way, he knows that you are referring to him.

First-Century Christianity

In first century Christianity, the members of the almighty God's Church *never* prayed to any saints nor did they bow down to idols. They *never* prayed to the Virgin Mary. They only prayed to the almighty God, the Christ, and the Holy Spirit. They did not even pray to angels.

In first century Christianity, the dedicated ministers and elders in the Church of God were primarily husbands and fathers (**1** Timothy **3:1–5**; Titus **1:5–9**). They were taught that in "latter times" some would be *deceived* by "doctrines of demons" into thinking it was wrong for men—certainly including ministers—to marry (**1** Timothy **4:1–3**).

Meeting regularly in plain surroundings on the day God made holy, *His* Sabbath which is <u>Saturday</u>, God's ministers were instructed: "Preach the *word!* Be ready in season and out of season. Convince, rebuke, exhort, with all long-suffering and teaching.

The early Christians "took for granted that the gospel was <u>continuous</u> with [the religion of Moshe (Moses)]; for them the New Covenant, which Yahshua the Christ had set up at the Last Supper with His disciples… did not mean that the covenant made between Lord Yahweh and Israel was no longer in force. They still observed the feasts of Passover, Pentecost and Tabernacles; they also continued to keep the weekly Sabbath.

The biblical and historical facts show that Christianity was a <u>continuation</u>, an <u>enlargement</u>, and "<u>magnification</u>" of the teachings Lord Yahweh gave through Moshe (Moses), *not* something brand new!

So a basic part of the very "foundation" of Christianity was the writings and teachings of the Old Testament prophets—those writings which Christ and the Apostles referred to as "Scripture" again and again!

First century Christianity was squarely based on the teachings of the "law and prophets"—except for those animal sacrifices and washings which pre-figured the sacrifice of Christ and the cleansing of the Holy Spirit. These sacrifices and washings were made obsolete (Hebrews **9:9–12**).

I hope and pray that all of you are, or will soon be, fully Judeo-Christian enough to enjoy Heaven for all eternity.

The First Book of Moshe (Moses), called
Genesis

CHAPTER 1

YHWH(Yahweh) the almighty God, created the heavens and the earth in the very beginning.

2 And the earth was without form, and void; and darkness was upon the face of the deep. And the Spirit of Lord Yahweh moved upon the face of the water.

3 And Lord Yahweh said, Let there be light; and there was light.

4 And Lord Yahweh saw that the light was good; and Lord Yahweh separated the light from the darkness.

5 And Lord Yahweh called the light: Day, and He called the darkness: Night. And there was evening and there was morning, the first day.

6 And Lord Yahweh said, Let there be a firmament in the midst of the waters, and let it divide the waters from the waters.

7 And Lord Yahweh made the firmament, and divided the waters that were under the firmament from the waters that were above the firmament; and it was so.

8 And Lord Yahweh called the firmament: Sky. And there was evening and there was morning, the second day.

9 And Lord Yahweh said, Let the waters that are under the sky be gathered together in one place, and let the dry land appear; and it was so.

10 And Lord Yahweh called the dry land: Earth; and the gathering together of the waters He called: Seas; and Lord Yahweh saw that it was good.

11 And Lord Yahweh said, Let the earth bring forth vegetation, the herb yielding seed after its kind, and the fruit tree yielding fruit after its kind, wherein is their seed, upon the earth; and it was so.

12 And the earth brought forth vegetation, the herb yielding seed after its kind, and the tree bearing fruit, wherein is its seed, after its kind; and Lord Yahweh saw that it was good.

13 And there was evening and there was morning, the third day.

14 Then Lord Yahweh said, Let there be lights in the firmament of the (second) heaven to seperate the day from the night; and let them be for signs, and for seasons, and and for days, and years.

15 And let them be for lights in the firmament of the (second) heaven to give light upon the earth (first heaven); and it was so.

16 And Lord Yahweh made two great lights, the greater light (the sun) to rule the day, and the smaller light (the moon) to rule the night; and the stars also.

17 And Lord Yahweh set them in the firmament of the (second) heaven to give light upon the earth,

18 And to rule over the day and over the night, and to separate the light from the darkness; and Lord Yahweh saw that it was good.

19 And there was evening and there was morning, the fourth day.

20 And Lord Yahweh said, Let the waters bring forth swarms of living creatures, and let fowl fly above the earth in the open firmament of the (first) heaven.

21 And Lord Yahweh created great great sea monsters, and every living creature that moves, which the waters brought forth abundantly after their kind; and every winged fowl after its kind; and Lord Yahweh saw that it was good.

22 And Lord Yahweh blessed them, saying, Be fruitful and multiply, and fill the waters in the seas, and let fowl multiply on the earth.

23 And there was evening and there was morning, the fifth day.

24 Then Lord Yahweh said, Let the earth bring forth living creatures after their kind, cattle, and creeping things, and beasts of the earth after their kind; and it was so.

25 And Lord Yahweh made the beasts of the earth after their kind, and the cattle after their kind, and everything that creeps upon the earth after its kind; and Lord Yahweh saw that it was good.

26 Then Lord Yahweh said, Let us make man in our image, after our likeness; and let them have dominion over the fish of the sea, and over the fowl of the air, and over the cattle, and over all the wild beasts of the earth, and over every creeping thing that creeps upon the earth.

27 So Lord Yahweh created man (mankind) in his own image, in the image of Lord Yahweh He created him; male and female, He created them.

28 And Lord Yahweh blessed them, and Lord Yahweh said to them, Be fruitful, and multiply, and fill the earth, and subdue it; and have dominion over the fish of the sea, and over the fowl of the air, and over the cattle, and over all the wild beasts that move upon the earth.

29 And Lord Yahweh said, Behold, I have given you every herb yielding seed, which is upon the face of all the earth, and every tree which bears fruit yielding seed; to you it shall be food.

30 And to every beast of the earth, and to every fowl of the air, and to everything that creeps upon the earth, wherein there is life, I have given every green herb for food; and it was so.

31 And Lord Yahweh saw everything that He had made, and, behold, it was very good. And there was evening and there was morning, the sixth day.

CHAPTER 2

Thus the heavens and the earth were finished, and all the host of them.

2 And on the sixth day, Lord Yahweh finished his works which He had made; and He rested on the seventh day from all his works which He had made.

3 So Lord Yahweh blessed the seventh day, and sanctified it; because in it, He had rested from all the works which Lord Yahweh created and made.

4 These are the generations of the heavens and of the earth when they were created, in the day that Lord Yahweh made the heavens and the earth.

5 And all the trees of the field were not yet in the ground, and every herb of the field had not yet sprung up; for the Lord had not caused it to rain upon the earth, and there was no man to till the ground.

6 But powerful spring gushed out of the earth, and watered all the face of the ground.

7 And Lord Yahweh formed Adam out of the soil of the earth, and breathed into his nostrils the breath of life; and man became a living soul.

8 And Lord Yahweh planted a garden eastward in Eden; and there He put the man whom He had formed.

9 And out of the ground Lord Yahweh made to grow every tree that is pleasant to the sight and good for food; the tree of life also in the midst of the garden, and the tree of the knowledge of good and evil.

10 And a river flowed out of Eden to water the garden; and from thence it divided and became into four heads.

11 The name of the first is Pishon; it is the one which encircles the whole land of Havilah, where there is gold;

12 And the gold of that land is good; there is also beryllium and the onyx stone.

13 And the name of the second river is is Gihon, the one which encircles the whole land of Ethiopia.

14 And the name of the third river is is Deklat (Tigris); it is the one which flows east of Assyria. And the fourth river is the Euphrates.

15 And Lord Yahweh took the man, and put him in the garden of Eden to till it and to keep it.

16 And Lord Yahwed commanded the man, saying, Of every tree of the garden you may freely eat;

17 But of the tree of the knowledge of good and evil, you shall not eat; for in the day that you eat of it you shall surely die.

18 Then Lord Yahweh said, It is not good that the man should not be alone; I will make him a helper who is like him.

19 And out of the ground, Lord Yahweh formed every beast of the field, and every fowl of the air; and brought them to Adam to see what he would call them; and whatever Adam called every living creature, that was its name.

20 And Adam gave names to all cattle, and to all fowl of the air, and to all wild beasts; but for Adam there was not found a helper who was equal to him.

21 So Lord Yahweh caused a deep sleep to fall upon Adam, and he slept; and Lord Yahweh took one of Adam's ribs, and closed up the place with flesh in its stead;

22 And of the rib which Lord Yahweh had taken from Adam He made a woman, and brought her to Adam.

23 And Adam said, This is now bone of my bones, and flesh of my flesh; she shall be called: Woman, because she was taken out of Man.

24 Therefore shall a man leave his father and his mother, and shall cleave unto his wife, and they shall be one flesh.

25 And they were both naked, Adam and his wife, and were not ashamed.

CHAPTER 3

Now the serpent was more subtle than all the wild beasts that Lord Yahweh had made. And the serpent said to the woman, Truly has Lord Yahweh said that you shall not eat of any tree of the garden?

2 And the woman said to the serpent, We may eat of the fruit of all the trees of the garden;

3 But of the fruit of the tree of the knowledge of good and evil which is in the midst of the garden, Lord Yahweh has said, You shall not eat of it, neither shall you touch it, lest you die.

4 And the serpent said to the woman, You shall not surely die;

5 For Lord Yahweh knows that in the day you eat of it, your eyes shall be opened and you shall be like gods, knowing good and evil.

6 So when the woman saw that the tree was good for food, and that it was pleasant to the eyes, and that the tree was delightful to look at, she took of the fruit thereof, and did eat, and she also gave to her husband with her; and he did eat.

7 Then the eyes of them both were opened, and they knew that they were naked; and they sewed fig leaves together, and made aprons for themselves.

8 And they heard the voice of Lord Yahweh walking in the garden in the cool of the day; and Adam and his wife hid themselves from the presence of Lord Yahweh among the trees of the garden.

9 And Lord Yahweh called to Adam, and said to him, Where are you, Adam?

10 And Adam said, I heard thy voice in the garden, and when I saw that I was naked, I hid myself.

11 And Lord Yahweh said to him, Who told you that you were naked? Have you eaten of the tree of which I commanded you that you should not eat?

12 And Adam said, The woman whom Thou gave to be with me, she gave me of the fruit of the tree, and I did eat.

13 And Lord Yahweh said to the woman, What is this that you have done? And the woman said, The serpent beguiled me, and I did eat.

14 And Lord Yahweh said to the serpent, Because you have done this thing, cursed are you above all cattle and above all beasts of the field; on your belly shall you go, and dust shall you "eat" all the days of your life;

15 And I will put enmity between you and the woman, and between your posterity and her posterity; her posterity shall tread your head under foot, and you shall strike him in his heel.

16 To the woman He said, I will greatly multiply your pain and your conception; in pain you shall bring forth children, and you shall be dependent on your husband, and he shall rule over you.

17 And to Adam He said, Because you have listened to the voice of your wife, and have eaten of the tree of which I commanded you, saying, You shall not eat of it, cursed is the ground for your sake; in sorrow shall you eat the fruits of it all the days of your life;

18 Thorns also and thistles shall it bring forth to you; and you shall eat the herb of the field;

19 In the sweat of your face shall you eat bread, until you return to the ground; out of it you were taken; for dust you are, and to dust shall you return.

20 So Adam called his wife's name: Havah (Eve) because she was the mother of all living.

21 And Lord Yahweh made for Adam and for his wife coats of skin, and clothed them.

22 Then Lord Yahweh said, Behold, the man has become like one of us, to know good and evil; and now, lest he put forth his hand, and take also of the tree of life, and eat, and live forever;

23 Therefore Lord Yahweh sent him forth from the garden of Eden, to till the ground from whence he was taken.

24 So Lord Yahweh drove out the man; and He placed at the east of the garden of Eden, Cherubim and a flaming sword which turned every way, to guard the path to the tree of life.

CHAPTER 6

And it came to pass, when man began to multiply on the face of the earth and daughters were born to them,

2 That the fallen angels saw that the daughters of man were fair; so they took them as wives of all whom they chose.

3 Then Lord Yahweh said, My Spirit shall not dwell in man forever, because he is flesh; let his days be a hundred and twenty years.

4 There were giants (born from human wives of fallen angels) on the earth in those days; and also after that, for the sons (angels) of Lord Yahweh came in unto the daughters of man, and they bore children to them, and the children became giants who in the olden days were mighty men of renown.

5 And Lord Yahweh saw that the wickedness of man was great in the earth, and that every imagination of the thoughts of his heart was evil continually.

6 And Lord Yahweh was sorry that He had made man on the earth, and it grieved Him in his heart.

7 So the Lord said, I will destroy man whom I have created from the face of the earth;

8 But Noach found mercy in the eyes of the Lord.

13 So Lord Yahweh said to Noach, the end of all flesh is come before me; for the earth is full of wickedness through man; and, behold, I will destroy them with the earth.

14 Make yourself an ark of gopher wood; make rooms in the ark and daub it outside and inside with pitch.

17 And, behold, I will bring a flood of waters upon the earth, to destroy all flesh that has the breath of life in it from under heaven; and everything that is on the earth shall die.

18 But I will establish my covenant with you; and you shall enter into the ark, you, and your sons, and your wife, and your sons' wives with you.

19 And of every living thing of all flesh, bring two of every kind into the ark, to keep them alive with you; they shall be male and female.

22 Thus did Noach; according to all that Lord Yahweh commanded him, so he did.

CHAPTER 7

Then Lord Yahweh said to Noach, Enter into the ark; you and all your household, for you alone have I seen righteous before Me in this generation.

5 And Noach did according to all that the Lord commanded him.

6 And Noach was six hundred years old when the flood of waters came upon the earth.

11 In the six hundredth year of Noach's life, in the second month, the seventeenth day of the month; on that very day, all the fountains of the great deep burst forth and the windows of heaven were opened.

12 And the rain fell upon the earth for forty days and forty nights.

24 And the waters prevailed upon the earth for a hundred and fifty days.

Chapter 8

2 The fountains of the deep and the windows of heaven were closed, and the rain from the sky was restrained;

3 And the waters receded from the earth gradually; and after the end of a hundred and fifty days, the waters abated.

14 And in the second month, on the twenty-seventh day of the month, the earth was dry.

15 And Lord Yahweh spoke to Noach, saying,

16 Go forth out of the ark, you and your wife, and your sons, and your sons' wives with you.

17 Bring forth with you every beast of every kind that is with you, both fowl and cattle, and every creeping thing that creeps on the earth; so that they may breed abundantly on the earth and be fruitful and multiply upon the face of the earth.

Chapter 9

And Lord Yahweh blessed Noach and his sons, and said to them, Be fruitful, and multiply, and replenish the earth.

2 And the fear of you, and the dread of you, shall be upon every beast of the earth, and upon every fowl of the air, upon all that moves upon the earth, and all the fish of the sea; into your hand they are delivered.

3 Every moving thing that is alive shall be food for you; even as the green herb have I given you all things.

4 Only flesh with the life thereof, that is, the blood thereof, you shall not eat.

6 Whoever sheds the blood of man, by man shall his blood be shed; for man was made in the image of Lord Yahweh.

7 As for you, be fruitful, and multiply; bring forth abundantly on the earth, and multiply in it.

8 And Lord Yahweh spoke to Noach and to his sons with him, saying,

9 As for Me, behold, I will establish my covenant with you and with your descendants after after you;

10 And with every living creature that is with you, the fowl, the cattle, and every wild beast of the earth with you; with all that come out of the ark, and with every beast of the earth.

11 And I will establish my covenant with you; so that never again shall all flesh perish by the waters of a flood; neither shall there any more be a flood to destroy the earth.

12 And Lord Yahweh said to Noach, This is the sign of the covenant which I make between Me and you and every living creature that is with you, for perpetual generations:

13 I set my bow (rainbow) in the clouds, and it shall be for a sign of a covenant between Me and the earth.

The Second Book of Moshe (Moses), called
Exodus

CHAPTER 19

In the third month after the departure of the children of Israel out of the land of Egypt, on same day they came to the wilderness of Seen.

2 Then they journeyed from Rephidim and came to the wilderness of Sinai, and they encamped in the wilderness; and there Israel camped before the mountain.

3 And Moshe went up to Lord Yahweh, and Lord Yahweh called to him out of the mountain and said to him, Thus shall you say to the house of Jacob, and tell the children of Israel:

4 You have seen what I did to the Egyptians, and how I bore you as though you were on eagles' wings and brought you to Myself.

5 Now therefore, if you will obey my voice indeed and keep my covenant, then you shall be my beloved ones above all peoples, for all the earth is mine;

6 And you shall be to Me a kingdom and priests and a holy people. These are the words which yo0u shall speak to the children of Israel.

7 And Moshe came and called for the eloders of the people, and said in their presence all these words which the Lord commanded him.

8 And all the people answered together and said, All that the Lord has spoken we will do. And Moshe returned the words of the people to Lord Yahweh.

9 And the Lord said to Moshe, Lo, I am coming to you in a thick cloud, so that the people may hear when I speak with you and also believe you forever. And Moshe told the words of the people before the Lord.

10 And Lord Yahweh said to Moshe, Go to the people and sanctify them today and tomorrow, and let them wash their clothes,

11 And be ready by the third day; for on the third day, Lord Yahweh will come down in the sight of all the people upon Mount Sinai.

12 And you shall publish a warning among the people, saying, Take heed to yourselves, neither go up into the mountain; nor draw near to the border of it; whoever draws near to the mountain shall be put to death;

13 No hand shall touch it, but he shall surely be stoned and hurled down; whether it be beast or man, it shall not live; when the trumpet is silent, then you are permitted to ascend the mountain.

14 And Moshe went down from the mountain to the people and sanctified the people; and they washed their clothes.

15 And he said to the people, Be ready on the third day; do not touch your wives.

16 And it came to pass, on the third day in the morning, that there were thunders and lightnings and a thick cloud appeared upon the mountain and the sound of the trumpet exceedingly loud so that all the people that were in the camp, trembled.

17 Then Moshe brought forth the people out of the camp to meet Lord Yahweh; and they stood at the base of the mountain.

18 And the whole mountain of Sinai was smoking because Lord Yahweh descended upon it in fire; and the smoke thereof ascended like the smoke of a furnace, and the whole mountain quaked greatly.

19 and when the blast of the trumpet sounded long and grew louder and louder, Moshe spoke, and Lord Yahweh answered him by a voice.

20 And Lord Yahweh came down upon Mount Sinai, to the very top of the mountain; and the Lord called Moshe up to the top of the mountain, and Moshe went up.

21 And Lord Yahweh said to Moshe: Go down, warn the people, lest they break through to Me to gaze, and many of them perish;

22 And let the priests also who come near to Me sanctify themselves, lest I the Lord break forth upon them.

23 And Moshe said to Lord Yahweh, The people cannot come up to Mount Sinai; for Thou did warn us, saying, Set bounds about the mountain and sanctify it.

24 And Lord Yahweh said to Moshe: Hasten, go down, and then come up, you, and Aharon (Aaron) your brother with you; but let not the priests and the other people break through to come up before I the Lord, lest I break forth upon them.

25 So Moshe went down to the people and told them.

CHAPTER 20

And Lord Yahweh spoke all these words, saying,

2 I am the Lord your God, who brought you out of Egypt, out of the house of bondage.

3 You shall have no other gods except Me.

4 You shall not make for yourself any graven image, or any likeness of anything that is in heaven above or that is in the earth beneath or that is in the water under the earth;

5 You shall not worship them nor serve them; for I, the Lord your God, am a jealous God, visiting the offences (sins?) of the fathers upon their children to the third and fourth generations of those who hate Me;

6 And showing mercy to thousands of generations of those who love Me and keep my commandments.

7 You shall not take a false oath in the name of the Lord your God; for I, the Lord, will not declare him innocent who takes an oath in my name falsely.

8 Remember the Sabbath day to keep it holy.

9 Six days shall you labor and do all your work;

10 But the seventh day (Saturday) is a Sabbath to the Lord your God; in it you shall not do any work, you, nor your son, nor your daughter, nor your manservant, nor your maidservant, nor your cattle, nor the stranger who is within your gates;

11 For in six days Lord Yahweh made heaven and earth, the seas, and all things that are in them, and rested on the seventh day; therefore the Lord blessed the Sabbath day and sanctified it.

12 Honor your father and your mother, so that your days may be long upon the land which the Lord your God gives you.

13 You shall not murder.

14 You shall not commit adultery.

15 You shall not steal.

16 You shall not bear false witness.

17 You shall not covet (desire) your neighbor's house, you shall not covet your neighbor's wife, nor his manservant, nor his maidservant, nor his ox, nor his donkey, nor anything that is your neighbor's.

18 And all the people observed the thunderings, the lightning flashes, the sound of the trumpet, and the mountain smoking; and when the people saw all of this, they were afraid and they stood afar off.

19 And they said to Moshe, You speak to us and we will listen; but let not Lord Yahweh speak with us, lest we die.

20 And Moshe said to the people, Fear not; for Lord Yahweh is come to prove you, so that his worship may be before your faces, and so that you may not sin.

21 And the people stood afar off, and Moshe drew near to the thick darkness where Lord Yahweh was.

22 And the Lord said to Moshe, Thus you shall say to the children of Israel: You have seen that I (Lord Yahweh) have talked with you from heaven.

23 You shall not make for yourselves, "gods" of gold to be worshipped along with Lord Yahweh, neither shall you make for yourselves "gods" of silver.

CHAPTER 21

15 He who strikes his father or his mother shall surely be put to death.

16 He who steals a person and sells him, or he is found in his possession, he shall surely be put to death.

(contrary to popular opinion, slavery is obviously NOT approved by the Bible)

CHAPTER 22

16 And if a man entices a virgin who is not betrothed, and lays with her, he shall surely marry her.

17 If her father refuses to give her to him, he shall pay money according to the dowry of a virgin.

18 You shall not allow a witch to live.   (unless she asks Lord Yahshua for forgiveness, and repents from any witchcraft)

19 Whoever lays with an animal shall surely be put to death.

20 He who sacrifices to idols shall be utterly destroyed.

25 If you lend money to any of my people who are poor among you, you shall not be to him as an usurer, neither shall you take any usury from him.

CHAPTER 23

4 If you meet your enemy's ox or his donkey going astray, you shall surely bring it back to him again.

5 If you should see the donkey of your enemy lying under its burden, and you are unwilling to help him lift it up, you should surely help him to lift it up nevertheless.

13 Take heed of all things that I have said to you; and make no mention of the name of any of the false idols, neither think of them.

CHAPTER 24

12 And the Lord said to Moshe: Come up to the mountain to Me, and present yourself there; and I will give you tablets of stone, and the laws and commandments which I have written; that you may teach them.

16 And the glory of Lord Yahweh rested upon Mount Sinai, and the cloud covered it for six days; and on the seventh day, the Lord called to Moshe out of the midst of the cloud.

17 And in the sight of all the children of Israel, he saw the glory of Lord Yahweh like a burning fire on the top of the mountain.

CHAPTER 32

15 And Moshe turned and went down from the mountain, and the two stone tablets of the testimony were in his hand, the tablets that were written on both sides;

16 The tablets were the work of Lord Yahweh, and the writing was the writing of Lord Yahweh engraved upon the tablets.

17 And when Y'hoshua (Joshua) heard the noise of the people fighting, he said to Moshe, There is a noise of war in the camp.

18 Moshe said to him, it is not the sound of the cry of mighty men, neither is it the sound of the cry of weak men; but it is the sound of sin that I hear.

19 And it came to pass as soon as they came near to the camp, Moshe saw the calf (which was made of gold to be a false god) and the cymbals; Moshe's anger raged and he threw the tablets out of his hand and broke them at the foot of the mountain.

20 and he took the calf (false god) which they had made, and burned it in the fire, and filed it with a file until it was ground into dust, and he scattered it upon the water and made the children of Israel drink of it.

CHAPTER 34

And Lord Yahweh said to Moshe, Hew two tablets of stone like the first ones; and write upon the tablets the words that were on the first tablets, which you broke.

4 And Moshe hewed two tablets of stone like the first ones; and he arose early in the morning and went up to the top of Mount Sinai, as the Lord commanded him, and he took in his hand the two stone tablets.

12 (Lord Yahweh said:) Take heed to yourself lest you make a covenant with the inhabitants of the land whither you go, lest they become a stumbling block to you.

13 but you must destroy their altars, break their images, and cut down their idols.

14 For you shall worship no other god; for Lord Yahweh is a jealous God.

28 And Moshe was there with the Lord forty days and forty nights; he neither ate bread nor drank water. And he wrote upon the tablets the words of the covenant, the ten commandments.

The Third Book of Moshe (Moses), called

Leviticus

Chapter 18

And the Lord spoke to Moshe, saying,

2 Speak to the children of Israel and say to them, I (Lord Yahweh) am the Lord your God.

3 You shall not do according to the doings of the land of Egypt wherein you dwelt, neither shall you do according to the doings of the land of Canaan whither I bring you; neither shall you walk in their ordinances.

4 But you shall do my judgments and keep my commandments and walk in them; I am the Lord your God.

5 You shall therefore keep my commandments and my judgments, which if a man do, he shall live in them; I am the Lord.

6 None of you shall be sexually intimate with any that is near near of kin to you to uncover his or her nakedness; I am the Lord.

7 You shall not shame your father by sexually approaching your mother; she is your mother, you shall not uncover her nakedness.

8 You shall not sexually approach your father's wife; it is your father's nakedness.

9 You shall not sexually approach your sister or brother, the daughter or son of your father or the daughter or son of your mother.

10 You shall not sexually approach your son's daughter or son, or your daughter's daughter or son, because they are your own kin.

11 You shall not sexually approach your step-sister or step-son, she or he is your sibling; you you shall not uncover her or his nakedness.

12 You shall not sexually approach your father's sister or brother, they are your father's near kin.

13 You shall not sexually approach your mother's sister or brother, they are your mother's near kin.

14 You shall not put to shame your father's brother; You shall not sexually approach his wife, for she is your aunt. you shall not uncover her nakedness. (this rule also applies to your uncle)

15 You shall not sexually approach your daughter-in-law; for she is your son's wife; you shall not uncover her nakedness.

16 You shall not sexually approach your sibling's spouse, it is your sibling's nakedness.

17 You shall not sexually approach a woman and her daughter;

18 You shall not take to wife a sister of your wife, to distress her, to uncover her nakedness beside the other in her lifetime.

19 You shall not be intimate with a woman while she is unclean during her menstruation.

20 Moreover, you shall not lie carnally with your neighbor's (or anyone else's) wife or husband to defile yourself with her or him.

21 You shall not let any of your reproductive fluid be cast into a strange woman to cause her to be pregnant; neither shall you profane the name of your God; I am the Lord.

22 A male shall not lie with a male as with a woman (also: a female shall not lie with a female as with a man); because it is an abomination.

23 Neither shall you (male or female) lie with any beast to defile yourself with it; because it is an abomination.

30 Therefore you shall keep my ordinances, and you shall not commit any of these abominable customs which were committed before you, and you shall not defile yourselves by them; I am the Lord your God.

Chapter 19

And Lord Yahweh spoke to Moshe, saying,

2 Speak to all the congregation of the children of Israel and say to them: You shall be holy; for I, the Lord your God, am holy.

3 You must revere every man his father and his mother, and keep my commandments; for I am the Lord your God.

4 You shall not turn to idols nor make yourselves molten "gods"; I am the Lord your God.

18 You shall not bear any enmity against the children of your own people, but you shall love your neighbor as yourself; I am the Lord your God.

19 You shall keep my statutes. You shall not let your cattle breed with a diverse kind; you shall not sow your field with mixed seed; neither shall you wear a mantle of mixed materials.

26 You shall not eat blood; neither shall you use any enchantment, nor shall you consult an oracle.

27 You shall not let the hair of your beards grow, neither shall you trim the corners of your beard.

28 You shall not make any cuttings in your flesh for the dead, nor inscribe any marks upon you; I am the Lord your God.

29 You shall not permit your daughter to become a whore, lest the land fall to whoredom and become full of wickedness.

30 You shall keep my commandments and reverence my sanctuary; I am the Lord.

31 You shall not go after diviners, neither after soothsayers, nor shall you consult them to be defiled by them; I am the Lord your God.

32 You shall rise up before an elder, and honor the person who is older than you and revere your God; I am the Lord your God.

33 And when a new convert sojourns with you in your land, you shall not wrong him;

34 But let him or her be among you as one of you; and the new converts who sojourn among you, you must love them as yourselves; for you also were new converts in the land of Egypt; I am the Lord your God.

35 You shall do no injustices in judgment, in balances, in weight, or in measure.

37 Therefore you shall keep all my commandments and all my judgments, and do them; I am Lord Yahweh your God.

Chapter 21

7 A man shall not marry a harlot or any unclean woman; neither shall he marry a woman who has been divorced from her husband; for he is holy to his God.

13 And he shall take a wife in her virginity.

14 A widow or a woman who is divorced or is defiled by whoredom, these he shall not take; but he shall take a virgin of his own people to wife.

The Fifth Book of Moshe (Moses), called

Deuteronomy

Chapter 4

29 But if you shall seek the Lord your God, you shall find Him if you search for Him with all your heart and with all your soul.

30 When you are in tribulation, and all these things are come upon you, even in the latter days, if you turn to the Lord your God and be obedient to his voice;

31 For the Lord your God is a merciful God, He will not destroy you, nor forsake you, nor forget the covenant which He swore to their fathers.

35 You saw and knew that Lord Yahweh is the God; there is none else besides Him.

39 Know therefore this day and cause your heart to repent, for it is Lord Yahweh who is the God in heaven above and upon the earth beneath; there is none else besides Him.

40 You must keep therefore his statutes and his commandments, which I (Moshe) command you this day, so that it may be well with you and with your children after you, and that you may prolong your days in the land which the Lord Your God gives you forever.

Chapter 6

4 Hear, O Israel: Lord Yahweh our God is one Lord;

5 And you shall love Lord Yahweh your God, with all your heart and with all of the soul which you are, and with all your might.

6 And these words (from Lord Yahweh) which I (Moshe) command you this day shall be in your hearts;

7 And you shall repeat them diligently to your children, and shall talk of them when you sit in your house, when you walk by the way, when you lie down, and when you rise up.

25 And it shall be our righteousness, if we observe and do all these commandments before the Lord our God, as He has commanded us.

CHAPTER 10

12 And now, Israel, what does the Lord Your God require of you, but to revere the Lord your God, to walk in his ways, and to love Him, and to serve the Lord your God with all your heart and with all of your self (soul),

13 To keep the commandments of Lord Yahweh your God, and his statutes, which I command you this day for your good.

14 Behold, the heaven, and the heaven of heavens belong to the Lord your God, the earth also belongs to Him with all that therein is.

16 Circumcise therefore the "foreskin" of your heart, and be no more stiffnecked.

CHAPTER 22

5 A woman shall not wear any garment that pertains to a man, neither shall a man put on a woman's garments; for whosoever does these things is an abomination in the sight of the Lord your God.

Chapter 23

21 When you shall vow a vow to the Lord your God, you shall not be slack to pay it; for the Lord your God will surely require it of you; and it would be a sin in you.

Chapter 26

16 This day, the Lord your God has commanded you to do these statutes and judgments; you shall therefore keep and do them with all your heart and with all of yourself the soul.

17 You have confessed Lord Yahweh this day to be your God, and promised to walk in his ways and to keep his statutes and his judgments and his commandments, and to harken to his voice;

18 And the Lord has promised you again this day to be his beloved people, as He had promised you, that you should keep and do his commandments;

19 And that He shall exalt you above all nations which He has made, in praise, in name, and in honor; and that you may be a holy people to the Lord your God, as He has spoken.

The First Book of The
Kings

Chapter 8

22   And Solomon stood before the altar of Lord Yahweh in the presence of all the congregation of Israel, and spread forth his hands toward heaven and prayed;

23   And he said: O Lord, God of Israel, there is no one like Thee in heaven above or on earth beneath, who keeps covenant and mercy with thy servants who walk before Thee in truth with all their hearts and with all their souls, selves.

24   Who has kept with thy servant David, my father, what Thou did promise him; Thou did speak with thy mouth, and has fulfilled it with thy hand, as it is this day.

25   Therefore, now, O Lord, God of Israel, keep with thy servant David, my father, what Thou did promise him, saying, There shall not fail you a man in my sight to sit on the throne of Israel; if only your sons take heed to their way, to walk before Me in truth as you have walked before Me.

26   And now O Lord, God of Israel, let thy word be confirmed, which Thou has sworn to thy servant David my father.

27   But will Lord Yahweh indeed dwell on the earth? Behold, the heaven, and the heaven of heavens, cannot contain Thee; how much less this house that I have built?

56   Blessed be Lord Yahweh who has given rest to his people of Israel, according to all that He promised; there has not failed even one word of all his good promises which He promised by the hand of Moshe his servant.

57 The Lord our God be with us, as He was with our fathers; let Him not leave us nor forsake us;

58 That Lord Yahweh may incline our hearts unto Him, to walk in all his ways and to keep his commandments, his statutes, and his judgments, which He commanded our fathers.

The Book of
Psalms

Psalm 1

Blessed is the one who walks not in the way of the ungodly, nor abides in the counsel of sinners, nor sits in the company of mockers;

2 But ones' delight is in the law of Lord Yahweh, and on his law does one meditate day and night.

3 And one shall be like a tree planted by a stream of water, that brings forth its fruit in its season, whose leaves do not fall off; and whatsoever one begins, one accomplishes.

4 The ungodly are not so, but are like the chaff which the wind drives away.

5 Therefore the ungodly shall not be justified in the judgment, nor sinners in the congregation of the righteous;

6 For the Lord knows the way of the righteous; but the way of the ungodly shall perish.

Psalm 2

Why do the heathen rage, and the peoples imagine vain things?

2 The kings of the earth, and the rulers, have conspired and have taken counsel together against Lord Yahweh and against his anointed (Yahshua the Son), saying,

3 Let us break their bands asunder, and let us cast away their yoke from us.

4 He that dwells in heaven shall laugh, and the Lord shall ridicule them.

5 Then shall He speak to them in his anger, and terrify them in his wrath and say,

6 I have appointed my king (Yahshua the Christ) over Zion, my holy mountain.

7 I will declare my decree; the Lord has said to me (Yahshua), You are my Son; this day I have begotten you.

8 Ask of Me, and I shall give you the heathen for your inheritance and the uttermost parts of the earth for your dominion.

9 You (Yahshua the Christ) shall shepherd them with a rod of iron; you shall break them pieces like a potter's vessel. (this verse is confirmed by Revelation 2:27)

10 Be wise now, therefore, O kings; be instructed, O judges of the earth.

11 Serve the Lord with reverence, and uphold Him with trembling.

12 Kiss the Son, lest he be angry, and you perish from his way while his wrath is kindled but a little. Blessed are all that put their trust in him.

PSALM 5

4 For Thou are not a God that has pleasure in wickedness; neither shall evil dwell with Thee.

5 The proud shall not stand in thy sight; Thou hate all workers of iniquity.

6 Thou shall destroy them that speak falsehood; the Lord will reject the bloody and deceitful man.

7 But as for me, I will come into thy house in the multitude of thy mercy; and I will enter into thy house and worship in thy holy temple.

11 But let all those that put their trust in Thee rejoice; they shall glorify Thee forever, and Thou shall dwell among them; and all that love thy name shall be strengthened by Thee.

12 For Thou, O Lord, will bless the righteous; with favor will Thou adorn him as with a perfect shield.

PSALM 7

O Lord Yahweh my God, in Thee do I put my trust; save me from all them that persecute me, deliver me,

2 Lest I, a human soul, be torn as by a lion, and there is no one to save and deliver me.

3 O Lord my God, if I have done evil and there be iniquity on my hands,

4 If I have been vengeful to whoever has done me evil, and if I have oppressed my enemies without a cause;

5 Let the enemy pursue me and overtake me, yea, let my enemy tread down my life upon the earth and lay my honor in the dust.

PSALM 11

5 The Lord tries the righteous; but the Almighty Soul Lord Yahweh hates the wicked and whoever loves violence.

6 Snares have come down upon the wicked like rain; fire and brimstone, and a destructive tempest, shall be the portion of their cup.

7 For the Lord is righteous, and He loves righteousness; his countenance beholds the upright.

Psalm 14

The fool has said in his heart, There is no God. They are corrupt, they have been defiled by their own devices; there is none that does good.

2 Lord Yahweh looked down from heaven upon the children of man to see if there were any that did understand and seek Lord Yahweh.

Psalm 15

Lord Yahweh, who shall dwell in thy tabernacle? who shall inhabit thy holy mountain?

2 He that walks in righteousness and speaks the truth in his heart.

3 He that does not deceive with his tongue, nor does evil to his neighbor, nor accepts a bribe from his neighbor;

4 In whose eyes a detestable person is despised; but he honors them that worship the Lord; he swears to his neighbor and does not lie;

5 He lends out his money without interest, nor takes a bribe. He is upright and shall never be moved.

Psalm 23

The Lord is my shepherd; I shall not want.

2 He makes me to rest in green pastures; He leads me beside still waters.

3 He restores the soul that I am. He leads me in the paths of righteousness for his name's sake.

4 Yea, though I walk through the valley of the shadow of death, I will fear no evil; for Thou are with me; thy rod and thy staff they comfort me.

THE BIBLICAL TEXTBOOK OF SALVATION

5 Thou prepare a table before me in the presence of my enemies; Thou anoint my head with oil; my cup runneth over.

PSALM 25

Unto Thee, O Lord Yahweh, do I lift up my self, a soul.

2 O my God, I trust in Thee; let me not be ashamed, let not my enemies triumph over me.

3 Yea, let none that trust in Thee be ashamed; let the wicked be ashamed with their vanity.

4 Show me thy ways, O Lord Yahweh; teach me thy paths.

5 Lead me in thy truth, and teach me; for Thou are my God and my Savior; on Thee do I wait all the day.

6 Remember, O Lord, thy tender mercies and the love and kindness; for they are from the beginning of the world.

7 Remember not the sins of my youth; but remember me according to your abundant mercy because of thy goodness' sake, O Lord Yahweh.

8 Good and upright is the Lord; therefore will He direct sinners in the way.

9 He will guide the meek in judgment, and He will teach the poor his way.

10 All the paths of Lord Yahweh are mercy and truth unto those who keep his covenant and his testimonies.

14 Lord Yahweh is mindful of them who worship Him, and He will show them his covenant.

PSALM 32

Blessed is the person whose transgression is forgiven, and whose sin is blotted out.

7 Thou are my refuge; Thou shall protect me from my enemies, Thou will direct me about with glory and deliverance.

10 The wicked has many sorrows; but he that trusts in the Lord, mercy shall surround him.

11 Be glad in the Lord and rejoice, you righteous; and praise Him, all you that are upright in heart.

n Psalm 33

11 The counsel of the Lord stands forever, the thoughts of his heart to all generations.

12 Blessed is the nation whose God is Lord Yahweh; and the people whom He has chosen for his own inheritance.

18 Behold, the eye of the Lord is upon the righteous, upon those who hope in his mercy;

19 To deliver those souls from death and to keep them alive in famine.

20 We souls wait for the Lord; He is our help and our shield.

Psalm **37**

Fret not because of evildoers, neither be envious of the workers of iniquity,

2 For they shall soon wither like grass, and fade away as the green herbs.

3 Trust in Lord Yahweh, and do good; dwell in the land, and seek after faithfulness.

4 Trust in the Lord; and He shall give you the desires of your heart.

5 Commit your way to the Lord; also trust in Him, and He shall bring it to pass.

PSALM 50

7 Hear, O my people, and I will speak to you; O Israel, I will testify to thee: I am Lord Yahweh, your God.

8 I reproved you not for your sacrifices or your burnt offerings; to have been continually before Me.

13 I (Lord Yahweh) eat not the flesh of bulls, neither do I drink the blood of goats.

14 Offer to Lord Yahweh the sacrifice of thanksgiving; and fulfill your vows to the Most High.

15 Call upon Me in the day of trouble; I will strengthen you, and you shall glorify Me.

PSALM 91

He who dwells in the protection of the Most High shall abide under the shadow of Lord Yahweh who is the Most High.

2 I will say of the Lord, He is my refuge and my fortress; my God; in Him will I trust.

3 Surely He shall deliver you from the snare of the hunter, and from vain gossip.

4 He will cover you with his "feathers," and under his "wings" you shall trust; his truth shall be your shield and buckler.

5 You shall not be afraid of the terror by night, nor of the arrow that flies by day,

6 Nor of the conspiracy that spreads in darkness; nor of the pestilence that wastes at noonday.

7 Thousands shall fall at your side, and ten thousand at your right hand; but it shall not come near you.

8 Only with your eyes shall you behold the reward of the wicked.

9 For Thou, O Lord Yahweh, are my trust; Thou has established thy habitation in the highest.

10 No evil shall befall you, neither shall any plague come near your dwelling.

11 For He shall give his angels charge over you to keep you in all your ways.

12 They shall bear you up in their hands, lest you dash your foot against a stone.

14 Because you have loved Me, Lord Yahweh, therefore I will deliver you; I will set you on high because you have known my (most holy) name.

15 You shall call upon Me, and I will answer you; I will be with you in trouble; I will deliver you and honor you.

16 With long life will I satisfy you, and show you my salvation.

Psalm 92

It is a good thing to give thanks to Lord Yahweh, and to sing praises to his name, O Most High,

4 For Thou, O Lord, have made me glad through thy work; I will triumph in the works of thy hands.

5 O Lord, how great are thy works! and thy thoughts are very deep.

Psalm **100**

Make a joyful noise to Lord Yahweh, all you lands.

2 Serve the Lord with gladness; come before his presence with singing.

3 Know that He is the Lord our God; it is He who has made us, and not we ourselves; we are his people, and the "sheep" of his pasture.

4 Enter into his gates with thanksgiving, and into his courts with praise; be thankful to Him, and bless his name;

5 For the Lord is good; his mercy is everlasting; and his truth endures to all generations.

PSALM 105

O give thanks to Lord Yahweh, call upon his name, make known his deeds among the people.

2 Sing to Him, sing psalms to Him, talk of all his wondrous works.

3 Glory to his holy name; let the heart of them rejoice that seek the Lord.

4 Seek the Lord, and be strong, seek his face evermore.

5 Remember his marvelous works that He has done, his wonders, and the judgments of his mouth;

PSALM 110

Lord Yahweh said unto Lord Yahshua the Christ, sit thou at my right hand until I make thine enemies thy footstool.

2 The Lord Yahshua will send forth the scepter of his power out of Zion, and he will rule over thine enemies.

3 Thy people shall be glorious in the day of thy power; arrayed in the beauty of holiness from the womb, I have begotten thee (Yahshua the Christ) as a child from the ages.

4 Lord Yahweh has sworn, and will not lie; saying, You are a priest forever after the order of Melchizedek.

5 Lord Yahshua the Christ at your (Lord Yahwehs') right hand will defeat the kings in the day of his wrath.

6 Yahshua the Christ will judge among the nations, he will count the slain; he will cut off the heads of many on earth.

PSALM 112

Praise Lord Yahweh. Blessed is the man who fears the Lord, who is vigilant in his commandments.

2 His descendants shall be mighty upon earth; he shall be blessed in the generation of the upright.

3 Wealth and riches shall be in his house; and his righteousness endures forever.

4 To the upright there shines a light in the darkness; he is gracious and full of compassion upon the righteous.

5 Blessed is the man who shows mercy and lends; he shall proclaim his words with judgment.

6 Surely he shall not be moved forever; the righteous shall be in everlasting remembrance.

7 He shall not be afraid of evil tidings; his heart is fixed, trusting in the Lord.

8 His heart is strengthened; he shall not be afraid until he sees his desire upon his enemies.

9 He has given generously, he has given to the poor; his righteousness endures forever and ever; his horn shall be exalted with honor.

10 The wicked shall see it, and be grieved; the wicked shall gnash his teeth and be confounded; the desire of the wicked shall perish.

Aleph

Blessed are the undefiled in the way, who walk in the law of Lord Yahweh.

2 Blessed are they who keep his testimonies, and seek the Lord with their whole hearts.

3 They also do no iniquity; they walk in the Lords' ways.

4 Thou has commanded them to keep thy precepts diligently.

5 O that my ways were directed to keep thy statutes!

6 Then shall I not be ashamed, when I have observed all thy commandments.

7 I will praise Thee with uprightness of heart, when I shall have learned thy righteous judgments.

8 I will keep thy statutes; O forsake me not utterly.

33 Teach me, O Lord Yahweh, the way of thy commandments; and I shall keep them unto the end.

34 Give me understanding and I shall keep thy law; yea, I shall observe it with my whole heart.

35 Make me to go in the path of thy commandments; for therein do I delight.

36 Incline my heart unto thy testimonies, and not to fables.

37 Turn away my eyes so that they may not behold falsehood; and quicken me in thy way.

38 Strengthen thy word unto I thy servant who is devoted to Thee.

39 Turn away my reproach; because thy judgments are good.

40 Behold, I have delighted in thy precepts; quicken me in thy righteousness.

Semketh

113 I hate wicked thoughts; but thy law I do love.

114 Thou are my shelter and my refuge; I hope in thy word.

115 Depart from me, O you evildoers, so that I may keep the commandments of my God.

116 Uphold me according to thy word, and I shall live; and let me not be ashamed of my hope.

117 Help me and I shall be safe, and I will be continually mindful of thy commandments.

118 Thou has rejected all them that stray from Thee; for their thoughts are ungodly.

119 Sustain me, and I shall be safe; and I will always meditate on thy commandments.

120 My flesh shrinks for fear of Thee; and I am afraid of thy judgments.

The Proverbs

Chapter 1

The proverbs of Solomon, the son of David, king of Israel;

2 To know wisdom and instruction; to perceive the words of understanding;

3 To receive discipline, reverence, righteousness, justice, and equity;

4 To give subtlety to the simple, to the young men: knowledge and discretion.

5 A wise man will listen and will increase learning; and a man of understanding shall attain to leadership;

7 The reverence of Lord Yahweh is the beginning of knowledge and instruction.

Chapter 2

My son, if you receive my (Lord Yahweh's) words and hide my commandments in your heart.

2 And incline your ear to wisdom and apply your heart to understanding,

3 Yea, if you cry after knowledge and lift up your voice to understanding,

4 If you seek it as silver, and search for it as for hidden treasure;

5 Then you will understand how to worship the Lord and find the knowledge of Lord Yahweh.

6 For it is Lord Yahweh who gives wisdom; out of his mouth come knowledge and understanding.

7 He stores up hope for the upright; He helps those who walk without blemish.

8 He keeps the paths of justice, and preserves the ways of his saints.

9 Then you will understand righteousness, justice, and the uprightness of all good ways.

10 When wisdom enters into your heart, and knowledge is pleasant to you the soul,

11 Intelligence shall preserve you, and the understanding of the pious men shall deliver you;

12 That you may be delivered from evil ways, from men who speak perverse things,

13 Who forsake the path of uprightness to walk in the way of darkness;

14 Who rejoice to do evil, and delight in the perverseness of evil things;

16 Wisdom shall deliver you from a strange woman who flatters with her words,

17 Who has forsaken the mother of her youth, and has forgotten the covenant of her God.

20 Therefore you must walk in the way of good people and keep the path of the righteous.

21 For the upright shall dwell in the land, and those who are unblemished shall remain in it.

22 But the wicked shall be cut off from the earth, and the ungodly shall be rooted out of it.

CHAPTER 3

My son, do not forget my law; but let your heart keep my commandments;

2 For the length of days and long life will they add to you;

3 And peace, mercy, and truth will not forsake you; bind them about your neck; write them upon the tablets of your heart;

4 So you shall find favor, grace, and understanding in the sight of Lord Yahweh and men.

5 Trust in the Lord with all your heart, and rely not on your own wisdom.

6 In all your ways acknowledge Lord Yahweh, and He shall direct your paths.

7 Be not wise in your own eyes; revere the Lord, and depart from evil.

9 Honor the Lord with your substance and with the first fruits of all your crops;

11 My son, despise not the chastening of the Lord, neither be weary of his corrections.

12 For whom the Lord loves, He corrects; even as a father corrects his son.

19 Lord Yahweh, by his wisdom, has founded the earth; by his understanding, He established the heavens.

20 By his knowledge, the depths are broken up and the clouds drop down the dew.

27 Do not refuse to do that which is good, when it is in the power of your hand to do it.

CHAPTER 16

The reasoning of the mind is from man; but the answer of the tongue is from Lord Yahweh.

2 All the ways of a man are clean in his own eyes, but the Lord directs his way.

3 Commit your works to Lord Yahweh, and He will establish your thoughts.

4 All the works of the Lord are for those who will harken to Him; but the wicked are reserved for the day of calamity.

5 Every one who is proud in his heart is an abomination to the Lord; and he who stretches out his hand against his neighbor shall not be pardoned because of this evil.

6 By mercy and truth, iniquity is purged; and reverence of Lord Yahweh causes men to depart from evil.

8 Better is a little with righteousness than great ingathering acquired unjustly.

CHAPTER 21

3 He who does righteousness and justice is more acceptable to Lord Yahweh than he who offers a sacrifice.

13 He who closes his ears at the cry of the poor, he also shall cry to Lord Yahweh, but He shall not answer him.

CHAPTER 24

Be not envious of evil men, neither desire to be with them.

2 For their hearts devise evil, and their lips talk of iniquity.

3 Through wisdom, a house is built; and by understanding, it is established;

4 And by knowledge, the inner chambers are filled with all precious and pleasant riches.

5 A wise man is strong; yea, wisdom increases strength.

16 For a righteous man falls several times and rises up again; but the wicked shall fall into mischief.

17 Do not rejoice when your enemy falls, and let not your heart be glad when the enemy is overthrown,

23 These things I say to the wise: It is not good to show partiality in judgement.

CHAPTER 28

4 Those who forsake the law glory in wickedness; but those who keep the law, receive strength.

6 It is better to be poor and walk in righteousness, than to be rich and walk in perverse ways.

9 He who closes his ears from hearing the law, even his prayer is an abomination.

10 He who causes the righteous to go astray in an evil path, shall fall himself into the pit; but the upright shall inherit good things.

11 The rich man is wise in his own eyes; but a poor man of understanding will reprove the rich man.

13 He who hides his sins shall not prosper; but he who confesses his sins and forsakes them, Lord Yahweh will have mercy upon him.

14 Blessed is he who is always reverent; but he who hardens his heart shall fall into mischief.

23 He who rebukes someone shall find more favor afterwards than he who flatters with his tongue.

27 He who gives to the poor shall not lack; but he who turns his eyes away from the needy shall have many a curse.

CHAPTER 30

5 Every word of Lord Yahweh is pure; He is a shield to those who put their trust in Him.

Ecclesiastes

CHAPTER 5

2 Be not rash with your mouth, and let not your heart be hasty to utter a word before Lord Yahweh; for Lord Yahweh is in heaven, and you are upon the earth; therefore let your words be few.

4 When you vow a vow to Lord Yahweh, do not delay in fulfilling it; for He has no pleasure in fools; but as for you, pay that which you have vowed.

5 It is much better that you should not vow than that you should vow and not fulfill it.

6 Do not allow your mouth to cause your flesh to sin; neither say before Lord Yahweh that your vow was an error, lest Lord Yahweh be angry at your voice and destroy the work of your hands.

7 For within the multitude of dreams, vain things, and many words is false worship; but you should worship Lord Yahweh.

CHAPTER 7

5 It is better for a man to hear the rebuke of the wise than to hear the song of fools.

11 Wisdom is better than weapons; yea, it is better for those who see the light of the truth.

12 For the protection of wisdom is like the protection of money; and the advantage of knowledge is that wisdom gives life to him who possesses it.

16 Be not "over-righteous;" neither make yourself "over-wise;" lest you should become stupid.

The Book of The Prophet Yeshayah (Isaiah)

CHAPTER 1

10 Hear the word of Lord Yahweh, you rulers of Sodom; give ear to the law of our God, you people of Gomorrah.

11 Of what purpose is the multitude of sacrifices to Me? says the Lord Yahweh; I am full of the burnt offerings of rams, and the fat of fed beasts; and I do not delight in the blood of bullocks, of lambs, or of goats.

14 (Lord Yahweh continues): Your new moons and your appointed feasts I hate; they are a burden to Me; I am weary to bear them.

17 Learn to do good; seek justice, do good for the oppressed, plead for the fatherless, plead for the widows.

18 Come now, and let us reason together, says the Lord; though your sins be as scarlet, they shall be as white as snow; though they be red as crimson, they shall be like wool.

CHAPTER 2

The word that Yeshayah (Isaiah), the son of Amoz, saw concerning Judah and Jerusalem:

2 And it shall come to pass in the last days, that the mountain of the Lord's house shall be established above the mountains, and shall be exalted above the hills; and all nations shall look to it.

3 And many people shall go and say, Come, let us go up to the mountain of Lord Yahweh, to the house of the God of Ya'akov; and He will teach us his ways, and we will walk in his paths; for out of Zion shall go forth the law, and the word of the Lord from Jerusalem.

4 And the Lord shall judge among the nations, and shall rebuke many peoples who are far off; and they shall beat their swords into plowshares, and their spears into sickles; nation shall not lift up sword against nation, neither shall they learn war anymore.

12 For the day of the Lord shall be against every one that is proud and lofty, and against every one that is lifted up, that he shall be brought low;

17 And the loftiness of man shall be humbled, and the haughtiness of man shall be brought low; and the Lord alone shall be exalted in that day.

18 And the idols shall utterly pass away.

19 And the people shall go into the holes of the rocks, and into the caves of the earth, for fear of Lord Yahweh, and for the glory of his majesty when He arises to shake the earth.

20 In that day, a man shall cast away to the moles and to the bats his idols of gold and his idols of silver which they made each one for themselves to worship.

22 Shun the man who is hasty, for of what account is he?

Chapter 4

2 In that day shall the glory and honor of Lord Yahweh shine forth, and the fruit of the earth shall be excellent and comely for the remnant of Israel.

3 And it shall come to pass; that he who is left in Zion, and he who remains in Jerusalem, shall be called holy, even every one who is written among the living in Jerusalem,

4 When the Lord shall have washed away the filth of the daughters of Zion, and have shall purged the bloodshed from the midst of Jerusalem, by the spirit of judgement, and by the spirit of purging.

5 And the Lord will create upon every dwelling place of mount Zion, round about, a cloud by day, and the smoke and shining of a flaming fire by night; for the glory of the Lord shall be a shelter over all.

6 And there shall be a shelter for a shade in the daytime from the heat, and for a place of refuge, and for a shelter from the storm and from the rain.

Chapter 5

11 Woe to them who rise up early in the morning, and run after strong drink; that continue drinking until night, until wine inflames them!

12 They drink wine while listening to the harps, timbrels, tambourines, and flutes; but they do not regard the works of Lord Yahweh, neither consider the deeds of his hands.

13 Therefore my people are gone into captivity because they have no knowledge; and their dead are multiplied because of the famine, and have been overcome with thirst.

14 Therefore hell has enlarged itself, and opened its mouth without measure; and the "glorious" men, the "honorable" men, and the mighty men shall descend into it.

15 And the mean man shall be humbled, the mighty man shall be brought down, and the eyes of the lofty shall be humbled;

16 But the Holy God shall be exalted in judgement, and the Holy God shall be sanctified in righteousness.

20 Woe to them who call evil: good, and call good: evil; who put darkness for light, and light for darkness; who put bitter for sweet, and sweet for bitter!

21 Woe to those who are wise in their eyes, and prudent in their own sight!

22 Woe to those who are mighty to drink wine, and strong men who mix strong drink;

23 Woe to those who justify the guilty because of his bribe, and take away justice from the righteous!

24 Therefore, as the fire devours the stubble and the flame consumes the chaff, so they shall be consumed by the flame, and their root shall be as dust; and their blossom shall go up like chaff because they have rejected the law of Lord Yahweh who is the Lord hosts, and because they despised the command of Yahshua the Christ who is the Holy One of Israel.

25 Therefore the anger of Lord Yahweh is kindled against his people, and He has stretched forth his hand against them, and has smite them, and the mountains trembled; and their carcasses were like mud in the streets. For all his anger has not turned away, and his hand is stretched out still.

26 And He will lift up an ensign to the nations from afar, and will whistle to them from the end of the earth; and, behold, they shall come swiftly with speed.

CHAPTER 7

14 Therefore, Lord Yahweh Himself shall give you a sign; Behold, a virgin shall conceive and bear a son, and shall call his name: Yahshua.

CHAPTER 8

19 And when they shall say to you: Inquire of men who have familiar spirits, and of "wise" men who chirp and mutter, these men are not Lord Yahweh's people, these men who inquire of the dead concerning the living.

20 As for the law and the testimony, if they do not speak according to this word, it is because they do not receive a bribe for it.

Chapter 9

6 For to us a child is born, to us a son is given; and the government will be upon his shoulder; and his name is called Wonderful Counselor, The Mighty One, The Everlasting God, The Prince of Peace (Yahshua the Christ).

7 Of the increase of his government and of his peace there shall be no end, upon the throne of David and upon his kingdom, to establish it and to sustain it with justice and with righteousness from henceforth even for ever. The zeal of the Lord of hosts will perform this.

8 Lord Yahweh has sent a word to Ya'akov, and it has lighted upon Israel.

Chapter 10

Woe to those who decree unrighteous decrees, and who write unjust decrees;

2 To turn aside the needy from justice and to take away the right from the poor of my people, that they may plunder the widows and that they may rob the fatherless!

23 For the Lord, God of hosts, shall bring destruction and make decrees throughout all the earth.

33 Behold, the Lord, God of hosts, shall overthrow the "glorious" ones with might; and the ones who are high of stature shall be humbled, and the haughty shall be brought down.

Chapter 11

2 And he shall be at peace, and the Spirit of Lord Yahweh shall rest upon him, the spirit of wisdom and understanding, the spirit of counsel and might, the spirit of knowledge and of the reverence of the Lord;

3 And shall shine forth in the reverence of the Lord; and He shall not judge after that which his eyes see, neither reprove after that which his ears hear;

4 But with justice shall He judge the poor, and reprove with uprightness for the meek of the earth; and He shall smite the earth with the rod of his mouth, and with the breath of his lips shall He slay the wicked.

5 Righteousness shall be the girdle of his loins, and faithfulness shall be the girdle of of his waist.

6 the wolf shall dwell with the lamb, and the leopard shall lie down with the goat; and the calf and the young lion and the ox shall feed together; and a little child shall lead them.

7 And the cow and the bear shall feed together; and their young ones shall grow up together; and the lion shall eat straw like the ox.

8 And the suckling child shall play with the serpent, and the weaned child shall put his hand into the hole of the asp (a snake which is presently poisonous).

CHAPTER 53

3 He is despised and humbled of men; a man of sorrows and acquainted with grief; and we turned our faces away from him; we despised him, and we esteemed him not.

4 Surely he has borne our sorrows and carried our griefs; but we considered him stricken, smitten of Lord Yahweh, and afflicted.

5 But he, Yahshua the Christ, was slain for our sins; he was afflicted for our iniquities. The chastisement of our peace was upon him, and with his wounds we are healed.

6 All we like sheep have strayed; we have turned many to his own way; and Lord Yahweh has laid upon Yahshua the sins of us all.

9 He made his grave with the wicked, and with the rich in his death, although he had done no iniquity, neither was there any deceit in his mouth.

12 Therefore I, Lord Yahweh, will divide him a portion with the great, and he shall divide the spoil with the strong because he has poured out his life to death; and he was numbered with the transgressors; and he bore the sins of many, and died the death of transgressors.

CHAPTER 55

3 Incline your ear, and come to Me (Lord Yahweh); listen to Me, and the soul yourself shall live; and I will make an everlasting covenant with you, even the sure mercies of David.

4 Behold, I have given you for a witness to the Gentiles, a ruler and leader to the nations.

5 For you shall call nations that you know not, and nations that knew you not shall run to you because of the Lord your God (Lord Yahweh), and because of the Holy One of Israel (Yahshua the Christ); for he has glorified you.

6 Seek Lord Yahshua the Christ; and when you find him, call upon him while he is near;

7 Let the sinner forsake his way, and let the wicked man forsake his wicked thoughts; and let him return to Lord Yahshua, and he will have mercy upon him; and let him return to our God Lord Yahweh, for He will abundantly pardon.

8 For my thoughts are not like your thoughts, neither are my ways like your ways, says, Lord Yahweh.

9 For as the heavens are higher than the earth, so are my ways higher than your ways, so are my thoughts higher than your thoughts.

CHAPTER 59

Behold, Lord Yahweh's hand is not so unable that it cannot save; neither is his ear dull that it cannot hear;

2 But it is your iniquities that have separated you and your God; and your sins have hid his face from you, so that He will not hear.

12 For our transgressions are multiplied before Lord Yahweh, and our sins testify against us; our iniquities are with us, and our sins are well known;

20 And a savior shall come to Zion, and to those who turn from transgression, says the Lord.

The book of the Prophet Yechezk'el (Ezekiel)

Chapter 2

18 When I, Lord Yahweh, say to the sinner: You shall surely die; but you (Yechezk'el) have not warned him, nor have you spoken to warn the sinner from his wicked way to save his life; the same sinner shall die in his iniquity; and his blood will I require at your hand.

19 But if you warn the sinner, and he does not turn from his sin nor from his evil way, he shall die in his sins; but you have delivered the soul which you are.

21 Nevertheless, if you warn the righteous man so that he may not sin, and he does not sin, the righteous man shall surely live because he is warned; and you have delivered the soul which you are.

Chapter 6

And the word of Lord Yahweh came to me, saying,

4 Your altars shall be desolate, and your images shall be broken; and I (Lord Yahweh) will cast down your slain men before your idols.

6 In all your dwelling places, the cities shall be laid waste, and the high places shall be desolate so that your altars may be destroyed and made desolate, and your idols may be broken and made desolate, and your images may be cut down, and your works may cease.

CHAPTER 38

And the word of Lord Yahweh came to me saying,

2 Thou son of man, set you face against the country of Turkey, the chief prince of Meshech and Tubal, and prophesy against him and say,

3 Thus says Lord Yahweh: Behold, I am against you O Turkey, the chief prince of Meshech and Tubal:

4 I will gather your people together and put a bridle in your jaws, and I will bring you forth out of your country, both you and all your army, horses and horsemen, all of them clothed in armor, a great host with spears and shields, all of them handling swords;

5 Iranians (Persians), Ethiopians, and Lybians with them, all of them with shields and helmets.

6 Gomar, which is in northeast Turkey, and all her army, the house of Togarmah, which is in eastern Turkey, and the uttermost parts of the north with all their hosts, and many other people who are with you.

14 Therefore, thou son of man, prophesy and say to Turkey; Thus says Lord Yahweh: On that day when my people of Israel shall dwell in tranquillity, you shall know it.

15 And you shall come from your place out of the north parts, you, and many people with you, all of them riding on horses, a great host and a mighty army;

16 And you shall come up against my people of Israel, like a cloud to cover the land; it shall be in the latter days, and I will bring you against my land, and the nations will know Me when I shall be sanctified through your defeat.

The book of Daniel

CHAPTER 7

13 I saw in the night visions, and behold, one like the Son of man came upon the clouds of heaven, and came to the Ancient of days, brought him before Lord Yahweh.

14 And there was given him, Yahshua the Christ, dominion and glory and a kingdom, so that all the peoples, nations, and languages should serve him; his dominion is an everlasting dominion which shall not pass away, and his kingdom is one that shall not be destroyed.

17 Then he (a ministering spirit) said to me: These four "great beasts" which you saw are four kings which shall arise out of the earth.

18 But the saints of the Most High shall receive the kingdom and possess it forever and ever.

19 Then I wanted to know the truth concerning the fourth "beast" which was different from all the others, exceedingly dreadful,...

23 Thus he (a ministering spirit) said to me: The fourth "beast" shall be the fourth kingdom upon the earth, which shall be greater than all the kingdoms and shall devour the entire earth, and shall tread it down and break it in pieces.

24 And as for the ten "horns" out of the fourth kingdom, they are ten kings that shall arise; and another king shall arise after them, and he shall be greater than the first and he shall defeat the three kings.

25 And he shall speak words against the Most High, and shall plot against the saints of the Most High, and think to change times and laws; and they shall be given into his hand for a time, times, and half a time.

26 But when the judge is seated in judgment, they shall take away his dominion, to consume and to destroy it to the end of his kingdom.

27 And the dominions and the greatness of the kingdom under the entire heaven shall be given to the holy people of the Most High, whose kingdom is an everlasting kingdom, and all dominions shall serve and obey Him.

CHAPTER 8

13 Then I heard a saint speaking, and another saint said to that certain saint who spoke, How long shall be the vision concerning the continual sacrifice, and how soon will the iniquity and corruption be over and the holy thing be and host be trodden under foot?

14 And he said to him, For two thousand and three hundred days; then righteousness shall prevail.

15 And it came to pass when I, Daniel, has seen this vision and sought to understand it, then behold, there stood before me as it were the appearance of a man.

16 And I heard what sounded like a man's voice between the banks of Ulai, who called and said: Gavri'el, make this man to understand the vision.

17 So Gavri'el came near where I stood; and when he came, I was afraid and fell upon my face; but he said to me, Understand O thou son of man; for at the time of the end shall be the vision.

19 And he said to me, Behold, I will show you what shall be at the latter end of the indignation; for at the expiration of the time appointed the end shall be.

20 The ram which you saw with two horns represents the kings of Media (North-west Iran) and Persia (Iran).

21 And the he-goat is the king of Greece, and the great horn that is between his eyes is the first king.

22 And as for the horn that was broken, and there rose four others under it, four kings shall rise up out of the nation, but not by their own power.

23 And at the latter end of their kingdom, when the transgressions are come to an end, a king of fierce countenance who understands riddles shall arise.

27 And he shall confirm the covenant with many for seven weeks and half of seven weeks, then he shall cause the sacrifice and gift offerings to cease; and upon the horns of the altar the abomination of desolation, and the desolation shall continue until the appointed time; the city shall remain desolate.

27 And he shall confirm the covenant with many for seven weeks and half of seven weeks, then he shall cause the sacrifice and gift offerings to cease; and upon the horns of the altar the abomination of desolation, and the desolation shall continue until the appointed time; the city shall remain desolate.

CHAPTER 11

2 And the angel said, Now I will show you the truth. Behold, there shall arise yet three kings in Persia (Iran); and the fourth king shall be far richer than all of them; and when he has become powerful in his own country, he shall stir up all the kingdoms of Greece.

3 And a mighty king shall arise, and he shall rule with great dominion, and do according to his will.

4 And when he has risen, his kingdom shall be broken and shall be scattered toward the four winds of heaven; but it will not extend to its former borders nor according to his dominion which he ruled; for his kingdom shall be uprooted, and there shall be no kingdoms beside the divisions of this kingdom.

5 And the king of the south and his princes shall be strong, and the people shall follow him, and he shall rule over a great dominion.

6 And after some years they shall come to an agreement, and the daughter of the king of the south shall come to the king of the north to make peace between them; but she will not be able to achieve her purpose because of fear; and she shall surrender together with those who had brought her, her maids, and her allies at that time.

16 But he who comes against the king of the north (Turkey) shall do according to his own will, and none shall stand before him; and he shall invade the land of Israel, and it shall be delivered into his hands.

19 (afterwards) Then he shall turn his face toward the fortified places of the earth; but he shall be overthrown and fall, and shall not be found.

20 Then shall rise up in his place a weak ruler and a vassal of the kingdoms; but within a short time he shall be destroyed, neither in anger nor in battle.

21 And in his place shall rise up a vile person, to whom they shall not bestow the royal honor; but he shall come suddenly and seize the kingdom by fraud.

26 Yea, those who eat of his delicacies shall destroy him, and his army shall be scattered; and many shall fall down slain.

28 Then he shall return to his own land with a great army; and his heart shall be against the holy covenant..

29 And he shall do as at the former time, even so in the latter time.

30 For the hosts of Turkey shall come against him; and they shall defeat him, and he shall return, and have indignation against the holy covenant; he shall have an understanding with those who had forsaken the holy covenant.

36 And the king shall do according to his will; and he shall exalt himself and magnify himself above every god, and shall speak great vain things against the God of "gods," and shall prosper till the indignation is accomplished; for that which is determined shall be done.

37 Neither shall he regard the God of his fathers nor the desire of women, nor regard and god; for he shall magnify himself above all.

40 And at the time of the end, the king of the south shall fight against him; and the king of the north shall march against him with "chariots" and with horsemen and with many ships; and he shall invade the land.

41 He shall reach also the land of Israel, and many people shall be slain; but these shall be delivered out of his hands, even Edom and Moab and the remnant of the children of Ammon.

CHAPTER 12

And at that time shall Michael arise, the great angel who has charge over your people; and there shall be a time of trouble such as never has been like it since the beginning of the world; and at that very time some of your people shall be delivered, every one whose name shall be found written in the book of life.

2 And many of those who sleep in the dust of the earth shall awake; some to everlasting life, and some (at a later time) to shame and everlasting contempt.

3 And those who have done good, and the men of understanding, shall shine as the brightness of the firmament; and those who have turned many to righteousness shall shine and stand like stars forever and ever.

4 But you, O Daniel, seal these words and be silent, and seal this book even to the time of the end; many shall want to know the end, and knowledge shall be increased.

Hosea

CHAPTER 4

3 Therefore the land shall mourn, and all its inhabitants shall languish, even the beasts of the field and the fowls of the air; and the fish of the sea shall also perish.

Joel

Chapter 2

Blow the trumpet in Zion, and sound an alarm in my holy mountain; let all the inhabitants of the land tremble; for the day of the Lord is come;

10 The earth quakes before them; the heavens tremble; the sun and the moon are darkened, and the stars have withdrawn their shining.

11 The Lord has shouted before his army; for his host is very great; mighty is the work executed by his word; for the day of the Lord is great and very terrible; who can endure it?

12 Therefore now, says the Lord, return to Me with all your heart, and with fasting and with weeping and with mourning;

13 And rend your hearts and not your garments, and turn to the Lord your God; for He is gracious and merciful, patient and of great kindness, and He averts disaster.

28 And it shall come to pass afterward that I will pour out my Spirit upon all flesh; and your sons and your daughters shall prophesy, your old men shall dream dreams, your young men shall see visions;

30 And I will show wonders in the heavens and on the earth; blood and fire, and pillars of smoke.

31 The sun shall be turned into darkness and the moon into blood, before the great and terrible day of the Lord comes.

32 And it shall come to pass that whosoever shall call on the name of the Lord shall be delivered; for in Mount Zion and in Jerusalem shall be deliverance, as the Lord has said to the remnant whom the Lord has called.

CHAPTER 3

2 I will also gather all nations and will bring them down into the valley of Y'hoshafat (Jehoshaphat), and I will enter into judgment with them there for the sake of my people and for the sake of my heritage Israel, whom they have scattered among the nations, and because they have divided up my land.

16 The Lord also shall roar out of Zion, and utter his voice from Jerusalem; and the heavens and the earth shall shake; but the Lord will have pity upon his people, and will strengthen the children of Israel.

17 Then you shall know that I am Lord Yahweh your God, dwelling in Zion, my holy mountain; then Jerusalem shall be holy, and there shall no foreigners sojourn in it anymore.

Amos

Chapter 4

11 I (Lord Yahweh) have overthrown you (Israel) as I overthrew Sodom and Gomorrah, and you have become like a firebrand which is plucked out of the burning; yet you did not return to I the Lord.

12 Therefore thus will I do to you, O Israel, at the end; and because I will do this to you, prepare, O Israel, that you may call to your God.

Chapter 5

14 Seek good and not evil so that you may live; and so the Lord, the God of hosts, shall be with you, as you have spoken.

15 Hate the evil and love the good, and establish justice in the gate; it may be that the Lord, God of hosts, will be gracious to the remnant of Yosef (Joseph).

18 Woe to you who desire the day of the Lord! To what end is it to you? The day of the Lord? For it is a day of darkness and not light.

19 As when a man fled from a lion and a bear met him; or went into the house and leaned his hand on the wall and a serpent bit him.

20 Such is the day of the Lord; it is darkness and not light; yea, it is a day of thick darkness and no brightness is in it.

Chapter 8

Thus has Lord Yahweh showed me: and behold, a sign of the end.

2 And the Lord said to me, Amos, what do you see? And I said, A sign of the end. Then the Lord said to me, The end is come upon my people Israel; I will not again cause it to pass by them anymore.

4 Hear this, O you who wrong the poor, and cause the needy of the land to come to an end,

5 Saying, When the month be over, so that we may sell grain? When will the Sabbath be over so that we may open storehouses and make our measures small, and enlarge weights and make deceitful balances?

9 And it shall come to pass in that day, says the Lord, that I will cause the sun to go down at noon, and I will darken the earth in the daylight.

11 Behold, the days are coming, says the Lord, when I will send a famine in the land; not a famine of bread, nor a thirst for water, but of hearing the word of the Lord;

12 And they shall gather together from sea to sea and from the north even to the east; they shall run to and fro to seek the word of the Lord, and shall not find it.

Mikhah (Micah)

CHAPTER 3

5 Thus says the Lord concerning the prophets who lead my people astray, who bite with their teeth preach peace; and when one puts not bread into their mouths, they preach war against him.

6 Therefore it shall be night to you, that you should not have a vision; and it shall be dark to you so that you shall not divine; and the sun shall go down upon the prophets, and the day shall be dark over them.

7 Then the seers shall be ashamed, and the diviners confounded; yea, they shall all cover their lips because Lord Yahweh will not answer them.

8 But truly I (Mikhah) am full of power by the Spirit of the Lord, and of justice and of might, to declare to Ya'akov his transgression, and to Israel his sin.

9 Now hear this, O you chiefs of the house of Ya'akov and princes of the house of Israel who abhor justice and pervert all equity;

11 The chiefs thereof judge for a bribe, and its priests teach for hire, and its prophets divine for money; yet they rely upon the Lord, saying, The Lord is among us, no evil can come upon us;

12 Therefore, because of you, Zion shall be ploughed as a field, and Jerusalem shall become desolate, and the mountain of the temple like a forest.

CHAPTER 4

But it shall come to pass in the latter days, that the mountain of Lord Yahweh shall be established in the top of the mountains, and the mountain of Lord Yahweh shall be exalted above the hills; and all people shall gather to it.

2 Any many nations shall come and say, Come, let us go up to the mountain of the Lord, to the house of the God of Ya'akov; and He will teach us of his ways, and we will walk in his paths; for the law shall go forth out of Zion, and the word of the Lord of Jerusalem.

Nahum

CHAPTEr 1

2 Lord Yahweh is jealous (when He has a strong reason to be), and the Lord is avenging; the Lord is avenging and is furious; the Lord will take action on his adversaries, and He reserves wrath for his enemies.

3 Lord Yahweh is slow to anger and great in power, and will not at all acquit the wicked; the Lord's way is in the whirlwind and in the tempest, and the clouds are the dust of his feet.

6 Who can stand before his indignation? Who can endure in the fierceness of his wrath? His fury burns like fire, and the mountains melt at his presence.

7 Lord Yahweh is good, a great help in the day od trouble; and He knows those who trust in Him.

CHAPTER 2

2 For the Lord will restore the excellency of Ya'akov, as the excellency of Israel; for the oppressors have trampled upon them and destroyed their branches.

Tz'fanyah (Zephaniah)

Chapter 1

2 I (Lord Yahweh) will utterly remove all things from off the face of the earth, says the Lord.

14 The great day of Lord Yahweh is near, it is very near, and hastens fast; even the voice of the day of the Lord; yea, it is bitter, harsh, and severe.

15 That day is a day of wrath, a day of trouble and distress, a day of confusion and desolation, a day of darkness and gloominess, a day of clouds and thick darkness,

16 A day of trumpet and shouting against the fenced cities and against the high towers.

17 And I (Lord Yahweh) will bring distress upon men, so that they shall walk like blind men, because they have sinned against the Lord; and their blood shall be poured out like dust, and their flesh like dung.

18 Neither their silver nor their gold shall be able to deliver them in the day of the Lord's wrath; but the whole land shall be consumed in the fire of his indignation against all the inhabitants of the earth.

Chapter 2

Gather yourselves, bind yourselves together, O people without discipline;

2 Before you become like the chaff which is driven away, before the fierce anger of the Lord comes upon you, before the day of the Lord's anger reaches you.

3 Seek Lord Yahweh, all you meek of the earth, execute justice; seek righteousness and meekness; perhaps you may find refuge in the day of the Lord's anger.

CHAPTER 3

9 For then, Lord Yahweh will restore to the people a pure speech so that they may call upon the name of YHWH, to serve Him with one consent.

13 The remnant of Israel shall not do iniquity, nor speak lies; neither shall a deceitful tongue be found in their mouth; for they shall feed and lie down, and none shall harm them.

15 The Lord has taken away your judgments, He has cast out your enemies; the King of Israel, even the Lord, is in the midst of you; you shall not see evil anymore.

17 The Lord your God in the midst of you is a mighty Savior; He will make you to rejoice with gladness; He will renew you with his love, He will make you joyful with a praise as in the day of a feast.

20 At that time I will bring you again, and at that very time I will gather you; for I will make you a name and a praise among all the people of the earth, when I bring back your captivity in the presence of your enemies, says Lord Yahweh.

Z'kharyah (Zechariah)

CHAPTER 1

3 Therefore (Z'kharyah) say to them, Thus says the Lord of hosts: Return to Me, and I will return to you, says the Lord of hosts.

4 Be not like your fathers, to whom the former prophets preached, saying, Thus says the Lord of Hosts: Turn now from your evil ways and from your evil doings; but but they did not listen, nor give ear to Me, says the Lord.

14 So the angel who spoke with me, said to me: Proclaim and say, Thus says the Lord of hosts: I am zealous for Jerusalem and for Zion with a great zeal.

15 And I am very angry with the nations who are raging; for while I was but a little angry, they helped to carry the disaster to the extreme.

16 Therefore thus says the Lord: I am returned to Jerusalem with mercies; my house shall be built in it, says the Lord of Hosts, and a measuring line shall be stretched forth over Jerusalem.   n   Chapter **8**

16 These are the things that you shall do: Speak the truth everyone to his neighbor; to fully carry out the truth, justice and peace in your gates;

17 And let none of you devise evil in your heart against his neighbor; and love no false oaths; for all these are things that I hate, says the Lord of hosts.

CHAPTER 14

Behold, the day of Lord Yahshua the Messiah is coming! and your spoil shall be divided in the midst of you.

2 For I will gather all nations against Jerusalem to battle; and the city shall be taken and the houses plundered and the women seized; and a half of the city shall go into captivity, but half of the people shall not perish from the city.

3 Then Yahshua the Christ shall go forth and fight against those nations as when he fought in the day of battle.

4 And his feet shall stand upon the Mount of Olives, which is opposite Jerusalem on the east, and the Mount of Olives shall split in two, half toward the east and the other half toward the west, and there shall be in it a great valley; and half of the mountain shall be left toward the north, and half of it toward the south.

5 And you shall flee to the valley of the mountains; for the valley of the mountains shall reach the place of disaster, and you shall flee as you fled from the earthquake in the days of Uzziah the king of Judah; and the Lord my God shall come in, and all his saints with Him.

6 And it shall come to pass in that day there shall be no light, but cold and ice.

7 It shall be a day which is known to Lord Yahweh; it shall be neither night nor day; and it shall come to pass that at evening time, it shall be light.

8 And it shall be in that day, that living waters shall go out from Jerusalem; half of them toward the eastern sea, and half of them toward the western sea; they shall continue to flow in summer and in winter.

9 And Lord Yahshua shall be king all the earth; on that day shall there be one Lord, and his name one.

16 And it shall come to pass that every one that is left of all the nations which come against Jerusalem, shall even go up from year to year to worship the King, the Lord of hosts (Lord Yahweh), and to keep the feast of tabernacles.

Mal'akhi (Malachi)

Chapter 3

Behold, I, Lord Yahweh, will send my messenger and he shall prepare the way before Me; and he for whom you are waiting shall suddenly come to the temple of the Lord, even the messenger of the covenant, in whom you delight; behold, he shall come, says the Lord of hosts.

2 But who can endure the day of his coming? And who can stand when he appears? For he is like a refiner's fire and like fuller's soap;

3 For he shall return to refine and purify the people like silver; and he who is Lord Yahshua the Christ shall cleanse the sons of Levi and purge them like gold and silver, so that they may offer to the Lord an offering in righteousness.

Chapter 4

For behold, the days are coming when my (Lord Yahweh's) anger shall burn as an oven; and all the wicked and all who do iniquity shall be stubble; and the day that comes shall burn them up, says the Lord of hosts, that it shall leave them neither root nor branch.

2 But for you who revere my name shall the sun of righteousness arise with healing upon his lips; and you shall go forth and leap for joy like the calves of the heard.

3 And you shall tread down the wicked; for they shall be ashes under the soles of your feet in the day that I shall do this, says the Lord of hosts.

4 Remember the law of Moshe (Moses) my servant, which I commanded to him in Horeb for all Israel, with the statutes and judgments.

5 Behold, I will send you Eliyah (Elijah) the prophet before the coming of the great and dreadful day of the Lord;

6 And he shall turn the heart of the fathers to the children, and the heart of the children to their fathers, before I come and smite the earth to ruin.

Each of the four apostles (Mattityahu, Mark, Luke, and Yochanan) wrote the same story which is repeated three times but each one has written some details which the other three did not, so I have removed the repeated words but included ALL the details from All four apostles.

THE GOSPEL OF MATTITYAHU/MARK/LUKE/YOCHANAN

LUKE 1

5 There was in the days of Herod, king of Judea, a priest whose name was Z'kharyah (Zachariah), of the order of ministry of the house of Aviyah (Abijah); and his wife was of the daughters of Aharon (Aaron), and her name was Elisheva (Elizabeth).

6 They were both righteous before the almighty God, Lord YHWH (Yahweh), and walked in all His commandments, and in the righteousness of the Lord Yahweh without blame.

7 But they had no son, because Elisheva was barren, and they were both well on in years.

8 And it came to pass while Z'kharyah was ministering in the order of his ministry before the almighty God: Lord Yahweh,

9 According to the custom of the priesthood, his turn came to burn incense; so he entered the temple of the Lord.

10 And all the congregation of the people prayed outside, at the time of incense.

11 And the angel Gavri'el (Gabriel) of the Lord appeared to Z'kharyah, standing on the right of the altar of incense.

12 And when Z'kharyah saw him, he became dumbfounded, and fear came upon him.

13 And the angel said to him, Fear not, Z'kharyah; for your prayer has been heard, and your wife will bear you a son, and you will call his name Yochanan (John).

14 And you will have joy and gladness; and a great many will rejoice at his birth.

15 For he will be great before the Lord, and he will not drink wine and strong drink; and he will be filled with the Holy Spirit, while he is still in the womb of his mother.

16 And many Israelites he will cause to turn to the Lord their God.

17 And he will go before them with the spirit and the power of Eliyahu (Elijah), to turn the hearts of parents to their children, and those who are disobedient to the wisdom of the righteous; and he will prepare a true people for the Lord.

18 And Z'kharyah said to the angel, How will I understand this? for I am an old man, and my wife is well on in years.

19 And the angel answered, saying to him, I am Gavri'el, who stand in the presence of the almighty God, Lord Yahweh; and I am sent to speak to you, and to bring you the glad tidings.

20 From henceforth you will be dumb (unable to speak), and not able to speak till the day these things happen, because you did not believe these my words which are to be fulfilled in their time.

26 Now in the sixth month (of Elisheva's pregnancy) the angel Gavri'el was sent from Lord Yahweh to Galilee, to a city called Nazareth,

27 To a virgin who was acquired for a dowry for a man named Yosef (Joseph), of the house of David; and the name of the virgin was Miryam (Mary).

28 And the angel Gavri'el went in and said to her, Peace be to you, O full of grace; our Lord is with you, O blessed one among women.

30 And the angel said to her, Fear not, Miryam; for you have found grace with the Lord God Yahweh.

31 For behold, you will conceive and give birth to a son, and you will call his name Yahshua (Jesus).

32 He will be great, and he will be called the Son of the Highest; and Lord Yahweh will give him the throne of his father David.

33 And he will rule over the house of Ya'akov (Jacob) for ever; and there will be no limit to his kingdom.

34 Then Miryam said to the angel, How can this be, for no man has "known" me.

35 The angel answered and said to her, The Holy Spirit will come, and the power of the Highest will rest upon you; therefore the one who is to be born of you is holy, and he will be called the Son of Lord Yahweh.

37 For nothing is impossible for the almighty God, Lord Yahweh.

38 Miryam said, here I am, a handmaid of the Lord; let it be to me according to your word. And the angel went away from her.

MATTHEW 1

19 But Yosef her husband was a pious man, and did not wish to make it (Miryam's pregnancy not of Yosef) public; so he was thinking of divorcing her secretly.

20 While he was considering this, the angel of the Lord appeared to him in a dream, and said to him, O, Yosef, son of David, do not be afraid to take your wife Miryam, because he that is to be born of her is of the Holy Spirit.

21 She will give birth to a son, and you will call his name Yahshua; for he shall save his people from their sins.

YOCHANAN (JOHN) 3

16 For the almighty God, Lord Yahweh, so loved the world that He even gave his only begotten Son, so that whoever believes in him should not perish, but have eternal life.

MATTITYAHU (MATTHEW) 1

24 When Yosef rose up from his sleep, he did just as the angel of the Lord commanded him, and he took his wife.

25 And he did not "know" her until she gave birth to her first-born son; and she called his name Yahshua.

(MATTHEW) 3

1 In those (later) days came Yochanan (John) the Baptist; and he was preaching in the wilderness of Judea,

2 Saying, Repent, for the kingdom of heaven is near.

MARK 1

4 Yochanan was in the wilderness, baptizing and preaching the baptism of repentance for the forgiveness of sins,

7 And he preached, saying, Behold, there is coming after me one who is mightier than I am, even the strings of whose shoes I am not good enough to untie.

8 I have baptized you with water; but he will baptize you with the Holy Spirit.

MATTHEW 3

13 Then Yahshua came from Galilee to the Jordan River to Yochanan, to be baptized by him.

14 But Yochanan tried to stop him, saying, I need to be baptized by you, and yet have you come to me?

15 But Yahshua answered and said to him, Permit it now, for this is necessary for us so that all righteousness may be fulfilled; and then he permitted him.

16 When Yahshua was baptized, he immediately went up out of the water; and the heavens were opened to him, and he saw the Spirit of Lord Yahweh descending like a dove, and coming upon him;

17 And behold, a voice from heaven which said, This is my beloved Son, with whom I am well pleased.

MATTHEW 4

4 ...(Yahshua said:) It is written that it is not by bread alone that man can live, but by every word which proceeds from the mouth of the almighty God.

MATTHEW 5

3 (Yahshua said:) Blessed are the humble, for theirs is the kingdom of heaven.

4 Blessed are they who mourn, for they shall be comforted.

5 Blessed are the meek, for they shall inherit the earth.

6 Blessed are those who hunger and thirst for righteousness, for they shall be well satisfied.

7 Blessed are the merciful, for they shall have mercy.

8 Blessed are the pure in heart, for they shall see the almighty God.

9 Blessed are the peacemakers, for they shall be called sons of the almighty God.

10 Blessed are those who are persecuted for the sake of righteousness, for theirs is the kingdom of heaven.

11 Blessed are you when men reproach you and persecute you and speak against you every kind of evil, falsely for my sake,

12 Then be glad and rejoice, for your reward is increased in heaven; for in this very manner they persecuted the prophets who were before you.

16 Let you light so shine before men that they may see your good works and glorify your Father in heaven.

17 Do not suppose that I (Yahshua) have come to weaken (or end) the law or the prophets; I have not come to weaken (or end) , but to fulfill.

21 You have heard that it was said to those who were before you, You shall not murder, and whoever murders is guilty before the court.

22 But I say to you that whoever becomes angry with his brother for no reason is guilty before the court; and whoever should say to his brother, Raca (which means, I spit on you) is guilty before the congregation; and whoever says to his brother, you are brutish or abnormal, is condemned to hell fire.

27 You have heard that it is said, you shall not commit adultery.

28 But I say to you that whoever looks at a woman with lust, has already committed adultery with her in his heart.

29 If your right eye should cause you to stumble, pluck it out and throw it away from you; for it is better for you to lose one of your members, and not have all your body fall into hell.

42 Whoever asks of you, give him; and whoever wishes to borrow from you, do not refuse him.

44 But I say to you, Love your enemies, bless anyone who curses you, do good to anyone who hates you, and pray for those who carry you away by force and persecute you,

45 So that you may become sons of your Father who is in heaven, who causes the sun to shine upon the good and the bad, and who pours down his rain upon the just and the unjust.

48 Therefore become perfect, just as your Father in heaven is perfect.

Matthew 6

1 Be careful concerning your alms, do not do them in the presence of men, merely that they may see them; otherwise you have no reward with your Father in heaven.

2 Therefore when you give alms, do not blow a trumpet before you, just as the hypocrites do in the synagogues and in the market places, so that they may be glorified by men. Truly I say to you that they have already received their reward.

5 And when you pray, do not be like the hypocrites, who like to pray, standing in the synagogues and at the street corners.

6 But as for you, when you pray, enter into your inner chamber and lock your door, and pray to your Father who is in secret, and your Father who sees in secret shall Himself reward you openly.

7 And when you pray, do not repeat your words like the pagans, for they think that for their much talking they will be heard.

8 Do not be like them, for your Father knows what you need before you ask Him;

9 Therefore pray in this manner: Our Father in heaven, hallowed by thy name.

10 Thy kingdom come. Thy will be done, as in heaven so on earth.

11 Give us bread for our needs from day to day.

12 And forgive us our offenses (sins), as we have forgiven our offenders (those whom sin against us).

13 And do not let us enter into temptation, but deliver us from evil. For thine is the kingdom and the power and the glory for ever and ever. Amen.

14 For if you forgive men their offenses, your Father in heaven will also forgive you.

15 But if you do not forgive men, neither will your Father forgive even your offenses.

19 Do not lay up for yourselves treasures buried in the ground, a place where rust and moth may destroy and where thieves break through and steal.

20 But lay up for yourselves a treasure in heaven, where neither rust nor moth destroys and where thieves do not break through and steal.

21 For where your treasure is, there also is your heart.

33 But first seek the kingdom of the almighty God, Lord Yahweh, and his righteousness, and all these things will be added to you.

MATTHEW 7

1 Judge not, that you may not be judged.

2 For with the same judgment that you judge, you will be judged, and with the same measure with which you measure, it will be measured to you.

3 Why do you see the splinter which is in your brother's eye, and do not feel the (wooden) beam which is in your own eye?

4 Or how can you say to your brother, Let me take out the splinter from your eye, and behold there is a beam in your own eye?

5 O hypocrites, first take out the beam from your own eye, and then you will see clearly to get out the splinter from your brother's eye.

6:12 Whatever you wish men to do for you, do likewise also for them; for this is the law and the prophets.

13 Enter in through the narrow door, for wide is the door and broad is the road which leads to destruction, and many are those who travel on it.

14 O how narrow is the door and how difficult is the road which leads to life, and few are those who are found on it.

15 Be careful of false prophets who come to you in lamb's clothing, but within are ravening wolves.

16 You will know them by their fruits. Do they gather grapes from thorns or figs from thistles?

17 So every good tree bears good fruit; but a bad tree bears bad fruit.

18 A good tree cannot bear bad fruit, neither can a bad tree bear good fruit.

19 Every tree which does not bear good fruit will be cut down and cast into the fire.

20 Thus by their fruit you will know them.

21 It is not everyone who merely says to me, My Lord, my Lord, who will enter into the kingdom of heaven, but he who does the will of my Father in heaven.

22 A great many will say to me in that day, My Lord, my Lord, did we not prophesy in your name and in your name cast out devils and in your name do many wonders?

23 Then I will declare to them, I have never known you; keep away from me, O you that work iniquity.

MATTHEW 8

2 And behold, a leper came and worshipped him (Yahshua), and said, My Lord, if you wish, you can cleanse me.

3 And Yahshua stretched out his hand and touched him, and he said, I do wish it, be cleansed. And in that hour his leprosy was cleansed.

6 (a centurion) Saying, My Lord, my boy is lying in the house paralyzed and suffering greatly.

7 Yahshua said to him, I will come and heal him.

13 So Yahshua said to the centurion, Go, let it be done to you according to your belief. And his boy was healed in that very hour.

MATTHEW 9

2 And they brought to him a paralytic, lying on a quilt; and Yahshua saw their faith, and he said to the paralytic, Have courage, my son; your sins have been forgiven.

6 But that you might know that the Son of man has authority on earth to forgive sins, then he said to the paralytic, Arise, take up your quilt and go to your home.

7 And he rose up and went to his home.

MARK 1

21 When they entered into Capernaum, straightway he taught in their synagogues on the Sabbaths.

22 And they were amazed at his teaching; for he taught them as one with authority, and not as their scribes.

23 And there was in their synagogue a man who had in him an unclean spirit; and he cried out,

24 Saying, Yahshua of Nazereth, what have we in common? Have you come to destroy us? I know who you are, Holy One of Lord Yahweh.

25 And Yahshua rebuked him, saying, Be silent and come out of him.

26 And the unclean spirit threw him down and cried out in a loud voice and left him.

27 And they were all astonished, and kept asking one another, saying, What does this mean? and what is this new teaching, that with such a power he commands even unclean spirits and they obey him?

39 And he preached in all their synagogues throughout Galilee, and cast out demons.

LUKE 6

6 And it came to pass on another Sabbath he entered into the synagogue and taught; and there was there a man whose right hand was withered.

7 And the scribes and the pharisees watched him to see if he would heal on the Sabbath, so they might find an accusation against him.

8 But he knew their thoughts, and said to the man whose hand was withered, Rise up and come to the center of the synagogue. And when he came and stood up,

9 Yahshua said to them, I will ask you, what is lawful to do on the Sabbath, that which is good or that which is bad? to save a life or to destroy it?

10 And he looked at all of them, and said to him, Stretch out your hand. And he stretched it out; and his hand was restored like the other.

11 But they were filled with bitterness, and discussed with each other what to do with Yahshua.

8:11 This is the parable: the seed is the word of the almighty God.

12 Those on the roadside are those who hear the word, and the enemy comes and takes away the word from their hearts, so that they may not believe and be saved.

13 Those on the rock are those who when they have heard, receive word with joy; and yet they have no root, but their belief is for a while, and in time of trial they stumble.

14 That which fell among the thistles are those who hear the word, and then choke themselves with worries and riches and worldly covetousness, and bear no fruit.

15 But that in good soil, these are those who hear the word with a pure and good heart, and keep it, and bear fruit with patience.

MATTHEW 10

16 Behold, I am sending you like lambs among wolves; therefore be wise as serpents and pure as doves.

19 But when they deliver you up, do not worry as to how or what you will speak; for it will be given to you in that very hour what you are to speak.

20 For it is not you who speak, but the Spirit of your Father, which speaks through you.

28 Do not be afraid of those who kill the body but who cannot kill the soul; but above all, be afraid of Him who can destroy both the soul and the body in hell.

32 Everyone therefore who will acknowledge me before men, I will also acknowledge him before my Father in heaven.

33 But whoever will deny me before men, I will also deny him before my Father in heaven.

34 Do not suppose that I have come to bring peace on earth; I have not come to bring peace but a division.

35 For I have come to set a man against his father and daughter against her mother and a daughter-in-law against her mother-in-law.

36 And a man's enemies will be the members of his own household.

37 Whoever loves father or mother more than me is not worthy of me; and whoever loves son or daughter more than me is not worthy of me.

MATTHEW 24

3 While Yahshua sat on the mount of Olives, his disciples…said to him, Tell us when these things will happen and what is the sign of your coming and of the end of the world?

4 Yahshua answered, saying to them, Be careful that no man deceives you.

5 For many will come in my name, and say, I am the Christ, and they will deceive many.

6 You are bound to hear of revolutions and rumors of wars; watch out and do not be disturbed; for all of these things must come to pass, but the end is not yet.

7 For nation will rise against nation, and kingdom against kingdom; and there will be famines and plagues and earthquakes in different places.

8 But all these things are just the beginning of travail.

9 Then they will deliver you over to be oppressed, and they will kill you; and you will be hated by all nations for my name's sake.

10 Then many will stumble, and they will hate one another and betray one another.

11 And many false prophets will rise and will mislead a great many.

12 And because of the growth of iniquity, the love of many will become cold.

13 But he who has endured to the end will be saved.

14 And this gospel of the kingdom shall be preached throughout the world as a testimony to all the nations; then the end will come.

21 For then there will be great suffering such as has never happened from the beginning of the world until now, and never will again.

22 And if those days were not shortened, no flesh would survive; but for the sake of the chosen ones, those days will be shortened.

23 Then if any man should say to you, Behold, here is the Christ, or there; do not believe it.

24 For there will rise false christs and lying prophets, and they will show signs and great wonders, so as to mislead, if possible, even the chosen ones.

27 For just as lightning comes out from the east, and is seen even in the west, so will be the coming of the Son of man.

29 Immediately after the tribulation of those days, the sun will be darkened and the moon will not give its light and the stars will fall from the sky and the powers of the universe will be shaken.

30 Then the sign of the Son of man will appear in the sky; and all the generations of the earth will mourn, and they will see the Son of man coming on the clouds of the sky with power and great glory.

31 And he will send his angels with a large trumpet, and they will gather his chosen ones from the four winds, from one end of the (1st?) heaven to the other.

MARK 12

30 And you must love the Lord your God with all your heart and with all your soul and with all your mind and with all your might; this is the first commandment.

MATTHEW 12

31 Therefore I say to you that all sins and blasphemies will be forgiven to men; but the blasphemy against the Holy Spirit shall not be forgiven to men.

32 And whoever speaks a word against the Son of man will be forgiven; but whoever speaks against the Holy Spirit shall not be forgiven, neither in this world nor in the world to come.

MATTHEW 15:

17 Do you not know that what enters into the mouth goes into the stomach, and thence, through the intestines, is cast out?

18 But what comes out of the mouth comes out from the heart; and that is what defiles a man.

19 For from the heart come out evil thoughts, such as fornication, murder, adultery, theft, false witness, blasphemy.

MATTHEW 19

9 But I say to you, Whoever leaves his wife without a charge of adultery and marries another commits adultery; and he who marries a woman thus separated commits adultery.

MARK 10

9 What therefore the almighty God has joined, let no man separate.

1ST CORINTHIANS 7

27 If you are married, do not seek divorce. If you are divorced from a wife, do not seek a wife.

MARK 10

10 And his disciples again asked him about this in the house.

11 And he said to them, Whoever divorces his wife and marries another commits adultery.

12 And if a woman divorces her husband and marries another, she commits adultery.

MATTHEW 22

30 For at the resurrection of the dead, men neither marry women, nor are women given in marriage, but they are like the angels of the

almighty God in heaven.

MARK 10

15 Truly I say to you, whoever does not receive the kingdom of the almighty God like a little child shall not enter it.

MARK 11

25 And if you stand up and pray, forgive whatever you have against any man, so that your Father in heaven will forgive you your offenses.

26 But if you will not forgive, even your Father in heaven will not forgive you your offenses.

MARK 9

17 One of the multitude answered, saying, Teacher, I brought my son to you, for he has a spirit of dumbness.

18 And whenever it seizes him, it troubles him; and he foams and gnashes his teeth and faints. And I asked your disciples to cast it out, but they could not.

25 he rebuked the unclean spirit and said to it, O deaf and dumb spirit, I command you, come out of him and do not enter him again.

26 And the epileptic cried out violently and was tortured, and the spirit went out; then the boy became as if dead, so that many said, He is dead.

27 Then Yahshua took him by the hand and lifted him up.

28 When Yahshua entered the house, his disciples asked him privately, Why could we not cast it out?

29 He said to them, This kind cannot be cast out by anything except by fasting and prayer.

MARK 5

25 And there was a woman who had had a hemorrhage for twelve years,

26 Who had suffered much at the hands of many doctors, and had spent everything she had and was not helped at all, but rather became worse.

27 When she heard about Yahshua, she came through the dense crowd from behind him, and touched his cloak;

28 For she said, If I can only touch his cloak, I shall live.

29 And immediately the hemorrhage was dried up; and she felt in her body that she was healed of her disease.

30 Yahshua instantly knew that some power had gone out of him; so he turned around to the people and said, Who touched my garments?

33 But the woman, frightened and trembling, because she knew what had happened to her, came and fell before him and told him the whole truth.

34 He said to her, my daughter, your faith has healed you; go in peace and be healed of your disease.

JOHN 11

14 Then Yahshua said to them plainly, Lazar is dead;

17 So Yahsha came to Bethany, and he found that Lazar had been four days in the tomb.

23 Yahshua said to her, your brother will rise up.

24 Martha said to him, I know he will rise up in the resurrection at the last day.

25 Yahshua said to her, I am the resurrection and the life; he who believes in me, even though he die, he shall live.

41 So they took away the stone (of the tomb). And Yahshua lifted his eyes upwards and said, O Father, I thank Thee for Thou hast heard me,

43 ...he cried with a loud voice, Lazar, come out.

44 And the dead man came out, his hands and feet bound with burial clothes, and his face bound with a burial napkin. Yahshua said to them, Loose him and let him go.

MATTHEW 23

8 (Yahshua said) But you should not be called Rabbi; for one is your master, and all you are brethren.

9 And call no one on earth, father, for one is your Father in heaven.

12 For whoever exalts himself shall be humbled; and whoever humbles himself shall be exalted.

MARK 12

41 And when Yahshua sat in front of the treasury, he watched how the people cast their alms into the treasury; and many rich men were casting in a great deal.

42 And there came a poor widow, and she cast in two coins, which are a few pennies.

43 And Yahshua called his disciples and said to them, Truly I say to you that this poor widow has cast into the treasury more than all the men who are casting;

44 For all of them cast in of their abundance; but she of her poverty cast everything she had, even all of her possessions.

MATTHEW 20

17 Now Yahshua was ready to go up to Jerusalem; and he took his twelve disciples apart on the road, and he said to them,

18 Behold, we are going up to Jerusalem, and the Son of man will be delivered to the high priests and the scribes, and they will condemn him to death.

19 And they will deliver him to the Gentiles and they will mock him and scourge him and crucify him; and on the third day he will rise up.

40 For as Jonah was in the whale's belly three days and three nights, so the Son of man will be in the heart of the earth three days and three nights. (the location of hell?)

(Perhaps, all the righteous who have died before Yahshua provided the way for sins to be forgiven, could not enter heaven so they were placed in hell but NOT in the fire. Perhaps, Yahshua taught them how to accept the sacrifice which Yahshua would provide so that when it is completed, those righteous will be able to enter heaven.)

LUKE 22

14 And when it was time, Yahshua came and sat down, and the twelve apostles with him.

15 And he said to them, I have greatly desired to eat this passover with you before I suffer;

16 For I say to you that henceforth I will not eat it until it is fulfilled in the kingdom of the almighty God.

17 And he took the cup and gave thanks and said, Take this and divide it among yourselves.

18 For I say to you, I will not drink of the fruit of the wine until the kingdom of the almighty God comes.

19 And he took bread and gave thanks and broke it, and gave it to them and said, This is my body, which is given for your sake; this do in remembrance of me.

20 And likewise also he took the cup, after they had eaten supper, and he said, This is the cup of the new covenant in my blood which is shed for you.

1st Corinthians 11

26 For whenever you eat this bread and drink this cup, you commemorate our Lord's death until his coming.

27 Therefore whosoever shall eat of the Lord's bread and drink of his cup unworthily shall be guilty of the blood and the body of the Lord.

28 For this reason, let a man examine himself and eat of this bread and drink of this cup.

29 For he who eats and drinks unworthily, eats and drinks to his condemnation; for he does not discern the Lord's body.

Mark 15:24 And when they had crucified him, they divided his clothes and cast lots on them, to see what each man should take.

25 It was the third hour when they crucified him.

Matthew 27

37 And they placed above his head in writing the reason for his death: THIS IS YAHSHUA THE KING OF THE JEWS.

Mark 15

27 And they crucified with him two bandits, one on his right and one on his left.

28 And the scripture was fulfilled which said, He was reckoned with the wicked.

LUKE 23

39 Now one of the malefactors (bandits) who were crucified with him blasphemed against him, saying, If you are the Christ, save yourself and save us also.

40 But the other rebuked him and said to him, Do you not fear even the almighty God, for you are also in the same judgment?

41 And ours is just, for we are paid as we deserve and as we have done; but he has done nothing wrong.

42 And he said to Yahshua, Remember me, my Lord, when you come in your kingdom.

43 Yahshua said to him, Truly I say to you today, you will be with me in Paradise.

(Because of "Mattityahu 40": "For as Jonah was in the whale's belly three days and three nights, so the Son of man will be in the heart of the earth three days and three nights." Luke 23:43 originally said: "... today, You will be with me in Paradise. NOT: "... ,Today you will be with me in Paradise.)

44 Now it was about the sixth hour, and darkness fell upon the whole earth, and lasted until the ninth hour.

MATTHEW 27

46 And about the ninth hour, Yahshua cried out with a loud voice and said, Eli, Eli, lemana shabakthani! (which means): My God, my God, for this I was spared!

JOHN 19

30 When Yahshua drank the vinegar, he said, It is fulfilled; and he bowed his head and gave up his spirit.

31 Now since it was Friday, the Jews said, Let not these bodies remain on their crosses because the Sabbath is dawning; for that Sabbath was a great Sabbath. So they besought Pilate to have the legs of those who were crucified broken, and to have their bodies lowered down.

33 But when they came to Yahshua, they saw that he was dead already, so they did not break his legs.

34 But on of the soldiers pierced his side with a spear, and immediately blood and water came out.

36 For these things happened that the scripture may be fulfilled, which said, Not even a bone shall be broken in him.

Matthew 27

51 And immediately and the curtains at the door of the temple were torn in two, from the top to the bottom; and the earth quaked and rocks split;

52 And tombs were opened; and the bodies of a great many saints who were sleeping in death rose up

53 And went out; and after this resurrection, they entered into the holy city and appeared to a great many.

54 When the centurion and those who were with him watching Yahshua, saw the earthquake and all that had happened, they were frightened, and they said, Truly this man was the Son of Lord Yahweh.

57 When it was evening, there was came a rich man of Ramtha, whose name was Yosef who was also a disciple of Yahshua.

58 He went to Pilate and asked for the body of Yahshua. And Pilate commanded that the body should be given to him.

59 So Yosef took the body, and wrapped in a shroud of fine linen,

60 And laid it in his own new tomb which was hewn in a rock; and they rolled a large stone, and placed it against the door of the tomb and went away.

MATTHEW 28

2 And behold, a great earthquake took place; for the angel of the Lord came down from heaven, and went up and rolled the stone away from the door, and sat on it.

3 His appearance was like lightning, and his garments were white as snow.

4 And for fear of him the guards who were watching trembled and became as if they were dead.

5 But the angel answered, saying to the women (Miryam of Magdala and the other Miryam), You need not be afraid; for I know that you are seeking Yahshua who was crucified.

6 He is not here, for he has risen, just as he had said. Come, see the place where our Lord was laid.

7 And go quickly and tell his disciples that he has risen from the dead; and behold, he will go to Galilee; there you will see him; lo, I have told you.

17 And when they (the disciples) saw him, they worshipped him; but some of them were doubtful.

18 And Yahshua came up and spoke with them, and he said to them, All power in heaven and on earth has been given to me. Just as my Father has sent me I am also sending you.

19 Go, therefore, and convert all nations; and baptize them in the name of the Father and of the Son and of the Holy Spirit;

20 And teach them to obey everything that I have commanded you; and, lo, I am with you always, to the end of the world. Amen.

JOHN 15

1 I (Yahshua) am the vine, and my Father is the laborer.

2 Every branch in me that does not bear fruit, He cuts off; and the one which bears fruit, He prunes so that it may bring forth more fruit.

5 I am the vine, you are the branches. He who remains with me, and I with him, will bear abundant fruit; for without me you can do nothing.

3 You have already been pruned because of the word which I have spoken to you.

4 Remain with me and I with you. Just as a branch cannot give fruit by itself unless it remains in the vine, even so you cannot unless you remain with me.

6 Unless a man remains with me, he will be cast outside like a branch which is withered, which they pick up and throw into the fire to be burned.

8 In this the Father will be glorified, that you bear fruit and be my disciples.

9 If you keep my commandments, you will abide in my love, even as I have kept my Father's commandments and abide in his love.

MARK 16

19 Then our Lord Yahshua, after he had spoken to them, ascended to heaven and sat on the right hand of the almighty God, Lord Yahweh.

20 And they went out and preached in every place; and our Lord helped them (by sending the Holy Spirit) and strengthened their words by the miracles which they performed.

The Acts of The Apostles

CHAPTER 1

The first book have I written, O Theophilus, concerning all the things which our Lord Yahshua The Christ began to do and teach,

2 Until the day when he ascended, after he, through the Holy Spirit, had given commandments to the apostles whom he had chosen,

3 The very ones to whom he had also shown himself alive, after he had suffered, with many wonders during the forty days, while appearing to them and talking with them concerning the kingdom of Yahweh;

4 And as he ate bread with them, he commanded them not to depart from Jerusalem but to wait for the promise of the Father, the one of whom you have heard from me.

5 For, Yochanan baptized with water; but you shall be baptized with the Holy Spirit not many days hence.

6 While they were assembled, they asked him, saying, Our Lord, will you at this time restore the kingdom to Israel?

7 He said to them, It is not for you to know the time or times which the Father has put under his own authority;

8 But when the Holy Spirit comes upon you, you shall receive power and you shall be witnesses to me both in Jerusalem and in all Judea also in the province of Samaria and to the uttermost part of the earth.

9 And when he had spoken these things. he ascended while they were looking at him; a cloud received him and he was hidden from their sight.

10 And while they looked steadfastly toward heaven as he went up, behold to men stood by them in white robes;

11 And they said to them, Men of Galilee, why do you stand gazing up into heaven? This same Yahshua who has ascended from you into heaven shall so come in like manner as you have seen him ascend into heaven.

12 Then they returned to Jerusalem from the mount which is called Olivet, Place of Olives, which is near to Jerusalem, about a mile away.

13 And after they had entered into the city, they went into an upper room, where stayed Kefa and Yochanan and Ya'akov and Andrew, and also Philip and T'oma (Thomas) and Mattityahu and Bar-Talmai (Bartholomew) and Ya'akov the son of Alphaeus and Shim'on (Simon) the Zealot and Y'hudah (Judah) the son of Ya'akov.

14 These all continued together in prayer with one accord, also the women, and Miryam the mother of Yahshua, and his brothers.

15 And in those days Shim'on Kefa (Simon Peter) stood up in the midst of the disciples {the number of men together were about a hundred and twenty}, and said,

16 Men and brethren, it was proper that the scripture should be fulfilled, that which the Holy Spirit foretold by the mouth of David concerning Y'hudah, who was guide to them that seized Yahshua.

17 For he was numbered with us and had a vote in this ministry.

18 He is the one who earned for himself a field with the price of sin; and falling headlong, he burst open in the midst and all his bowels gushed out.

19 And this very thing is known to all who dwell in Jerusalem; so that the field is called in the language of the country, Khakal-Dema which is to say Koriath-dem, the field of blood.

20 For it is written in the book of Psalms, Let his habitation be desolate, and let no one dwell in it; and let his ministry be taken by another man.

21 It is necessary, therefore, that one of these men, who have been with us during all the time that our Lord Yahshua went in and out among us,

22 Beginning from the baptism of Yochanan until the day he ascended from among us, became a partner with us as a witness of his resurrection.

23 So they appointed two: Yosef called Barshabas, who was surnamed Justus, and Mattityahu.

24 And as they prayed, they said, O Lord, Thou knowest what is in the hearts of all men; show which of these two Thou dost choose,

25 That he may receive the lot to the ministry and apostleship, from which Y'hudah has been relieved to go his own way.

26 Then they cast lots, and the lot fell upon Matthias; and he was numbered with the eleven apostles.

CHAPTER 2

And when the day of Pentecost was fulfilled, while they were assembled together,

2 Suddenly there came a sound from heaven as of a rushing mighty wind and it filled all the house where they were sitting.

3 And there appeared to them tongues which were divided like flames of fire; and they rested upon each of them.

4 And they were all filled with the Holy Spirit, and they began to speak in various languages, according to whatever the Spirit gave them to speak.

5 Now there dwelt at Jerusalem, devout men and Jews from every nation under heaven.

6 And as the sound took place, all the people gathered together, and they were confused because every man heard them speak in his own language.

7 And they were all amazed and marveled, saying one to another, Behold, are not all these who speak, Galileans?

8 How is it that we hear every man in our own native language?

9 Parthians and Medes and Elamites and those who dwell in Mesopotamia, Jews and Cappadocians and those from Pontus and Asia Minor,

10 And those from the region of Phrygia and of Pamphylia and of Egypt, and of the regions of Lybia near Cyrene, and those who have come from Rome, both Jews and Proselytes,

11 And those from Crete, and Arabians, behold we hear them speak in our own tongues of the wonderful works of Lord Yahweh.

12 And they were all amazed and stunned, saying one to another, What does this mean?

13 Others mocking said, These men are full of new wine.

14 And afterwards, Shim'on Kefa stood up together with the eleven disciples, and lifted up his voice and said to them, Men of Jewish race, and all that dwell at Jerusalem, let this be known to you, and harken to my words;

15 For these men are not drunken as you suppose, for behold it is but the third hour of the day.

16 But this is that which was spoken by the prophet Yo'el (Joel):

17 It shall come to pass in the last days, said Lord Yahweh, I will pour my Spirit upon all flesh; and your sons and your daughters shall prophesy, and your young men shall see visions, and your old men shall dream dreams;

18 And upon my manservants, and upon my maidservants will I pour out my Spirit in those days; and they shall prophesy;

19 And I will show wonders in heaven and signs on the earth: blood and fire and vapor of smoke:

20 The sun shall be changed into darkness and the moon into blood, before that great and fearful day of the Lord shall come.

(ALSO) Mattityahu **24:29** ...and the stars will fall from the sky and the powers of the universe will be shaken.

21 And it shall come to pass that whoever shall call on the name of Lord Yahshua shall be saved.

22 Men of Israel, hear these words: Yahshua of Nazareth, The Son of Lord Yahweh, who appeared among you by miracles and signs and wonders which Lord Yahweh did by him among you, as you yourselves know,

23 The very one who was chosen for this purpose from the very beginning of knowledge and will of Lord Yahweh, you have delivered into the hands of wicked men, and you have crucified and murdered him;

24 Whom Lord Yahweh has raised up, having destroyed the pains of death, because it was not possible sheol to hold him.

36 Therefore let all the house of Israel know assuredly that Lord Yahweh has made this same Yahshua, whom you have crucified, both Lord and Christ.

37 When they heard these things, their hearts were touched and they said to Shim'on and the rest of the apostles, Our brethren, what shall we do?

38 Then Shim'on said to them, Repent and be baptized, every one of you in the name of the Lord Yahshua for the remission of sins, so that you may receive the gift of the Holy Spirit.

39 For the promise was made to you and to your children, and for all of those who are far off, even as many as the Lord Yahweh shall call.

40 And he testified to them with many other words and besought them, saying, Save yourselves from this sinful generation.

41 And those men among them who readily accepted his word and believed were baptized, and about three thousand souls were added in that day.

42 And they continued steadfastly in the teaching of the apostles, and they took part in prayer and in the breaking of bread.

43 And fear came upon every soul; and many miracles and wonders were done by the apostles in Jerusalem.

44 And all believers were together and had all things in common;

45 And those who had possessions sold them and divided to each man according to his need.

46 And they went to the temple every day with one accord; and at home they broke bread and received food with joy and with a pure heart,

47 Praising Lord Yahweh and finding favor with all the people. And our Lord daily increased the congregation of the church.

CHAPTER 3

It came to pass as Shim'on Kefa and Yochanan were going up together to the temple at the time of prayer, at the ninth hour,

2 Behold a certain man, lame from his mother's womb, was carried by men who were accustomed to bring him and lay him at the gate of the temple which is called Beautiful, so that he may ask alms from those who entered into the temple.

3 And when he saw Shim'on Kefa and Yochanan entering the temple, he begged of them to give him alms.

4 And Shim'on Kefa and Yochanan looked at him and said, Look at us.

5 And he looked at them, expecting to receive from them.

6 Then Shim'on Kefa said to him, Gold and silver have I none; but what I have I give to you. In the name of our Lord, Yahshua the Christ of Nazareth, rise up and walk.

7 And he took him by the right hand and lifted him up; and in that very hour, his legs and his feet received strength.

8 And he, leaping up, stood and walked, and entered with them into the temple, walking and leaping and praising Lord Yahweh.

9 And all the people saw him walking and praising Lord Yahweh;

10 And they recognized that he was the beggar who had sat daily and asked alms at the gate which is called Beautiful; and they were filled with amazement and wonder at what had happened.

11 And as he was assisted by Shim'on and Yochanan, all the people ran in astonishment towards them to the porch that is called Shlomo's.

12 And when Shim'on Kefa saw it, he said to them, Men of Israel, why are you wondering at this man or why are you looking at us as though by our own power or authority we had made this man to walk?

13 The God of Avraham and of Yitz'chak and of Ya'akov, the God of our fathers has glorified his Son Yahshua whom you delivered up and denied in the presence of Pilate when he was determined to let him go.

14 But you denied the Holy One and the Righteous and asked a murderer to be given to you,

15 And killed the Prince of Life, whom Lord Yahweh raised from the dead; all of us are his witnesses.

16 Faith in his name has healed this man whom you see and know, and made him strong; it is the faith in him which has granted this healing before you all.

17 But now, my brethren, I know that you did this through ignorance just as your leaders did it.

18 But those things which Lord Yahweh before had preached by the mouth of all the prophets that his Christ should suffer, he has so fulfilled.

19 Repent, therefore, and be converted, that your sins be blotted out when the times of tranquillity shall come to you from before the presence of the Lord;

20 And he shall send to you one who has been prepared for you, Yahshua the Christ,

21 Whom heaven must receive until all the things which Lord Yahweh has spoken by the mouth of his holy prophets since the world began should be fulfilled.

22 For Moshe (Moses) said, The Lord shall raise up a prophet like me for you from among your brethren; listen to him in all that he shall say to you.

23 And it shall come to pass that every person who will not listen to that prophet shall be lost from his people.

24 Yea, and all the prophets from Sh'mu'el (Samuel) and those that follow after as many as have spoken and preached, have likewise foretold of these days.

25 You are the children of the prophets and of the covenant which Lord Yahweh made with our fathers, saying to Avraham, By your seed shall all the kindred of the earth be blessed.

26 Now it was for you first, Lord Yahweh appointed and sent his Son to bless you if you turn and repent from your evils.

CHAPTER 4

And while they were speaking these words to the people, the priests and the Sadducees and the leaders of the temple rose up against them,

2 Being infuriated that they taught the people and preached through Yahshua the resurrection from the dead.

3 And they arrested them and detained them until the next day, for it was now eventide.

4 Howbeit many of them who heard the word believed; and the number of the men was about five thousand.

5 And the next day, the leaders and the elders and the scribes gathered together;

6 And also Annas the high priest, and Caiaphas and Yochanan and Alexander and those who were of the family of the high priest.

7 And when they had madethem to stand in the midst, they asked, By what power or by what name have you done this?

8 Then Shim'on Kefa, filled with the Holy Spirit, said to them, Leaders of the people and elders of the house of Israel, listen:

9 If we are convicted today by you, concerning the good which has been done to a sick man, on the ground of by what means he was healed;

10 Then let it be known to you and to all the people of Israel, By the name of Yahshua the Christ of Nazareth, whom you crucified, and whom Lord Yahweh raised from the dead, behold this man stands before you, healed.

11 This is the stone which you builders have rejected, which is become the corner-stone.

12 There is no salvation by any other man; for there is no other name under heaven given among men whereby we must be saved.

13 Now when they had heard the speech of Shim'on Kefa and Yochanan, which they had spoken boldly, and perceived that they were unlearned and ignorant men, they marveled; and they recognized them that they had been with Yahshua.

14 And because they saw the lame man who was healed standing with them they could say nothing against them.

15 But when they had commanded them to be taken aside out of the council, they conferred among themselves,

16 Saying, what shall we do to these men? For behold a miracle has openly been performed by them and it is known to all that dwell in Jerusalem; and we cannot deny it.

17 But, so that this news should not spread further among the people, let us threaten them, that they speak henceforth to no man in this name.

18 And they called them, and commanded them not to speak at all nor teach in the name of Yahshua.

19 But Shim'on Kefa and Yochanan answered, saying to them, Whether it be right before Lord Yahweh to listen to you more than to Lord Yahweh, you judge.

20 For we cannot stop speaking about the things which we have seen and heard.

21 So when they had further threatened them, they let them go; for they found no cause to punish them because of the people; for all men praised Lord Yahweh for that which was done.

22 For the man on whom this miracle of healing had been wrought was more than forty years old.

23 After they were released, they went to their brethren and told them all that the high priests and elders had said.

24 And when they heard this, they all together lifted up their voices to Lord Yahweh and said, O Lord, Thou art the God who hast made heaven and earth and the seas and all that is in them;

25 Thou art the One who spoke through the Holy Spirit by the mouth of thy servant David when he said, Why do the people rage and the nations devise worthless things?

26 The kings and the rulers of the earth have revolted and have taken counsel together against the Lord and against his anointed.

27 For truly, they assembled in this very city, together with both Herod and Pilate and with the Gentiles and with the people of Israel, against your holy Son Yahshua,

28 To execute whatever thy hand and thy will had previously decreed to take place.

29 And even now, O Lord, look and see their threatenings; and grant to thy servants that they may freely preach thy word,

30 Just as thy hand is freely stretched out for healing and wonders and thy miracles which are done in the name of thy holy Son Yahshua.

31 And when they had petitioned and made their supplications, the place in which they were assembled together was shaken, and they were all filled with the Holy Spirit and they spoke the word of Lord Yahweh boldly.

32 Now the congregation of the believers were of one soul and of one mind; not one of them spoke of the property he possessed as his own; but everything they had was in common.

33 And the Apostles testified with great power concerning the resurrection of Yahshua the Christ; and they were all greatly favored.

34 There was not a man among them who was destitute; for those who possessed houses, sold them and brought the money for the things that were sold,

35 And placed them at the disposal of the disciples; and the proceeds were then given to every man according to his needs.

36 Now Yosef whom the apostles surnamed Bar-Nabba (Barnabas) {which is, interpreted, the son of consolation}, a Levite of the country of Cyprus,

37 Had a field and he sold it and brought the money and placed it at the disposal of the apostles.

CHAPTER 5

But a certain man called Ananias, together with his wife named Shapphira, sold his field.

2 And he took some of the money and hid it, and his wife also knew of it, and he brought some of the money and placed it at the disposal of the apostles.

3 And Shim'on Kefa said to him, Ananias, why has Satan so filled your heart that you should lie to the Holy Spirit and hide part of the money of the price of the field?

4 Was it not your own before you sold it? And after it was sold, had you not the sole authority over its money? What made you think to do this thing? You have not only lied to men but to Lord Yahweh.

5 And when Ananias heard these words, he fell down and died; and great fear came upon all of those who heard these things.

6 The younger men among them arose and moved his body aside. Then they took him out and buried him.

7 Three hours later his wife also came in, not knowing what had happened.

8 Shim'on Kefa said to her, Tell me if you sold the field for this price? She said, Yes, for this price.

9 Then Shim'on Kefa said to her, Because you have been partners to tempt the Spirit of the Lord, behold the feet of the men who have buried your husband are at the door, and they shall carry you out also.

10 And in that very hour she fell down at their feet and died, and the young men came in and found her dead, and they picked her up and carried her away and buried her by the side of her husband.

11 And great fear came upon all the congregation and upon all who heard what had happened.

12 Many miracles and signs were wrought among the people by the apostles, and they were all gathered together in the portico of Shlomo.

13 And none of the unbelievers dared to interfere with them, but the people held them in respect.

14 And the number of those who believed in the Lord was greatly increased by multitudes both of men and women.

15 They even brought out the sick into the streets and laid them on quilts so that when Shim'on Kefa should happen to pass by, his shadow might fall upon them.

16 Many came to them from other cities around Jerusalem, bringing the sick and mentally afflicted, and they were all healed.

17 Then the high priest was filled with jealousy and all of those who were with him, for they were adherents to the teachings of the Sadducees,

18 So they laid hands on the apostles and arrested them and bound them in prison.

19 But during the night, the angel of the Lord opened the door of the prison and brought them forth and said to them,

20 Go, stand in the temple and speak to the people all these words of life.

21 Accordingly they went out early in the morning and entered into the temple and taught the people. But the high priest and those who were with him called their associates and the elders of Israel, and sent to the prison to bring the apostles.

22 And when those who were sent by them went and did not find them in the prison, they returned,

23 Saying, We found the prison carefully locked and also the guards standing at the doors; and we opened them but found no man there.

24 When the high priest and the leaders of the temple heard these words, they were astonished at them and they were reasoning how it could happen.

25 When a man came and informed them, behold! The men whom you put in prison are standing in the temple and teaching the people.

26 Then the leaders went with the soldiers to bring them, not by force, for they were afraid that the people might stone them.

27 And when they had brought them, they made them stand before the whole council, and the high priest proceeded,

28 Saying, Did we not strictly command you not to teach any man in this name? And behold, you have filled Jerusalem with your doctrine, and you intend to bring the blood of this man upon us.

29 Then Shim'on Kefa with the rest of the apostles answered, saying to them, We must obey Lord Yahweh rather than men.

30 The God of our fathers has raised up Yahshua whom you murdered when you nailed him on the cross.

31 This very one Lord Yahweh has appointed a Prince and a Saviour, and has lifted him up by his right hand so that he may grant repentance and forgiveness of sins to Israel.

32 And we are the witnesses of these words; so is also the Holy Spirit whom Lord Yahweh has given to those who believe in him.

33 When they heard these words, they were enraged and thought to murder the apostles.

34 Then one of the Pharisees whose name was Gamaliel, a teacher of the law and honored by all the people, rose up and ordered them to take the apostles outside for a little while;

38 So now I tell you, Keep away from these men and let them alone; for if this thought and this work is of men, it will fail and pass away.

39 But if it be of Lord Yahweh, you cannot suppress it, lest perchance you find yourself standing in opposition to Lord Yahweh.

40 And they listened to him, and they called the apostles and scourged them, and commanded them not to speak in the name of Yahshua, and let them go.

41 The apostles went out from the presence of the council, rejoicing that they had been worthy to suffer abuse for the sake of his name.

42 And they did not cease to teach daily in the temple and at home and to preach concerning our Lord Yahshua the Christ.

(Acts, chapters **6** and **7** are historical accounts with only a very small amount of theology which is much better explained in the preceding and later chapters)

CHAPTER 8

At that very time there was a severe persecution against The Church of Lord YHWH; and all, with the exception of the apostles, dispersed throughout the towns of Judea and Samaria.

5 Then Philip went down to a Samaritan city and preached to them about Yahshua the Christ.

6 And when the people of that place heard his word, they gave heed and listened attentively to everything Philip said, because they saw the miracles which he did.

7 Many who were mentally afflicted cried with loud voices and were restored; and others who were paralytic and lame were healed.

8 And there was great joy in that city.

9 Now there was a certain man called Shim'on, who had lived in that city for a long time, and who had deceived the Samaritan people by his magic, boasting of himself and saying, I am the greatest one.

10 And both the noblest and the least followed him saying, He is the greatest power of Lord Yahweh.

11 All of them listened to him, because for a long time he had bewitched them with his sorceries.

12 But when they believed Philip, preaching the things concerning the kingdom of Lord Yahweh in the name of our Lord Yahshua the Christ, they were baptized, both men and women.

13 Shim'on himself also believed and was baptized and attached himself to Philip, and as he saw the miracles and great signs performed by his hand, he marveled greatly.

14 Now when the apostles at Jerusalem heard that the Samaritan people had accepted the word of Lord Yahweh, they sent to them Shim'on Kefa and Yochanan,

15 Who, when they went down, prayed over them that they might receive the Holy Spirit.

16 For as yet it had not come upon them although they had been baptized in the name of our Lord Yahshua.

17 Then they laid their hands on them and they received the Holy Spirit.

18 And when Shim'on saw that the Holy Spirit was given by the laying on of the apostles' hands, he offered them money,

19 Saying, Give me also this authority so that on whomsoever I lay hands, he may receive the Holy Spirit.

20 Shim'on Kefa said to him, Let your money perish with you because you have thought that the gift of Lord Yahweh may be purchased with wealth.

21 You have no part nor lot in this faith because your heart is not right in the sight of Lord Yahweh.

22 Repent, therefore, of this evil of yours, and beseech Lord Yahweh that He may perhaps forgive you for the guile which is in your heart.

23 For I see your heart is as bitter as gall and you are in the bonds of iniquity.

24 Then Shim'on answered, saying, Pray to Lord Yahweh for me so that none of these things which you have spoken may come upon me.

25 Now when Shim'on Kefa and Yochanan had testified and taught them the word of Lord Yahweh, they returned to Jerusalem after they had preached in many Samaritan villages.

26 And the angel of the Lord spoke to Philip, saying, Arise and go south by way of the desert that leads down from Jerusalem to Gaza;

27 So he arose and went; and he was met by a eunuch, who had come from Ethiopia, an official of Candace, queen of the Ethiopians, who had the charge of all her treasure, and had come to worship at Jerusalem.

28 While he was returning, sitting in his chariot, he read the book of the prophet Yesha'yahu (Isaiah).

29 And the Spirit said to Philip, Go near and keep close to the chariot.

30 And as Philip drew near and heard him reading from the book of the prophet Yesha'yahu, he said to him, Do you understand what you are reading?

31 And the Ethiopian said, How can I understand unless someone teach me? and he invited Philip to come up and sit with him.

32 The portion of the scripture which he was reading was this: He was led like a lamb to the slaughter, and like a ewe lamb before the shearer, so he opened not his mouth.

33 In his humiliation, he suffered imprisonment and judgment; none can tell his struggle, for even his life is taken away from the earth.

34 And the eunuch said to Philip, I pray you, of whom does this prophet speak? of himself or of some other man?

35 Then Philip opened his mouth and began at that same scripture and preached to him concerning our Lord Yahshua.

36 And as they went on their way, they came to a place where there was water; and the eunuch said, Behold here is water; what prevents me from being baptized?

37 And Philip said, If you believe with all your heart, you may. And he answered, saying, I believe that Yahshua the Christ is the Son of Lord Yahweh.

38 And he commanded the chariot be stopped; and both went down into the water, and Philip baptized the eunuch.

39 And when they came up from the water, the Spirit of the Lord caught Philip away and the eunuch saw him no more; and he went on his way rejoicing.

40 Philip was found at Azotus; and from there he traveled around and preached in all the cities till he came to Caesarea.

CHAPTER 9

Now Sha'ul was still filled with anger and with threats of murder against the disciples of our Lord,

2 And he asked the high priests to give him letters to the synagogues at Damascus, that if he should find anyone, man or woman, following this faith he might bring them bound to Jerusalem.

3 And as he journeyed, he came near Damascus; and suddenly a light from the sky shone round about him;

4 And he fell to the ground and heard a voice saying to him, Sha'ul, Sha'ul, why do you persecute me? You make it hard for yourself by kicking against the pricks.

5 Sha'ul answered, saying, Who are you my Lord? And our Lord said, I am Yahshua of Nazareth whom you persecute;

6 Arise and go into the city, and there you will be told what you must do.

7 And the men who journeyed with him stood speechless, hearing only a voice, but seeing no man.

8 And Sha'ul arose from the ground, but he could not see even though his eyes were open; and they led him by the hand and brought him into Damascus.

9 And he was unable to see for three days, during which he neither ate nor drank.

10 Now there was in Damascus a disciple named Ananias, and the Lord said to him in a vision, Ananias. And he said, Behold, I am here, my Lord.

11 And our Lord said to him, Arise, and go into the street which is called Straight, and inquire at the house of Y'hudah for Sha'ul of the city of Tarsus; for behold, he is praying,

12 And he has seen in a vision, a man named Ananias coming in and laying his hand on him to restore his sight.

13 Then Ananias said, My Lord, I have heard from many concerning this man, how much misery he has brought to your saints in Jerusalem.

14 And behold here also he has authority from the high priests to bind all who call on your name.

15 But the Lord said to him, Arise and go; he is the agent whom I have chosen for myself to carry my name to the Gentiles and kings and the children of Israel;

16 For I will show him how great, things he must suffer for my name's sake.

17 Then Ananias went to him at the house, and laying his hands on him, said, Sha'ul, my brother, our Lord Yahshua who appeared to you on the way when you were coming, has sent me that you may receive your sight and be filled with the Holy Spirit.

18 And in that hour, there fell from his eyes something like scales; and his eyesight was restored, and he arose and was baptized.

19 And when he had received food, he was strengthened, and he remained several days with the disciples in Damascus.

20 From that time on, he preached in the Jewish synagogues concerning Yahshua, that he is the Son of Lord Yahweh.

21 But all those who heard him were amazed and said, Is this not he who persecuted those who called on his name in Jerusalem, and behold, he was sent here for that very purpose that he may bring them bound to the high priests?

22 But Sha'ul became more powerful, and he made the Jews who dwelt in Damascus tremble when he proved that Yahshua is the Christ.

23 After he had been there many days, the Jews plotted against him to kill him.

24 But their conspiracy was made known to Sha'ul, how they watched the gates of the city day and night to kill him.

25 Then the disciples placed him in a basket and let him down over the wall during the night.

26 Then Sha'ul went to Jerusalem, and wanted to join the disciples, but they were all afraid of him, and could not believe that he was a convert.

27 But Bar-Nabba took him and brought him to the apostles, and told them how he had seen the Lord on the way and how he had spoken to him, and how in Damascus he had spoken openly in the name of Yahshua.

28 So he went in and out with them at Jerusalem.

29 And he spoke openly in the name of Yahshua, and debated with the Jews who understood Greek; but they wanted to kill him.

30 And when the brethren knew it, they brought him by night to Caesarea, and from thence they sent him to Tarsus.

31 Then the church throughout Judea and Galilee and Samaria was at peace, and strengthened itself and developed obedience and reverence to Lord Yahweh, and by the consolation of the Holy Spirit it increased in numbers.

32 And it came to pass while Shim'on Kefa traveled to various cities, he came down also to the saints who dwelt at the city of Lydda.

33 And there he found a man named AEneas, who had been paralyzed and had lain in bed eight years.

34 And Shim'on Kefa said to him, AEneas, Yahshua the Christ heals you. Arise, and make your bed. And he arose immediately.

35 And all who dwelt at Lydda and Sharon saw him and turned to Lord Yahweh.

36 Now there was in the city of Joppa, a woman disciple called Tabitha which means gazelle; she was rich in good works and in charitable acts.

37 And it came to pass in those days that she fell sick, and died; they bathed her body and laid it in an upper room.

38 And the disciples heard that Shim'on Kefa was in the city of Lydda, which is beside Joppa; they sent to him two men, desiring him to come to them without delay.

39 Then Shim'on Kefa arose and went with them. And when he had arrived, they took him to the upper room where all the widows were gathered around him weeping and they showed him shirts and cloaks which Tabitha had given them when she was alive.

40 But Shim'on Kefa put all the people out and knelt down and prayed; then he turned to the body and said, Tabitha, arise. And she opened her eyes, and when she saw Shim'on Kefa, she sat up.

41 And he gave her his hand and lifted her up; then he called the saints and widows, and presented her to them alive.

42 And this was known throughout the city and many believed in our Lord.

43 And he remained in Joppa many days, staying at the house of Shim'on the tanner.

CHAPTER 10

There was in Caesarea a man called Cornelius, a centurion of the regiment which is called the Italian,

2 A man righteous and God-fearing, as were all his household; who gave alms to the people abundantly, and always sought after Lord Yahweh.

3 Very openly in a vision about three o'clock in the afternoon, he saw an angel of Lord Yahweh who came in to him, and said to him, Cornelius.

4 And he looked at the angel and was afraid, and he said, What is it, my lord? And the angel said to him, Your prayers and your alms have come up for a memorial before Lord Yahweh.

5 And now send men to the city of Joppa and bring here Shim'on who is called Kefa:

6 Behold he is staying with Shim'on the tanner, whose house is by the seaside.

7 And when the angel who spoke to him had departed, Cornelius called two of his household and a soldier who believed in Lord Yahweh and was obedient to Him.

8 And he related to them everything that he had seen, and sent them to Joppa.

9 The next day, while they were on their journey, drawing near to the city, Shim'on Kefa went up upon the housetop to pray about noontime.

10 And he became hungry, and wanted to eat; but while they were preparing food for him, he fell into a trance.

11 And he saw the heaven open and something fastened at the four corners, resembling a large linen cloth, was let down from heaven to the earth;

12 And there were in it all kinds of four-footed beasts and creeping things of the earth and birds of the air.

13 And there came a voice to him, saying, Shim'on Kefa, rise; kill and eat.

14 But Shim'on Kefa said, Far be it, my lord; for I have never eaten anything which was unclean and defiled.

15 And again the voice came to him a second time, What Lord Yahweh has cleansed, you should not call unclean.

16 This happened the third time; then the cloth was lifted up to the heaven.

17 Now while Shim'on Kefa was bewildered, wondering in himself what the vision he had seen should mean, the men who were sent by Cornelius arrived, and inquired for the house in which Shim'on Kefa had been staying, and they came and stood of the door of the courtyard.

18 And from there they called and asked if Shim'on who is called Kefa stayed there.

19 While Shim'on Kefa meditated about the vision, the Spirit said to him, Behold, three men seek you.

20 Arise, go down and go with them, without doubt in your mind; for I have sent them.

21 Then Shim'on Kefa went down to the men and said, I am the man you seek. What is the purpose of your mission?

22 They said to him, A man called Cornelius, a righteous and God-fearing centurion of whom all the Jewish people speak well, was told in a vision by a holy angel to send and bring you to his house and to hear words from you.

23 So Shim'on Kefa brought them into the place where he was staying and welcomed them. The next day he arose and went with them, and a few men from amongst the brethren of Joppa accompanied him.

24 And the next day they entered Caesarea. And Cornelius was waiting for them, and all his relatives and also his dear friends were assembled with him.

25 And just as Shim'on Kefa was entering, Cornelius met him and threw himself at his feet and worshipped him.

26 But Shim'on Kefa raised him, saying, Stand up; I am but a man also.

27 And after he had talked with him, he went in and found a great many people had come there.

28 So he said to them, You know well that it is unlawful for a Jew to associate with a stranger who is not of his tribe; but Lord Yahweh has showed me that I should not call any man common or unclean.

29 This is why I came at once when you sent for me; but now let me ask you, for what reason have you sent for me?

30 Then Cornelius said to him, Four days I have been fasting; and at three o'clock in the afternoon while I was praying in my house, a man dressed in white garments stood before me,

31 And said to me, Cornelius your prayer has been heard, and your alms are a memorial before Lord Yahweh.

32 But send to the city of Joppa and bring Shim'on, who is called Kefa; behold he is staying in the house of Shim'on the tanner, by the seaside; and he will come and talk with you.

33 At that very time I sent for you, and you have done well to come. Behold we are all here present before you, and we wish to hear everything commanded you from Lord Yahweh.

34 Then Shim'on Kefa opened his mouth and said, Of a truth I perceive that Lord Yahweh is not partial;

35 But among all people, he who fears Him and works righteousness is accepted with Him.

36 For Lord Yahweh sent the word to the children of Israel, preaching peace and tranquility by Yahshua the Christ; he is the Lord of all.

37 And you also are familiar with the news which was published throughout Judea, which sprang from Galilee, after the baptism preached by Yochanan,

38 Concerning Yahshua of Nazareth, whom Lord Yahweh anointed with the Holy Spirit and with power, and who, because Lord Yahweh was with him, went about doing good and healing all who were oppressed by the devil.

39 And we are witnesses of all things which he did throughout the land of Judea and in Jerusalem. This very one the Jews nailed on a cross and killed him;

40 Him, Lord Yahweh raised on the third day and made him seen openly;

41 Not to all the people, but to us who have been chosen by Lord Yahweh to be his witnesses, for we did eat and drink with him after his resurrection from the dead.

42 And he commanded us to preach to the people and to testify that it is he who was ordained by Lord Yahweh to be the judge of the living and of the dead.

43 Of him all the prophets testified that whosoever believes in his name shall receive remission of sins.

44 While Shim'on Kefa spoke these words, the Holy Spirit descended on all who heard the word.

45 And the Jewish converts who had come with him were seized with amazement because the gift of the Holy Spirit was poured out on the Gentiles also;

46 For they heard them speak with different tongues, and magnify Lord Yahweh.

47 Then Shim'on Kefa said to them, Can any man forbid water, that these people who have received the Holy Spirit, just as we have, should not be baptized?

48 And he commanded them to be baptized in the name of our Lord Yahshua the Christ. And they urged him to remain with them a few days.

CHAPTER 11

And the apostles and the brethren who were in Judea heard that the Gentiles also had received the word of Lord Yahweh.

2 And when Shim'on Kefa had come up to Jerusalem, those who upheld the circumcision contended with him,

3 Saying he had entered into the houses of uncircumcised men and had eaten with them.

4 Then Shim'on began to recite the facts one after another, saying,

5 As I was praying in Joppa, I saw in a vision something like a linen cloth descending from heaven, and it was tied at its four corners; and it came even to me.

6 And as I looked at it, I saw that there were in it four-footed beasts and creeping things of the earth, and birds of the air.

7 Then I heard a voice saying to me, Shim'on, arise, kill and eat.

8 And I said, Far be it, my Lord; for I have never eaten anything which was unclean and defiled.

9 And again the voice from heaven said to me, What Lord Yahweh has cleansed, do not call unclean.

10 This happened three times; then everything was lifted up into the heaven.

11 And in that very hour, three men who were sent to me by Cornelius from Caesarea came and stood at the door of the courtyard where I was staying.

12 And the spirit said to me, Go with them, doubting nothing. And these six brethren accompanied me, and we entered the man's house.

13 And he related to us how he had seen an angel in his house, who stood and said to him, Send to the city of Joppa and bring Shim'on who is called Kefa;

14 And he shall speak to you words by which you and all of your household shall be saved.

15 And as I began to speak, the Holy Spirit came on them, as on us at the beginning.

16 Then I remembered that word of our Lord, when he said, Yochanan indeed baptized with water; but you shall be baptized with the Holy Spirit.

17 Now, therefore, if Lord Yahweh has equally given the gifts to the Gentiles who believe in our Lord Yahshua the Christ, just as he gave to us, who am I that I should dispute Lord Yahweh?

18 When they heard these words, they held their peace and glorified Lord Yahweh, saying, Perhaps Lord Yahweh has also granted to the Gentiles repentance to life.

19 Now those who had been dispersed by the persecution which occurred on account of Stephen traveled as far as Phoenicia and even to the land of Cyprus and to Antioch, preaching the word to none but to the Jews only.

20 But there were some men among them from Cyprus and from Cyrene; these men entered into Antioch and spoke to the Greeks and preached concerning our Lord Yahshua.

21 And the hand of the Lord was with them; and a great number believed, and turned to the Lord.

22 Then tidings of these things came to the attention of the members of the congregation at Jerusalem; and they sent Bar-Nabba to Antioch.

23 When he came there and saw the grace of Lord Yahweh, he was glad, and he pleaded with them that they should follow our Lord with all their hearts.

24 For he was a good man, and full of the Holy Spirit and of faith; and many people were added to our Lord.

25 Then Bar-Nabba departed to Tarsus to seek for Sha'ul.

26 And when he had found him, he brought him to Antioch. And for the whole year they assembled together in the church and taught a great many people. The disciples were called Christians first at Antioch and from that time on.

27 And in those days came prophets from Jerusalem to Antioch.

28 And one of them named Agabus stood up and foretold by the spirit that a great famine was to come throughout the land, the famine which occurred in the days of Claudius Caesar.

29 Then the disciples, each one according to his ability, determined to set something aside for relief to the brethren who dwelt in Judea.

30 This they did, and sent it there to the elders by the hands of Bar-Nabba and Sha'ul.

CHAPTER 12

Now at that very time, Herod the king, surnamed Agrippa, seized some of the people of the church to oppress them.

2 And he killed Ya'akov, the brother of Yochanan, with the sword.

3 And when he saw that this pleased the Jews, proceeded to arrest Shim'on Kefa also. This happened during the days of unleavened bread.

4 So he seized him and put him in prison and delivered him to the care of sixteen soldiers to keep him, so that he may deliver him to the Jewish people after the Passover.

5 And while Shim'on Kefa was kept in the prison, continual prayer was offered for him to Lord Yahweh by the church.

6 And on that very night before the morning that he was to be delivered up, while Shim'on Kefa was sleeping between two soldiers, bound with two chains, and others were guarding the doors of the prison.

7 The angel of the Lord stood over him, and a light shone in all the prison; and the angel touched him on the side and woke him, and said, Rise up quickly. And the chains fell off from his hands.

8 And the angel said to him, Bind on your girdle and put on your sandals. And so he did. And again he said to him, Put on your robe and follow me.

9 And he went out and followed the angel, not knowing that what was done by the angel was true, but thought he saw a vision.

10 When they had passed the first and the second guard, they came to the iron gate and it opened to them of its own accord; and when they had gone out and had passed one street, the angel departed from him.

11 And when Shim'on Kefa came to himself he said, Now I surely know that the Lord has sent his angel and has delivered me out of the hand of Herod, the king, and from all that the Jews were conspiring against me.

12 And when he understood, he went to the house of Miryam the mother of Yochanan, whose surname was Mark, because many brethren were gathered there praying.

13 When he knocked at the door of the courtyard, a little girl named Rhoda came out to answer.

14 And when she recognized Shim'on's voice, because of her joy she did not open the door to him, but ran back and said, Behold, Shim'on Kefa stands at the gate of the courtyard.

15 They said to her, You are excited. But she argued that it was so. Then said they, Perhaps it is his angel.

16 But Shim'on Kefa continued knocking at the door; and they went out and saw him, and were astonished.

17 But he mentioned to them with his hand to keep quiet; then he entered and related to them how the Lord had brought him out of the prison. And he said, Tell these things to Ya'akov and to our brethren. And he went out and departed for another place.

18 Now when it was morning, there was great tumult among the soldiers as to what had become of Shim'on Kefa.

19 When Herod had sought him and could not find him, he sentenced the guards and commanded that they should be put to death. And Shim'on Kefa left Judea and stayed at Caesarea.

20 Herod was angry with the people of Tyre and Sidon, but they assembled together and came to him, and they appealed to Blastus, the king's chamberlain, and asked him that they may have peace, because their country was dependent upon the kingdom of Herod for food supplies.

21 Upon the set day Herod, arrayed in royal apparel, sat upon the throne and addressed the assembly.

22 And all the people shouted, saying, This sounds like the voice of Lord Yahweh speaking and not that of a man.

23 And because he did not give the glory to Lord Yahweh, in that very hour an angel of the Lord smote him, and he was eaten by disease and died.

24 But the gospel of Lord Yahweh continued to be preached and to reach many.

25 Bar-Nabba and Sha'ul, after they had fulfilled their ministry, returned from Jerusalem to Antioch, and took with them Yochanan whose surname was Mark.

CHAPTER 13

Now there were in the church at Antioch prophets and teachers: Bar-Nabba and Shim'on who was called Carpenter and Lucius from the city of Cyrene and Manael, who was the son of the man who brought up Herod the tetrarch, and Sha'ul.

2 As they fasted and prayed to Lord Yahweh, the Holy Spirit said to them, Appoint for me Sha'ul and Bar-Nabba for the work to which I have called them.

3 So, after they had fasted and prayed and laid their hands on them, they sent them away.

4 Thus these two were sent forth by the Holy Spirit, and they went down to Seleucia; and from there they sailed to Cyprus.

5 And when they had entered the city of Salamis, they preached the word of our Lord in the synagogues of the Jews; and Yochanan ministered to them.

6 And when they had traveled the whole island as far as the city of Paphos, they found a Jewish sorcerer, who was a false prophet and whose name was Bar-Shuma;

7 Who was a close friend to a wise man, the proconsul whose name was Sergius Paulus, who called for Sha'ul and Bar-Nabba and desired to hear from them the word of Lord Yahweh.

8 But Bar-Shuma the sorcerer {whose name is interpreted Elymas} withstood them, seeking to turn away the proconsul from the faith.

9 Then Sha'ul, who is called Saul, filled with the Holy Spirit, looked at him,

10 And said, O man full of every kind of subtlety and of all evil things, son of the devil and enemy of all righteousness, will you not cease to pervert the right ways of the Lord?

11 And now the hand of the Lord is against you, and you shall be blind and shall not see the sun for a time. And in that very hour, there fell on him a mist and darkness; and he went about seeking someone to lead him by the hand.

12 And when the proconsul saw what had happened, he was amazed and believed the teaching of the Lord.

13 Then Sha'ul and Bar-Nabba sailed from the city of Paphos, and came to Perga, a city in Pamphylia; and Yochanan separated from them and went to Jerusalem.

14 But they left Perga and came to Antioch, a city in Pisidia, and on the Sabbath day they went into the synagogue and sat down.

15 And after the reading of the law and the prophets, the elders of the synagogue sent to them, saying, O men and brethren, if you have a word of encouragement for the people, speak.

16 So Sha'ul stood up, and lifting his hands said, O men of Israel and those of you who fear Lord Yahweh, hear my words:

17 The Lord of this people of Israel chose our forefathers and exalted and multiplied them when they dwelt as strangers in the land of Egypt, and with a strong arm He brought them out of it.

18 And He fed them in the wilderness for forty years.

19 And He destroyed seven nations in the land of Canaan, and He gave them their land for an inheritance.

20 And for a period of four hundred and fifty years, He gave them judges until the time of the prophet Sh'mu'el.

21 Then they asked for a king, and Lord Yahweh gave them Sha'ul the son of Kish, a man of the tribe of Binyamin, for a period of forty years.

22 And when Lord Yahweh took Sha'ul away he raised up to them David to be their king, concerning whom he testified, saying, I have found David, the son of Yishai, a man after my own heart, to do my will.

23 Of this man's offspring Lord Yahweh has, according to his promise, raised to Israel the Saviour, Lord Yahshua,

24 Before whose coming, He had sent Yochanan to preach the baptism of repentance to all the people of Israel.

25 And as Yochanan fulfilled his ministry, he said, Who do you think I am? I am not he. But behold there comes one after me, the strings of whose shoes I am not worthy to untie.

26 O men and brethren, descendants of the family of Avraham, and whosoever reveres Lord Yahweh, to you is the word salvation sent.

27 For inasmuch as the inhabitants of Jerusalem and their leaders did not understand him nor the books of the prophets which are read every Sabbath day, they condemned him; but all the things which were written have been fulfilled.

28 And though they found no cause for his death, they asked Pilate that they may kill him.

29 And when they had fulfilled all that was written of him, they lowered him from the cross and laid him in a sepulchre.

30 But Lord Yahweh raised him from the dead;

31 And for many days he was seen by them who had come up with him from Galilee to Jerusalem, and they are now his witnesses to the people.

32 And behold we also preach to you that the very promise which was made by our fathers,

33 Behold Lord Yahweh has fulfilled it to us their children, for He has raised up Yahshua, just as it is written in the second psalm, You are my Son; this day I have begotten you.

34 And Lord Yahweh raised him from the dead, no more to return to corruption, as he said, I will give you the sure mercies of David.

35 And again he said in another place, You shall not suffer your Holy One to see corruption.

36 For David, after he had served his own generation according to the will of Lord Yahweh, died; though he was a greater man than his fathers, yet he saw corruption.

37 But he whom Lord Yahweh raised, did not see corruption.

38 Be it known to you, therefore, brethren, that through this very one is preached to you the forgiveness of sins:

39 And by him all that believe are justified by the law of Moshe.

40 Beware, therefore, lest that which is written in the prophets may come upon you.

41 Be careful, O you despisers, for you shall wonder and perish; for I will do a great work in your day which you will not believe even if a man tell it to you.

42 And as Sha'ul and Bar-Nabba were leaving them, the people besought them to speak these things to them the next Sabbath.

43 Now when the congregation was dismissed, a great many Jews, and also proselytes who feared Lord Yahweh, followed Sha'ul and Bar-Nabba, who, speaking to them, persuaded them to continue in the grace of Lord Yahweh.

44 And the next Sabbath day, the whole city gathered to hear the word of Lord Yahweh.

45 But when the Jews saw the great crowd, they were filled with envy, and they bitterly opposed the words of Sha'ul, and they blasphemed.

46 Then Sha'ul and Bar-Nabba said to them boldly, It was necessary that the word of Lord Yahweh should first be spoken to you; but because you reject it, you have decided against yourselves and you are unworthy of everlasting life, so behold, we turn to the Gentiles.

47 For so has our Lord commanded us, as it is written, I have set you to be a light to the Gentiles, that you should be for salvation to the ends of the earth.

48 And when the Gentiles heard this, they were glad and glorified Lord Yahweh; and as many as were ordained to eternal life believed.

49 And the word of the Lord was published throughout all that region.

50 But the Jews incited the chief men of the city and the rich women who worshipped Lord Yahweh with them, and they stirred up a persecution against Sha'ul and Bar-Nabba, and expelled them beyond their borders.

51 And as they went out, they shook off the dust of their feet against them, and they came to the city of Iconium.

52 And the disciples were filled with joy and with the Holy Spirit.

CHAPTER 14

And Sha'ul and Bar-Nabba entered into the Jewish synagogue and addressed the people in such manner, that a great many of the Jews and of the Greeks believed.

2 But the Jews who would not listen, stirred up the Gentiles to oppress the brethren.

3 So they remained there for a long time and spoke boldly concerning the Lord, which gave testimony to the word of his grace, and granted signs and wonders to be done by their hands.

4 But the people of the city were divided: part held with the Jews, and part followed the apostles.

5 And they were menaced by both the Gentiles and the Jews, and with their leaders who wanted to disgrace them and have them stoned.

6 And when they became aware of it, they departed and took refuge in Lystra and Derbe, cities of Lycaonia, and the villages nearby.

7 And there they preached the gospel.

8 And there dwelt in the city of Lystra, a cripple who had been lame from his mother's womb, who never had walked.

9 He heard Sha'ul speak; and when Sha'ul saw him and perceived that there was faith in him to be healed,

10 He said to him with a loud voice, I say to you, in the name of our Lord Yahshua the Christ, stand upright on your feet. And he leaped and walked.

11 And when the people saw what Sha'ul had done, they lifted their voices, saying in the language of the country, The gods have come down to us in the likeness of men.

12 So they called Bar-Nabba the chief of the gods; and Sha'ul they called Hermes, because he was the chief speaker.

13 Then the priest of Zeus, whose shrine was outside the city, brought oxen and garlands to the gate of the courtyard where they stayed, and he wanted to offer sacrifices to them.

14 When Bar-Nabba and Sha'ul heard of this, they tore their clothes and leaped to their feet and went out to the crowd, crying out,

15 And saying, Men, what are you doing? We also are ordinary human beings like you, who preach to you that you should turn from these useless things to the living God who made heaven and earth and the sea and all things that are therein,

16 Who in generations past, suffered all nations to walk in their own ways.

17 Nevertheless He did not leave Himself without testimony, in that He bestowed good on them from heaven and gave them rain and caused the fruits to grow in their seasons, and satisfied their hearts with food and gladness.

18 And even though they said these things, they had difficulty in restraining the people from offering sacrifice to them.

19 But there came certain Jews from Iconium and Antioch who stirred up the people against them, and they stoned Sha'ul and dragged him out of the city, supposing him to be dead.

20 Howbeit, as the disciples gathered around him, he rose up and entered again into the city; and the next day he departed from there with Bar-Nabba, and they came to the city of Derbe.

21 And when they had preached the gospel to the people of that city and had converted many, then they returned to the city of Lystra and to Iconium and Antioch,

22 Strengthening the souls of the converts and exhorting them to continue in the faith, and telling them that only through much tribulation, can we enter into the kingdom of Lord Yahweh.

23 And when they had ordained them elders in every church and had prayed with them with fasting, they commended them to our Lord, on whom they believe.

24 And after they had traveled through the country of Pisidia, they came to Pamphylia.

25 And when they had preached the word of the Lord in the city of Perga, they went down to Attalia;

26 And thence they sailed and came to Antioch, because from there they had been recommended to the grace of the Lord for the work which they fulfilled.

27 And as the whole congregation was gathered together, they related everything that Lord Yahweh had done them and how He had opened the door of faith to the Gentiles.

28 And there they remained a long time with the disciples.

CHAPTER 15

And certain men who had come down from Judea taught the brethren, Unless you are circumcised in accordance with the custom of the law, you cannot be saved.

2 And there was great dissension and controversy between them and Sha'ul and Bar-Nabba, and it reached such a point that it was necessary for

Sha'ul and Bar-Nabba, and others with them, to go up to Jerusalem to the apostles and elders concerning this question.

3 They were given an escort and sent on their way by the church, and they traveled through all Phoenicia and the territory of the Samaritans, declaring the conversion of the Gentiles; and they caused great joy to all the brethren.

4 On their arrival at Jerusalem, they were received by the church, and by the apostles and elders; and they reported everything that Lord Yahweh had done with them.

5 But some of the men who had been converted from the sect of the Pharisees rose up and said, You must circumcise them and command them to keep the law of Moshe.

6 Then the apostles and elders assembled to consider this matter.

7 And after much controversy, Shim'on Kefa rose up and said to them, Men and brethren, you know that from the early days Lord Yahweh chose that from my mouth of the Gentiles should hear the word of the gospel and believe.

8 And Lord Yahweh, who knows what is in the heart, has testified concerning them and has given them the Holy Spirit just as He did to us.

9 And He did not discriminate between us and them, because He purified their hearts by faith.

10 Now therefore why do you tempt Lord Yahweh by putting a yoke upon the necks of the disciples which neither our fathers nor were we able to bear?

11 But we believe that through the grace of the Lord Yahshua the Christ, we shall be saved even as they.

12 Then the whole congregation was silent and listened to Sha'ul and Bar-Nabba, who were declaring the miracles and signs among the Gentiles and everything which Lord Yahweh had wrought by their hands.

13 And when they had ceased speaking, Ya'akov rose up and said, Men and brethren, hear me:

14 Shim'on Kefa has told you how Lord Yahweh from the beginning chose a people from the Gentiles for his name.

15 And with this the words of the prophets agree, as it is written,

16 After this I will return, and I will set up again the tabernacle of David which has fallen down; and I will repair what has fallen from it, and I will set it up,

17 So that the men who remain may seek after the Lord, and also all the Gentiles upon whom my name is called; so said the Lord who does all these things.

18 The works of Lord Yahweh are known from the very beginning.

19 Because of this I say, Do not trouble those who turn to Lord Yahweh from among the Gentiles:

20 But let us send word to them that they abstain from defilement by sacrifices to idols and from fornication and from animals strangled and from blood.

21 For Moshe, from the very early centuries, had preachers in the synagogues in every city to read his books on every Sabbath day.

22 Then the apostles and elders, with the whole church, chose men from among themselves and sent them to Antioch with Sha'ul and Bar-Nabba; namely, Y'hudah who is call Bar-Nabba and Silas, men who were leaders among the brethren;

23 And they wrote a letter and sent it by them after this manner: The apostles and elders and brethren to the brethren of the Gentiles in Antioch and Syria and Cilicia, greetings:

24 We have heard that certain men have gone out and disturbed you with words, thus upsetting your souls, saying, You must be circumcised and keep the law; concerning these things we have never commanded them.

25 Therefore, we have considered the matter while we are assembled, and we have chosen and sent men to you with our beloved Sha'ul and Bar-Nabba,

26 Men who have dedicated their lives for the name of our Lord Yahshua the Christ.

27 And we have sent with them Y'hudah And Silas, so that they may tell you the same things by word of mouth.

28 For it is the will of the Holy Spirit, and of us, to lay upon you no additional burden than these necessary things:

29 That you abstain from sacrifices offered to idols and from blood and from animals strangled and from fornication; when you keep yourselves from these things, you will do well. Remain steadfast in our Lord.

30 Now when those who were sent came to Antioch and when the whole people were gathered together, they delivered the epistle;

31 And when they had read it, the people rejoiced and were comforted.

32 And Y'hudah and Silas, being prophets themselves also, confirmed the brethren with gracious words.

33 And after they had been there some time, the brethren let them go in peace to the apostles.

34 Notwithstanding, it pleased Silas to abide there still.

35 Sha'ul also and Bar-Nabba remained in Antioch, teaching and preaching the word of Lord Yahweh, with many others also.

36 And some days after, Sha'ul said to Bar-Nabba, Let us return and visit the brethren in every city where we have preached the word of Lord Yahweh and see how they do.

37 Now Bar-Nabba wanted to take Yochanan who was also called Mark.

38 But Sha'ul was unwilling to take him with them because he had left them when they were in Pamphylia and had not gone with them.

39 And because of this dispute, Sha'ul and Bar-Nabba separated from each other; and Bar-Nabba took Mark, and they sailed to Cyprus,

40 But Sha'ul chose Silas and departed, being commended by the brethren to the grace of Lord Yahweh.

41 And he traveled through Syria and Cilicia, establishing churches.

CHAPTER 16

Then he arrived at the city of Derbe and Lystra; there was there a disciple whose name was Timotheus, the son of a Jewess convert, but whose father was a Greek.

2 And all the disciples of Lystra and Iconium gave good testimony concerning him.

3 Sha'ul wanted to take this man with him, so he took him and circumcised him because of the Jews who were in that region; for they all knew that his father was a Greek.

4 And as they went through the cities, they preached and taught the people to obey the decrees which the apostles and elders had written at Jerusalem.

5 And so the churches were established in the faith, and increased in number daily.

6 Then they traveled through the countries of Phrygia and Galatia, and the Holy Spirit forbade them to speak the word of Lord Yahweh in Asia Minor.

7 And when they came to the country of Mysia, they wanted to go from thence to Bithynia; but the spirit of Yahshua permitted them not.

8 And when they had left Mysia, they came to the country of Troas.

9 And, in a vision of the night, there appeared to Sha'ul a man resembling a Macedonian, standing and begging him saying, Come over to Macedonia and help us.

10 And after Sha'ul had seen this vision, we were desirous to leave for Macedonia at once because we understood that our Lord had called us to preach the gospel to them.

11 When we sailed from Troas, we came in a direct course to Samothracia, and from thence on the following day, we came to Neapolis;

12 And from thence to Philippi, which is the capital of Macedonia, and is a colony; and we were in that city on certain holidays.

13 And on the Sabbath day we went outside the city gate to the river side because a house of prayer was seen there, and when we were seated, we spoke to the women who had gathered there.

14 And a certain woman, named Lydia, a seller of purple of the city of Thyatira, feared Lord Yahweh; her heart was so touched by our Lord that she listened to what Sha'ul said.

15 And she was baptized together with her household, and she begged us, saying, If you are sincerely convinced that I believe in our Lord, come and stay in my house; and she urged us strongly.

16 And it came to pass, as we went to the house of prayer, we were met by a young girl who was possessed of a spirit, and who brought her masters great gain by fortunetelling.

17 And she followed Sha'ul and us, crying and saying, These men are the servants of the Most High God, and they preach to you the way of salvation.

18 And she did this for many days. So Sha'ul was indignant and said to the spirit, I command you in the name of Yahshua the Christ to come out of her. And it left her the same hour.

19 And when her masters saw that the hope for their business was lost with her power, they seized Sha'ul and Silas and beat them and brought them to the market place.

20 And they brought them before the soldiers and the city magistrates, and said, These men are Jews, and they create disturbances in our city,

21 And they preach customs to us which are not lawful for us to accept and practice, because we are Romans.

22 And a large crowd gathered against them. Then the soldiers stripped them of their clothes and gave command to scourge them.

23 And when they had flogged them severely, they cast them into prison, charging the jailer to watch them carefully.

24 He, having received the charge, brought them in and put them into the inner chamber of the prison, and fastened their feet in the stocks.

25 Now at midnight, Sha'ul and Silas prayed and glorified Lord Yahweh; and the prisoners heard them.

26 And suddenly there was a great earthquake, so that the foundations of the prison were shaken, immediately all the doors were opened and the bands of all were loosed.

27 When the keeper of the prison awoke and saw that the prison doors were open, he took a sword and would have killed himself, for he thought the prisoners had escaped.

28 But Sha'ul cried with a loud voice, saying to him, Do not harm yourself, for we are all here.

29 Then he lighted a lamp and sprang in, trembling, and threw himself at the feet of Sha'ul and Silas.

30 And he brought them out, and said, Sirs, what must I do to be saved?

31 And they said to him, Believe in our Lord Yahshua the Christ, and both you and your household will be saved.

32 And they spoke to him the word of the Lord and to all who were of his household.

33 And he took them at that hour of the night and washed their wounds; and then was baptized in that very hour, he and all his household.

34 And when he had brought them up into his house, he set food before them; and he and all the members of his household rejoiced, believing in Lord Yahweh.

35 In the morning, the magistrates sent the soldiers to tell the prison warden to release those men.

36 And when the keeper of the prison heard this, he went in and told Sha'ul, saying, The soldiers have sent orders to release you; now therefore depart and go in peace.

37 But Sha'ul said to him, not having committed any offense, they flogged us, Roman citizens, in the presence of the people, and they cast us into prison; and now do they let us out secretly? No verily; let them come themselves and take us out.

38 And the soldiers went and told the magistrates these words which were told to them; and when they heard that Sha'ul and Silas were Roman citizens, they were afraid.

39 And they came to them and urged them to get out and depart from the city.

40 And they went out of the prison and entered into the house of Lydia where they saw the brethren and comforted them, and departed.

CHAPTER 17

Then they passed by the cities of Amphipolis and Apollonia, and came to Thessalonica, where there was a synagogue of the Jews.

2 And Sha'ul, as was his custom, went in to join them, and for three Sabbaths he spoke to them from the scriptures,

3 Interpreting and proving that the Christ had to suffer and rise again from the dead; and that he is the same Yahshua the Christ whom I preach to you.

4 And some of them believed and joined Sha'ul and Silas; and many of them were Greeks who revered Lord Yahweh, and many of them were well known women, a goodly number.

5 But the Jews, being jealous, secured a band of bad men from the streets of the city and formed a great mob, who caused disturbances in the city, and who came and assaulted the house of Jason and sought to bring them out from it and deliver them to the mob.

6 And when they failed to find them there, they dragged forth Jason and the brethren who were there and brought them before the authorities of the city, crying, These are the men who have created disturbances throughout the world, and behold, they have come here also,

7 And Jason had welcomed them; and all of them are against the decrees Caesar, saying that there is another king, Yahshua.

8 The authorities of the city and all the people were alarmed when they heard these things.

9 So they took bail from Jason and some of the brethren, and then let them go.

10 Then the brethren immediately sent away Sha'ul and Silas by night to the city of Berea; and when they arrived there, they entered into the synagogue of the Jews.

11 For the Jews there were more liberal than the Jews who were in Thessalonica, in that they gladly heard the word daily and searched the scriptures to find out if these things were so.

12 And many of them believed; and of the Greeks there were many men and notable women.

13 But when the Jews of Thessalonica found out that the word of Lord Yahweh was preached by Sha'ul in the city of Berea, they came there also, and ceased not to stir up and alarm the people.

14 Then the brethren sent Sha'ul away to go to the sea; but Silas and Timotheus remained in that city.

15 And those who escorted Sha'ul went with him as far as the city of Athens; and when they were leaving him, they received from him an epistle to Silas and Timotheus, requesting them to come to him in haste.

16 Now while Sha'ul waited for them at Athens, he saw the whole city full of idols, and he murmured thereat in his spirit.

17 And he spoke in the synagogue to the Jews and to those who feared Lord Yahweh, and in the market place daily with them who were there.

18 Philosophers, also, who were of the teaching of Epicurus, and others, who were called Stoics, argued with him. And some of them said, What does this babbler want? And others said, He preaches foreign gods, because he preached to them Yahshua and his resurrection.

19 So they arrested him and brought him to the courthouse which is called Areopagus, and said to him, May we know what is this new doctrine which you preach?

20 For you proclaim strange words to our ears, and we want to know what these things mean.

21 {For all the Athenians and the strangers who were there, uninterested in anything except something new to tell or to hear.}

22 When Sha'ul stood in the court at Areopagus, he said, Men of Athens, I see that above all things you are extravagant in the worship of idols.

23 For as I walked about, and viewed the house of your idols, I found an altar with this inscription: THIS IS THE ALTAR OF THE UNKNOWN GOD. He therefore, while you know Him not but yet worship Him, is the very one I am preaching to you.

24 For the God who made the world and all things therein, and who is the Lord of heaven and earth, does not dwell in temples made with human hands;

25 Neither is He ministered to by human hands, nor is He in need of anything, for it is He who gave life and breath to all men.

26 And He has made of one blood all nations of men to dwell on all the face of the earth, and He has appointed seasons by his command, and has set limits to the age of men;

27 So that they should seek and search after Lord Yahweh, and find Him by means of his creation, because He is not far from any one of us;

28 For in Him we live and move and have our being, as some of your own wise men have said, For we are his kindred.

29 Now therefore, man, being of the family of Lord Yahweh, is not bound to worship resemblances made of gold or silver or stone shapen by the skill and knowledge of man into resemblances of the Deity.

30 For the times of ignorance, Lord Yahweh has made to pass, and at this time He has commanded all men, everywhere, to repent.

31 For He has appointed a day in which He will judge all the earth with righteousness by the man whom He has chosen, and He has provided a guarantee to all men by resurrecting him from the dead.

32 And when they heard of the resurrection of the dead, some mocked, and others said, We will hear you again on this matter.

33 So Sha'ul left them.

34 Some of them, however, followed him and were converted; one of them was Dionysius, one of the judges of Areopagus, and another a woman named Damaris, and others with them.

(Acts, chapter 18 has historical accounts with almost no theology)

CHAPTER 19

And it came to pass that while Appollos (who had converted to the way of the Lord) was at Corinth, Sha'ul traveled through the northern countries and came to Ephesus, and inquired of the disciples whom he found there.

2 Have you received the Holy Spirit since you were converted? They answered, saying to him, We have not even heard that there is a Holy Spirit.

3 Then he said to them, By what baptism then were you baptized? They said, By the baptism of Yochanan.

4 Then said Sha'ul, Yochanan verily baptized the people with the baptism of repentance, saying to them that they should come after him, that is, Yahshua the Christ.

5 When they heard these things, they were baptized in the name of our Lord Yahshua the Christ.

6 And when Sha'ul laid his hands on them, the Holy Spirit came on them; and they spoke in different tongues, and prophesied.

7 And there were in all twelve persons.

8 Then Sha'ul entered into the synagogue and spoke openly for a period of three months, persuading the people concerning the kingdom of Lord Yahweh.

9 But some of them were stubborn, and they disputed and cursed the way of Lord Yahweh in the presence of the assembly. Then Sha'ul withdrew and separated the disciples from them, and he spoke to them daily in the school of a man named Tyrannus.

10 And this continued for two years until all who dwelt in Asia Minor, both Jews and Arameans {Syrians}, heard the word of Lord Yahweh.

11 And Lord Yahweh wrought great miracles by the hands of Sha'ul,

12 So that even when from the clothes on his body, pieces of garments were brought and laid upon the sick, diseases were cured and even the insane were restored.

13 Now certain Jews who went about exorcising evil spirits, invoked the name of our Lord Yahshua over those who were possessed, saying, We adjure you in the name of Yahshua whom Sha'ul preaches.

14 And there were seven sons of one Sceva, a Jew, and chief of the priests, who did this.

15 And the insane man answered, saying to them, Lord Yahshua I recognize and Sha'ul I know; but who are you?

16 Then the insane man leaped on them and overpowered them and prevailed against them, so they fled out of that house naked and wounded.

17 And this became known to all the Jews and Greeks who dwelt at Ephesus; and fear fell on them all, and the name of our Lord Yahshua the Christ was magnified.

18 And many of them that believed, came and told their faults and confessed what they had done.

19 Many magicians also gathered together their books and brought them and burned them before the presence of the people; and they counted the price of them, and it amounted to fifty thousand pieces of silver.

20 So mightily grew the faith of Lord Yahweh, and greatly increased in numbers.

(the rest of chapter 19 and the chapters of 20 through 25 are historical accounts with a very small amount of redundant theology)

CHAPTER 26

Then King Agrippa said to Sha'ul, You speak in your own behalf. Whereupon Sha'ul stretched forth his hand and answered, saying,

2 In view of all the things whereof I am accused by the Jews, I consider myself blessed, O King Agrippa, to defend myself today before you.

3 Especially because I know you are familiar with all the customs and questions and laws of the Jews; wherefore, I beg you to hear me patiently.

4 Even the Jews themselves, if they would be willing to testify, know well my manner of life from my childhood which started first among my own people at Jerusalem.

5 For they have been acquainted with me a long time, and know that I was brought up with the excellent doctrine of the Pharisees.

6 And now I stand and am on trial for the hope of the promise made by the God of our fathers.

7 It is to the fulfillment of this hope that our twelve tribes expect to arrive by means of earnest prayers day and night. And for this very hope's sake, I am accused by the Jews, O King Agrippa.

8 How can you judge? Is it improper to believe that Lord Yahweh can raise the dead?

9 For at the very beginning I was determined that I ought to many things contrary to the name of Yahshua of Nazareth,

10 Which I also did at Jerusalem; I cast many of the saints into prison, having received authority from the chief priests; and when some were put to death, I took part with those who condemned them.

11 And I tortured them in every synagogue, thus compelling them to blaspheme the name of Yahshua; and being exceedingly mad against them, I also went to other cities to persecute them.

12 I was on the way to Damascus for this purpose, with authority and commission from the chief priests, when,

13 At midday on the road, O king, I saw a light from heaven more powerful than that of the sun, shining round about me and upon those who journeyed with me.

14 When we all fell to the ground, then I heard a voice speaking to me, in the Hebrew tongue, Sha'ul, Sha'ul, why do you persecute me? It is hard for you to kick against the pricks.

15 And I said, My Lord, who are you? And our Lord said to me, I am Yahshua of Nazareth whom you persecute.

16 Then he said to me, Rise and stand upon your feet; for I have appeared to you for this purpose, to appoint you a minister and a witness both of those things in which you have seen me and of those things in which you will also see me again.

17 And I will deliver you from the Jewish people and from the other peoples to whom I send you,

18 To open their eyes, that they may turn from darkness to light, and from the power of Satan to Lord Yahweh and receive forgiveness of sins and a portion with the saints who are of the faith in me.

19 Whereupon, O King Agrippa, I did not disobey the heavenly vision;

20 But I preached first to them of Damascus and at Jerusalem, and throughout all the villages of Judea and then to the Gentiles that they may repent and turn to Lord Yahweh, and do works worthy of repentance.

21 For these causes, the Jews seized me in the temple and wanted to kill me.

22 But Lord Yahweh has helped me to this very day, and behold I stand and testify to the humble and to the great, saying nothing contrary to Moshe and the prophets, but the very things which they said were to happen,

23 That Christ should suffer and that he should be the first to rise from the dead, and that he should preach light to the people and to the Gentiles.

24 And while Sha'ul was pleading in this manner, Festus cried with a loud voice, Sha'ul, you are overwrought. Much study has made you mad.

25 But Sha'ul said to him, I am not mad, O most excellent Festus; but I speak the words of truth and soberness.

26 And King Agrippa is also familiar with these things, and this is why I am speaking openly before him, Because I think not one of these words has been hidden from him; for they were not done in secret.

27 King Agrippa, do you believe the prophets? I know that you believe.

28 Then King Agrippa said to him, With little effort you almost persuade me to become a Christian.

29 And Sha'ul said, I pray Lord Yahweh that not only you, but also all of those who hear me today were as I am, except for these bonds.

30 Then the king arose, and the governor and Bernice and they that sat with them;

31 And when they had departed, they talked between themselves, saying, This man has done nothing worthy of death or of imprisonment.

32 Then Agrippa said to Festus, This man could have been released had he not appealed to Caesar.

(chapters 27 and 28 are historical accounts with little, repeated theology)

The Epistle of Sha'ul The Apostle to The Romans

Chapter 1

Sha'ul, a servant of Yahshua the Christ, called to be an apostle and chosen to proclaim the gospel of Lord Yahweh,

2 Which was promised from early days by his prophets in the holy scriptures,

3 Concerning his Son who was born in the flesh of the seed of the house of David,

4 And who came to be known as the Son of Lord Yahweh with power and with the Holy Spirit, because he arose from the dead, and he is Yahshua the Christ our Lord;

5 And by him we have received grace and apostleship among all the Gentiles, so that they may hear the faith which bears his name,

6 And you also are of them, and are called by the name of Yahshua the Christ;

7 To all who are in Rome, beloved of Lord Yahweh, called and sanctified: Grace and peace to you from Lord Yahweh our Father, and from our Lord Yahshua the Christ.

8 First, I thank my God through Yahshua the Christ for you all, that your faith has been of throughout the world.

9 For Lord Yahweh, whom I serve in spirit in the gospel of his Son, is my witness that unceasingly I make mention of you in my prayers,

10 Beseeching that if the way is open to me by the will of Lord Yahweh, I may come to you.

11 For I long to see you, and to impart to you the gift of the Spirit, in order that you may be strengthened by the Spirit,

12 And that we may be comforted together by our mutual faith.

13 Now I want you to know, my brethren, that often I have wanted to come to you, but I have been prevented thus far, that I may have some fruit among you also, even as among other Gentiles,

14 Greeks and Barbarians, the wise and the unwise; for it is my duty to preach to everyone.

15 So I am eager to preach the gospel to you who are in Rome also.

16 For I am not ashamed of the gospel of the Christ; for it is the power of Lord Yahweh for salvation to everyone who believes, whether they are Jews first, or Greeks.

17 For therein is the righteousness of Lord Yahweh revealed from faith to faith; as it is written, The righteous shall live by faith.

18 For the wrath of Lord Yahweh is revealed from heaven against all the iniquity and wickedness of men who unjustly suppress the truth;

19 Because that which may be known of Lord Yahweh is manifested to them.

20 For, from the very creation of the world, the invisible things of Lord Yahweh have been clearly seen and understood by his creations, even his eternal power and Godhead; so that they are without excuse.

21 For they knew Lord Yahweh, and they did not glorify Him and give thanks to Him as the one true God, but became vain in their imaginations, and their hearts were darkened so that they could not understand.

22 And while they thought within themselves that they were wise, they became fools,

23 And they have changed the glory of the incorruptible God for an image made in the likeness of corruptible man, and in the likeness of birds and of four-footed beasts and of creeping things on the earth.

24 That is why Lord Yahweh also gave them up to uncleanness through the lusts of their hearts, to dishonor their own bodies among themselves;

25 And they have changed the truth of Lord Yahweh for lies, and worshipped and served the created things more than their Creator to whom belong glory and blessings for ever. Amen.

26 Therefore Lord Yahweh has given them up to vile passions; for even their women have changed the natural use of their sex into that which is unnatural;

27 And likewise also their men have left the natural use of the women and have run wild with lust toward one another, male with male committing shameful acts, and receiving in themselves the due recompense of their error.

28 And as they did not consent in themselves to know Lord Yahweh, Lord Yahweh has given them over to a weak mind, to do the things which should not be done; as,

29 Being filled with all manner of iniquity, fornication, bitterness, malice, extortion, envy, murder, strife, deceit, evil thoughts.

30 They are slanderers, backbiters, haters of Lord Yahweh, revilers, proud boasters, inventors of evil things, weak-minded, disobedient to their parents;

31 These have no respect for a covenant. They know neither love nor peace, nor is there mercy in them;

32 Knowing the judgment of Lord Yahweh, that those who commit such things, he condemns to death, they not only do them, but also associate with those who practice them.

Chapter 2

Therefore you are inexcusable, O man, to judge your neighbor; for in judging your neighbor, you condemn yourself; for even you who judge, practice the same things yourself.

2 But we know that the judgment of Lord Yahweh is rightly against those who commit such things.

3 What do you think, O man? Do you think that you who judge those who practice such things, while you commit them yourself, will escape the judgment of Lord Yahweh?

4 Do you stand against the riches of his goodness and forbearance, and the opportunity which He has given you, not knowing that the goodness of Lord Yahweh leads you to repentance?

5 Because of the hardness and impenitence of your heart you are laying up for yourself a treasure of wrath for the day of wrath and the revelation of the righteous judgment of Lord Yahweh,

6 Who will render to every man according to his deeds:

7 To those who continue patiently in good works, seeking glory and honor and immortality, He will give eternal life;

8 But to those who are stubborn and do not obey the truth, but obey iniquity, He will render indignation and wrath;

9 He will render suffering and affliction, for every man who does evil, for the Jews first, and also for the Gentiles;

10 But glory, honor and peace for everyone who does good, to the Jews first, and also for the Gentiles;

11 For there is no partiality with Lord Yahweh.

12 For those who have sinned without law shall also perish without law; and those who have sinned in the law shall be judged by the law,

13 For it is not the hearers of the law who are righteous before Lord Yahweh, but it is the doers of the law who shall be justified.

14 For if the Gentiles, who do not have the law, do by nature the things contained in the law, these having not the law are a law to themselves.

15 And they show the work of the law written in their hearts; and their conscience also bears them witness, when their thoughts either rebuke or defend one another,

16 In the day when Lord Yahweh shall judge the secrets of men according to my gospel by Yahshua the Christ.

17 Now if you who are called a Jew, trust on the law and boast of Lord Yahweh,

18 And because you know his will and know the things which must be observed, which you have learned from the law,

19 And you have confidence in yourself that you are a guide of the blind and a light to them who are in darkness,

20 An instructor of the foolish, a teacher of children, you are the pattern of knowledge and of truth as embodied in the law.

21 Now, therefore, you teach others but fail to teach yourself. You preach that men should not steal, yet you steal.

22 You say, Men must not commit adultery, yet you commit adultery. You despise idols, yet you rob the sanctuary.

23 You are proud of the law but you dishonor Lord Yahweh by breaking the law.

24 For the name of Lord Yahweh is blasphemed among the Gentiles through you, as it is written.

25 For circumcision is profitable only if you keep the law, but if you break the law, then circumcision becomes uncircumcision.

26 Therefore, if the uncircumcision keep the statutes of the law, behold would not the uncircumcision be counted for circumcision?

27 And the uncircumcision which fulfills the law naturally, will condemn you who, while in possession of the scripture and circumcision, transgress the law.

28 For it is not the one who is outwardly a Jew who is the real Jew; neither is circumcision that which is seen in the flesh.

29 But a real Jew is one who is inwardly so, and circumcision is of the heart, spiritually and not physically; whose praise is not from men but from Lord Yahweh.

CHAPTER 3

What then is the superiority of the Jew? or what is the importance of circumcision?

2 Much in every way; because the Jews were the first to believe in the words of Lord Yahweh.

3 For what if some had not believed, could their unbelief nullify the faith of Lord Yahweh?

4 Far be it; only Lord Yahweh is true and no man is wholly perfect; as it is written, That you may be justified by your words, and triumph when you are judged.

5 Now if our unrighteousness serves to highlight the righteousness of Lord Yahweh, what then shall we say? Is Lord Yahweh unjust when He inflicts his anger? I speak as a man.

6 Far be it; for then how would Lord Yahweh judge the world?

7 For if the truth of Lord Yahweh is made abundant through my falsehood to his glory, why then am I to be judged as a sinner?

8 As for those who blaspheme against us, saying that we say, Let us do evil that good may come; their condemnation is reserved for eternal justice.

9 What then do we uphold that is superior? We have already decided concerning both Jews and Gentiles, for they are all under sin.

10 As it is written, There is none righteous, no, not one;

11 There is none who understands, there is none who seeks after Lord Yahweh.

12 They are all gone astray and they have been rejected; there is none who does good, no, not one.

13 Their throats are like open sepulchres; their tongues are deceitful; the venom of asps is under their lips.

14 Their mouths are full of cursing and bitterness.

15 They are overquick to shed blood.

16 Destruction and misery are in their ways.

17 They have not known the path of peace.

18 There is no fear of Lord Yahweh before their eyes.

19 Now we know that whatever the law says, it is said to those who are under the law, so that every mouth may be shut, and all the world may become guilty before Lord Yahweh.

20 For by the deeds of the law, no flesh shall be justified before his presence; for by means of the law, sin is known.

21 But now the righteousness of Lord Yahweh without the law is manifested, and the very law and prophets testify to it;

22 But the righteousness of Lord Yahweh is by the faith of Yahshua the Christ to every one, also to every man who believes in him, for there is no discrimination;

23 For all have sinned and are short of the glory of Lord Yahweh;

24 For they are freely given righteousness by the grace of Lord Yahweh through the salvation which is in Yahshua the Christ,

25 Whom Lord Yahweh has foreordained to gain favor through faith in his blood for the remission of our sins that are past;

26 By the opportunity which Lord Yahweh has given us through his forbearance, for the manifestation of his righteousness at the present time, that he may be declared righteous; and for the justification of righteousness to him who is in the faith of our Lord Yahshua the Christ.

27 Where is boasting then? It is worthless. By what law? of works? No; but by the law of faith.

28 Therefore we conclude that it is by faith a man is justified and not by the works of the law.

29 Why? Is Lord Yahweh the God of the Jews only? Is he not also God of the Gentiles? Yes, he Is God of the Gentiles also;

30 For it is one God, who justifies the circumcision by faith, and uncircumcision by the same faith.

31 What, then? Do we nullify the law through faith? Far be it; on the contrary, we uphold the law.

CHAPTER 4

What then shall we say concerning Avraham, the chief of our forefathers, who lived according to the flesh before Lord Yahweh called him?

2 For if Avraham was justified by works, he has reason to be proud; but not before Lord Yahweh.

3 For what said the scripture? Avraham believed in Lord Yahweh, and it was counted to him for righteousness.

4 But to him who works, wages are not considered as a favor but as that which is due to him.

5 And to him who works not, but only believes in Him who justifies sinners, his faith is counted for righteousness.

6 Just as David also said about the blessedness of the man whom Lord Yahweh declared righteous without works,

7 Saying, Blessed are they whose iniquities are forgiven, and whose sins are wiped away.

8 Blessed is the man whose sins Lord Yahweh will not hold against him.

9 Now, therefore, is this blessedness on account of circumcision or an account of uncircumcision? For we say that Avraham's faith was accounted to him for righteousness.

10 How then was it given to him? by means of circumcision or in uncircumcision? It was not given in circumcision, but in uncircumcision.

11 For he received circumcision as a sign and a seal of the righteousness of his faith while he was uncircumcised, that he may become the father of all those who believe, though they be not circumcised, that righteousness may be reckoned also to them,

12 So that the father of circumcision is not only to those who are of circumcision, but also to those who walk in the steps of the faith of our father Avraham while he was yet uncircumcised.

13 For the promise to Avraham and his posterity that he should inherit the world was not made through the law, but through the righteousness of his faith.

14 For if they had become heirs by means of the law, then faith would have been empty and the promise made of no effect.

15 For the law causes provocation; for where there is no law, there is no transgression.

16 Therefore it is by faith that we will be justified by grace, so that the promise may be sure to all his posterity, not only to him who is of the law, but also to him who is of the faith of Avraham who is the father of us all;

17 As it is written, I have made you a father of many peoples, in the presence of the God in whom you have believed, who quickens the dead, and who invites those who are not yet in being, as though they were present.

18 For he who was hopeless trusted in hope, that he may become the father of many peoples; as it is written, So shall your descendants be.

19 His faith never weakened even when he examined his old body when he was a hundred years old, and the deadness of Sarah's womb.

20 He did not doubt the promise of Lord Yahweh as one who lacks faith; but his faith strengthened him, and he gave glory to Lord Yahweh.

21 He felt assured that what Lord Yahweh had promised him, Lord Yahweh was able to fulfill.

22 Therefore, his faith was reckoned to him for righteousness.

23 That his faith was reckoned for righteousness was not written for his sake alone,

24 But for us also; for He will number us also, who believe in Him who raised our Lord Yahshua the Christ from the dead;

25 Who was delivered up for our offenses (sins) and arose that he might justify us.

CHAPTER 5

Therefore, being justified by faith, let us have peace with Lord Yahweh through our Lord Yahshua the Christ;

2 Through him we have been brought by faith into the grace wherein we stand, and rejoice in the hope and the glory of Lord Yahweh.

3 And not only so, but we also glory in our tribulations; knowing that tribulation perfects patience in us;

4 And patience, experience; and experience, hope;

5 And hope causes no one to be ashamed; because the love of Lord Yahweh is poured into our hearts by the Holy Spirit which is given to us.

6 But Yahshua the Christ at this time, because of our weaknesses, died for the sake of the wicked.

7 Hardly would any man die for the sake of the wicked; but for the sake of the good, one might be willing to die.

8 Lord Yahweh has here manifested his love toward us, in that, while we were yet sinners, Yahshua died for us.

9 Much more then, being justified by his blood, we shall be delivered from wrath through him.

10 For if when we were enemies, we were reconciled to Lord Yahweh by the death of his Son, much more, being reconciled, we shall be saved by his life.

11 And not only so, but we also glory in Lord Yahweh through our Lord Yahshua the Christ, by whom we have now received the reconciliation.

12 Just as sin entered into the world by one man, and death by means of sin, so death was imposed upon all men, inasmuch as they all have sinned;

13 For until the law was given, though sin was in the world, it was not considered sin, because there was no law.

14 Nevertheless, death reigned from Adam to Moshe, even over them who had not sinned in the manner of the transgression of the law by Adam, who is the likeness of him that was to come.

15 But the measure of the gift of Lord Yahweh was not the measure of the fall. If therefore, because of the fall of one, many died, how much more will the grace and gift of Lord Yahweh, because of Yahshua the Christ, be increased for many?

16 And the effect of the gift of Lord Yahweh was greater than the effect of the sin of Adam; for while the judgment from one man's sin resulted in condemnation of many, the gift of Lord Yahweh in forgiveness of sins resulted in righteousness to many more.

17 For if by one man's sin, death reigned, how much more those who receive abundance of grace and of the gift of righteousness shall reign in life by one, Yahshua the Christ.

(Verses 18 and 19 are redundant and only repeat the preceding verses)

20 The introduction of the law caused sin to increase, and when sin had increased, grace became abundant.

21 Just as sin had reigned through death, so grace shall reign through righteousness to eternal life by our Lord Yahshua the Christ.

CHAPTER 6

What shall we then say? Shall we continue in sin that grace may abound?

2 Far be it. How shall we who are dead to sin continue to live in it?

3 Do you not know that those of us who have been baptized into Yahshua the Christ have been baptized into his death?

4 Therefore, we are buried with him by baptism into death, so that as Yahshua the Christ rose from the dead by the glory of his Father, even so we also shall walk in a new life.

5 For if we have been buried together with him in the likeness of his death, so shall we be also in the likeness of his resurrection:

6 For we know that our old selves are crucified with him, so that the sinful body might be destroyed, that henceforth we should not serve sin.

7 For he who is dead, is freed from sin.

8 Now if we are dead with Yahshua the Christ, let us believe that we shall also live with Yahshua the Christ.

9 We know that Yahshua rose from the dead, and dies no more; and that death has no more dominion over him.

10 For in dying he died once to sin; and in living he lives to Lord Yahweh.

11 Likewise, you also must consider yourself as being dead to sin, but alive to Lord Yahweh through Yahshua the Christ, our Lord.

12 Let not sin therefore reign in your mortal body, that you should obey it in the lusts thereof.

13 Neither should you yield your members as instruments of iniquity to sin; but yield yourselves to Lord Yahweh, just as if you were men who had risen from among the dead, and let your members be instruments of righteousness to Lord Yahweh.

14 Sin shall not have dominion over you; for you are no longer under the law, but under grace.

15 What then? Shall we sin because we are not under the law but under grace? Far be it.

16 Do you not know that to whom you yield yourselves as servants to obey, his servants you are; for you obey Him, whether it be to sin or whether to be of obedience to righteousness?

17 But thank Lord Yahweh that you, who were once the servants of sin, now obey from the heart, that form of doctrine which has been delivered to you.

18 Now, being made free from sin, you become the servants of righteousness.

19 I speak after the manner of men because of the weakness of your flesh; for as you have yielded your members to the servitude of uncleanness and iniquity, so now yield your members to the servitude of righteousness and holiness.

20 For when you were the servants of sin, you were free from righteousness.

21 What kind of fruit did you have then, in the things of which you are now ashamed? For the end thereof is death.

22 But now being made free from sin, and become servants of Lord Yahweh, your fruits are holy and the end thereof is life everlasting.

23 For the wages of sin is death; but the gift of Lord Yahweh is eternal life through our Lord Yahshua the Christ.

CHAPTER 7

Do you not know, my brethren, I speak to them who know the law, that the law has authority over a person as long as he lives?

2 Just as a woman is bound by the law to her husband as long as he lives; but if her husband should die, she is freed from the law of her husband.

3 Thus if, while her husband is alive, she should be attached to another man, she becomes an adulteress; but if her husband is dead, she is free from the law, so that she is not an adulteress though she becomes another man's wife.

4 Wherefore, my brethren, you also are become dead to the law by the body of the Christ, that you might become another's, even to him who arose from the dead, so that you may bring forth fruit to Lord Yahweh.

5 For when we were in the flesh, the pains of sin which were by the law, worked in our members to bring forth fruits to death.

6 But now we are freed from the law, being dead to that which had hold upon us; and we should henceforth serve in newness of spirit, and not in the oldness of the letter of the law.

7 What shall we say then? Is the law sin? Far be it. I would not have known the meaning of sin except by means of the law; for I would never have known the meaning of covetousness unless the law said, Thou shalt not covet.

8 So by means of this commandment, sin found an occasion and provoked in me every kind of desire. For without the law, sin was dead.

9 Formerly, I lived without the law; but when the commandment came, sin came to life and I died.

10 And the commandment which was ordained to life, I found to be for death.

11 For sin, finding occasion by the commandment, misled me, and by it killed me.

12 Wherefore, the law is holy and the commandment is holy and just and good.

13 Has then that which is good become death to me? Far be it. But sin that is exposed as sin, and works death in me for that which is good, will be the more condemned by means of the law.

14 For we know that the law is spiritual; but I am of the flesh enslaved to sin.

15 For I do not know what to do; and I do not do the thing which I want, but I do the thing which I hate. That is exactly what I do.

16 So then if I do that which I do not wish to do, I can testify that the law is good.

17 Now then it is not I who do it, but sin which dominates me.

18 Yet I know that it does not fully dominate me {that is in my flesh}; but as far as good is concerned, the choice is easy for me to make, but to do it is difficult for me.

19 For it is not the good that I wish to do, that I do; but it is the evil that I do not wish to do, that I do.

20 Now if I do that which I do not wish, then it is not I who do it, but the sin which dominates me.

21 I find therefore that the law agrees with my conscience when I wish to do good, but evil is always near, distracting me.

22 For I delight in the law of Lord Yahweh after the inward man;

23 But I see another law in my members, warring against the law of my mind, and it makes me a captive to the law of sin which is in my members.

24 O wretched man that I am! Who shall deliver me from this mortal body?

25 I thank Lord Yahweh for deliverance through our Lord Yahshua the Christ. Now therefore with my mind I am a servant of the law of Lord Yahweh; but with my flesh I am a servant of the law of sin.

CHAPTER 8

There is therefore no condemnation to those who are in union with Yahshua the Christ.

2 For the law of the spirit of life which is in Yahshua the Christ has made you free from the law of sin and death.

3 For the law was weak through the weakness of the flesh, so Lord Yahweh sent his own Son in the likeness of sinful flesh, on account of sin, in order to condemn sin by means of his flesh,

4 That the righteousness of the law might be fulfilled in us; for we do not walk after the things of the flesh, but after the Spirit.

5 For they who are after the flesh, mind the things of the flesh; but they who are after the Spirit, mind the things of the Spirit.

6 To be carnally minded is death; but to be spiritually minded is life and peace,

7 Because the carnal mind is enmity against Lord Yahweh; for it is not subject to the law of Lord Yahweh, because it cannot be.

8 So then, they who are in the flesh cannot please Lord Yahweh.

9 But you are not in the flesh but in the Spirit, if the Spirit of Lord Yahweh truly dwells within you. Now if any man does not have the Spirit of the Christ, he does not belong to him.

10 And if the Spirit of the Christ is within you, the body is dead because of sin; but the Spirit is life because of righteousness.

11 And if the Spirit of Him who raised our Lord Yahshua the Christ from the dead dwells within you, So He who raised Yahshua the Christ from the dead, will also quicken your mortal bodies by his Spirit that dwells within you.

12 Therefore, my brethren, we are not indebted to the flesh to live after the flesh.

13 For if you live after the flesh, you will die; but if you, though the Spirit, subdue the deeds of the body, you shall live.

14 Those who are led by the Spirit of Lord Yahweh, are the sons of Lord Yahweh.

15 For you have not received the spirit of bondage, to be in fear again; but you have received the Spirit of adoption, whereby we cry, Abba, Abon, Father, our Father.

16 And this Spirit bears witness to our spirit, that we are the children of Lord Yahweh;

17 And if children, then heirs, heirs of Lord Yahweh and joint heirs with Yahshua the Christ; so that if we suffer with him, we shall also be glorified with him.

18 For I think that the sufferings of the present time are not worthy to be compared with the glory which shall be revealed in us.

19 For the earnest expectation of all mankind waits for the manifestation of the sons of Lord Yahweh.

20 For man was made subject to vanity, not willingly, but by reason of Him who gave him free will in the hope that he would choose rightly,

21 Because man himself shall be delivered from the bondage of corruption into the glorious liberty of the children of Lord Yahweh.

22 For we know that the whole creation groans and labors in pain to this day.

23 And not only they, but ourselves also, who have the first fruits of the Spirit, even we groan within ourselves, waiting for the adoption, that is, the salvation of our bodies.

24 For we live in hope; but hope that is seen is not hope: for if we see it, why should we yet hope?

25 But if we hope for that which we do not see, then do we wait for it in patience.

26 Likewise the Spirit also helps our weaknesses; for we do not know what is right and proper for us to pray for; but the Spirit prays for us with that earnestness which cannot be described.

27 And he who searches the hearts knows what is the mind of the Spirit, for the Spirit prays for the saints according to the will of Lord Yahweh.

28 And we know that those who love Lord Yahweh, are helped by Him in everything for good.

29 He knew them in advance, and He marked them with the likeness of the image of his Son so that he might be the first-born among many brethren.

30 Moreover, those whom He marked in advance, He has called, and those whom He has called, He has declared righteous, and those whom He has declared righteous, He has glorified.

31 What then shall we say concerning these things? If Lord Yahweh be for us, who can be against us?

32 If He did not spare his own Son, but delivered him up for us all, why will He not freely give us all things with him?

33 Who is to complain against chosen ones of Lord Yahweh? It is Lord Yahweh who justifies.

34 Who is he who condemns? It is Yahshua the Christ who died and rose again, and he is at the right hand of Lord Yahweh and making intercession for us.

35 What shall separate me from the love of Yahshua the Christ? Tribulation or imprisonment or persecution or famine or nakedness or peril or sword?

36 As it is written, For your sake we die every day, and we are accounted as lambs for the slaughter.

37 But in all these things we are more than conquerors through him who loved us.

38 For I am persuaded that neither death nor life, nor angels, nor empires, nor armies, nor things present, nor things to come,

39 Nor height, nor depth, nor anything else created shall be able to separate me from the love of Lord Yahweh which is in Yahshua the Christ, our Lord.

CHAPTER 9

I tell the truth through Yahshua the Christ, and I do not lie, my conscience also bears me witness through the Holy Spirit,

2 That I am exceedingly sorrowful, and the pain which is in my heart never ceases.

3 For I have prayed that I myself may be accursed because of Yahshua for the sake of my brethren and my kinsmen according to the flesh,

4 Who are Israelites; to whom belongs the adoption and the glory and the covenants and the law, and the rituals therein, and the promises,

5 And the fathers, from among whom Yahshua appeared in the flesh, Lord Yahweh who is over all, to whom are due praises and thanksgiving, for ever and ever. Amen.

6 It is not as though the word of Lord Yahweh had actually failed. For not all from Israel are Israelites;

7 Neither, are they all children because they are Avraham's offspring; rather, in Yitz'chak shall your descendants be called.

8 That is, it is not the children of the flesh who are the children of Lord Yahweh; but the children of the promise who are reckoned as descendants.

9 For this is the word of the promise: I will come at this season, and Sarah shall have a son.

10 And not only this; but Rebecca also, even though she had intimacy with one only, our father Yitz'chak;

11 Before her children were born or had done good or evil, the choice of Lord Yahweh was made known in advance; that it might stand, not by means of works, but through Him who made the choice.

12 For it was said, The elder shall be the servant of the younger.

13 As it is written, Ya'akov have I loved but Esav have I set aside.

14 What shall we say then? Is there injustice with Lord Yahweh? Far be it.

15 For He said to Moshe also, I will have mercy on him whom I love, and I will have compassion on him whom I favor.

16 Therefore, it is not within reach of him who wishes, nor within the reach of him who strives, but it is within the reach of the merciful God.

17 For in the scripture, He said to Pharaoh, It was for this purpose that I have appointed you, that I may show my power in you, so that my name may be preached throughout all the earth.

18 Thus He has mercy on whom He pleases, and He hardens whom He pleases.

19 Perhaps you will say, Why then does He yet find fault? For who can resist his will?

20 However, O man, who are you to question Lord Yahweh? Shall the thing formed say to him who formed it, Why have you made me like this?

21 Does the potter have power over his clay, to make out of the same lump vessels, one for special occasions and the other for daily service?

22 Now then, if Lord Yahweh wanted to show his anger and make his power known, would He not then, after the abundance of his patience, bring wrath upon the vessels of wrath which were ready for destruction?

23 But He Poured his mercy upon the favored vessels, which were prepared for the glory of Lord Yahweh;

24 Namely, ourselves, the called ones, not of the Jews only but also of the Gentiles.

25 As He said also in Hoshea, I will call them my people, who were not my own people; and her beloved who was not beloved.

26 And it shall come to pass that in the place where it was said you are not my people, there shall they be called the children of the living God.

27 Yesha'yahu also preached concerning the children of Israel, Though the number of children of Israel should be as the sand of the sea, only a remnant shall be saved.

28 For whatever the Lord has determined and decreed, He shall bring to pass upon the earth.

29 Just as Yesha'yahu had said before, If the Lord of Hosts had not increased the remnant, we should have been like Sodom, and should have resembled Gomorrah.

30 What shall we say then? That the Gentiles who followed not after righteousness have attained to righteousness; that is, the righteousness which is the result of faith.

31 But Israel, who followed after the law of righteousness, has not attained to the law of righteousness.

32 Why? Because it was not sought by faith but by the works of the law. So they stumbled at that stumbling stone.

33 As it is written, Behold, the prophet I give to Zion becomes a stumbling-stone and rock of offense; but whoever believes in him (Yahshua the Christ) shall not be ashamed.

CHAPTER 10

My brethren, my heart's desire and prayer to Lord Yahweh for Israel is that they may be saved.

2 For I can testify for them that there is in them a zeal for Lord Yahweh, but not according to the true knowledge.

3 For they know not the righteousness of Lord Yahweh, but to seek establish their own righteousness, and because of this, they have not submitted themselves to the righteousness of Lord Yahweh.

4 For Yahshua the Christ is the end of the law for righteousness to everyone who believes.

5 For Moshe writes of the righteousness of the law thus: Whoever shall do these things shall live by them.

6 But the righteousness which is of faith, says thus: Do not say in your heart, Who has ascended to heaven and brought Yahshua down to earth?

7 And who has descended into the abyss of sheol and brought up Yahshua from the dead?

8 But what does it say? The answer is near to you, even in your mouth and in your heart, that is, the word of faith which we preach;

9 So if you will confess with your mouth our Lord Yahshua and will believe in your heart that Lord Yahweh raised him from the dead, you shall be saved.

10 For the heart which believes in him (Lord Yahshua) shall be declared righteous, and the mouth that confesses him shall live.

11 For the scripture says, Whosoever believes in him shall not be ashamed.

12 And in this, it does not discriminate between the Jews and the Greeks; for the same Lord over all is rich to all who call upon him.

13 For whoever shall call on the name of the Lord Yahshua shall be saved.

14 How then can they call on him in whom they have not believed? Or how can they hear without a preacher?

15 Or how can they preach if they are not sent forth? As it is written, How beautiful are the feet of those who preach peace, and those who bring good tidings!

16 But all have not heard the preaching of the gospel. For Yesha'yahu said, My Lord, who has believed the echoes of our voice?

17 So then faith comes by hearing, and hearing by the word of Lord Yahweh.

18 But I say, Have they not heard? And behold the echoes of their voices have gone out over all the earth, and their words to the ends of the world.

19 But I say, Did not Israel know? First Moshe spoke thus: I will provoke you to jealousy by a people that are not my people, and I will make you angry by a stubborn people.

20 Then Yesha'yahu dared to say, I appeared to those who did not seek me, and was found by those who did not ask for me.

21 But to Israel he said, All the day long I have stretched out my hands to a quarrelsome and disobedient people.

CHAPTER 11

I say, then, has Lord Yahweh rejected his people? Far be it. For I also am an Israelite, descendant of Avraham, of the tribe of Binyamin.

2 Lord Yahweh has not rejected his people whom He foreknew. Do you not know what the scripture says of Eliyahu? How he complained to Lord Yahweh against Israel, saying,

3 My Lord, they have killed thy prophets and demolished thine altars; and I am left alone, and they seek my life.

4 And it was said to him in a vision, Behold I have reserved for Myself seven thousand men who have not fallen on their knees to worship Baal.

5 Even so at the present time a remnant is preserved, elected by grace.

6 And if by grace, then it is not by works; otherwise grace is no more grace. But if by works, then it is not by grace; otherwise work is no more work.

7 What then? Israel has not obtained what is sought; but the elected ones have obtained it, and the rest were dulled in their minds.

8 As it is written, Lord Yahweh has given them a stubborn spirit, eyes that cannot see, and ears that cannot hear, to this very day.

9 And David said, Let their table become a snare and a trap and a stumbling-block and a reward to them.

10 Let their eyes be darkened, that they may not see, and let their backs be bowed down always.

11 I say then, Have they stumbled that they should fall? Far be it. But rather by their stumbling, salvation has come to the Gentiles, in order to make them zealous.

12 Now if their stumbling has resulted in riches to the world, and to their condemnation in riches to the Gentiles, how much more is their restoration?

13 It is to you Gentiles that I speak, inasmuch as I am the apostle to the Gentiles, and perhaps magnify my ministry;

14 But if I am able to make those who are my flesh zealous, I may thus save some of them.

15 And if their rejection has resulted in reconciliation of the world, how much more will their restoration be? Indeed it will be life from the dead.

16 For if the first fruit is holy, the rest of the lump is also holy; and if the root is holy, so are the branches.

17 And if some of the branches were cut off, and you who are a branch of a wild olive tree have been grafted in their place, and you have become a partaker of the root and fatness of the olive tree,

18 Do not boast over the branches. For if you boast, it is not you who sustains the root, but the root sustains you.

19 Perhaps you may say, The branches were cut off that I may be grafted in their place.

20 Well, they were cut off because of their unbelief, but you exist by faith. Be not high-minded, but reverence Lord Yahweh.

21 For if Lord Yahweh did not spare the natural branches, it may well be He will not spare you.

22 Consider therefore the goodness and severity of Lord Yahweh: on those who fell, severity; but on you, goodness, if you continue in his goodness; otherwise you also will be cut off.

23 And even they, if they do not abide in their unbelief, will be grafted in; for Lord Yahweh is able to graft them in again.

24 For if you who have been cut from the wild olive tree, which is natural to you, and grafted contrary to your nature to become a good olive tree; how much more fruitful would they be, if they were grafted into their natural olive tree?

25 I am desirous, my brethren, that you should know this mystery, so that you may not be wise in your own conceits; for blindness of heart has to some degree befallen Israel, until the end of the Gentiles shall come.

26 And then all Israel shall be saved; as it is written, A deliverer shall come out of Zion, and he shall remove ungodliness from Ya'akov;

27 And then they shall have the same covenant from Me, when I have forgiven their sins.

28 Now according to the gospel, they are enemies for your sake. But according to election, they are beloved for the patriarchs' sakes.

29 For Lord Yahweh does not withdraw his gift and his call.

30 Just as you were formerly disobedient to Lord Yahweh and have now obtained mercy because of their disobedience,

31 Likewise, they are also disobedient now to the mercy which is upon you, that there may be mercy upon them also.

32 For Lord Yahweh has included all men in disobedience, that He may have mercy on every man.

33 O the depth of the riches, the wisdom, and the knowledge of Lord Yahweh! For no man has searched his judgment, and his ways are inscrutable.

34 For who has known the mind of the Lord, or who has been his counselor?

35 Or who has first given to Him and then received from Him?

36 For of Him, and through Him, and to Him are all things. To Him be glory and blessing for ever and ever. Amen.

CHAPTER 12

I beseech you therefore, brethren, by the mercies of Lord Yahweh, that you present your bodies as a living sacrifice, holy and acceptable to Lord Yahweh, by means of reasonable service.

2 Do not imitate the way of this world, but be transformed by the renewing of your minds, that you may discern what is that good, and acceptable, and perfect will of Lord Yahweh.

3 For I say, through the grace which is given to me, to all of you, not to think of yourselves beyond what you ought to think; but to think soberly, every man according to the measure of faith which Lord Yahweh has distributed to him.

4 For as we have many members in one body, and all members have not the same function.

5 So we, being many, are one body in the Christ, and every one members one of another.

6 Having then, gifts differing according to the grace that is given to us, some have the gift of prophecy, according to the measure of faith,

7 Some have the gift of ministration, in their ministry; and some of teaching, in their doctrine.

8 Some of consolation, in consoling; he that gives, let him do it with sincerity; he that rules, with diligence; he that shows mercy, with cheerfulness.

9 Let not your love be deceitful. Abhor that which is evil; hold fast to that which is good.

10 Be kindly affectionate to one to another with brotherly love; in honor preferring one another;

11 Not slothful in business. Fervent in spirit, serving the Lord;

12 Rejoicing in hope, patient in tribulation, continuing instant in prayer.

13 Distributing to the necessity of saints, given to hospitality.

14 Bless them that persecute you; bless, and curse not.

15 Rejoice with them who rejoice, and weep with them who weep.

16 Be of the same mind, one toward another. Mind not vain glory, but associate with those who are humble. Be not wise in your own conceits.

17 Recompense to no man evil for evil. But be diligent to do good things before the presence of all men.

18 If it be possible, as much as lies in you, live peaceably with all men.

19 Dearly beloved, avenge not yourselves, but rather restrain your wrath; for it is written, Vengeance is mine; I will execute justice for you, said the Lord.

20 Therefore if your enemy hunger, feed him; if he thirst, give him drink; for in so doing, you shall heap coals of fire on his head.

21 Be not overcome by evil, but overcome evil with good.

CHAPTER 13

Let every soul be subject to the sovereign authorities. For there is no power which is not from Lord Yahweh; and those who are in authority are ordained by Lord Yahweh.

2 Whoever therefore resists the civil authority, resists the command of Lord Yahweh; and they who resist shall receive judgment to themselves.

3 For judges are not a menace to good works, but to evil. Now if you wish not to be afraid of authority, then do good, and you will be praised for it.

4 For the ruler is the minister of Lord Yahweh to you for good. But if you do that which is wrong, be afraid; for he is not girded with the sword in vain; for he is the minister of Lord Yahweh, and an avenger of wrath upon those who commit crime.

5 Wherefore, we must be obedient, not only in fear of wrath, but also for our conscience sake.

6 For this reason you pay head tax also; for they are ministers of Lord Yahweh who are in charge of these things.

7 Render therefore, to every one as is due to him, head tax to him who is in charge of head tax, duty to him who is in charge of taxes; reverence to whom reverence is due, and honor to whom honor is due.

8 Owe no man anything, but love one another; for he who loves his neighbor has fulfilled the law,

9 Which says, Thou shalt not murder, Thou shalt not commit adultery, Thou shalt not covet; and if there is any other commandment, it is fulfilled in this saying, namely, Thou shalt love thy neighbor as thyself.

10 Love does not work evil to his neighbor, because love is the fulfillment of the law.

11 Know this also, that now is the time and the hour that we should awake from our sleep, for now our salvation is nearer than we believed.

12 The night is far spent, the day is at hand; let us therefore cast off the works of darkness, and let us put on the armor of light.

13 Let us walk decently, as in the daylight; not in clamor and drunkenness, not in the practice of immorality, not in envy and strife.

14 But clothe yourselves with our Lord Yahshua the Christ, and disregard the lusts of the flesh.

THEOLOGY WITHIN CHAPTER 14

1 Assist him who is weak in the faith. And do not waver in your reasoning.

7 For none of us lives to himself, and none of us dies to himself.

8 For whether we live, we live to our Lord; and whether we die, we die to our Lord; whether we live therefore, or die, we belong to our Lord.

9 For to this end even Yahshua the Christ both died and came back to life, and rose to be Lord both of the dead and living.

17 For the kingdom of Lord Yahweh is not meat and drink, but righteousness and peace and joy in the Holy Spirit.

THEOLOGY WITHIN CHAPTER 15

1 We who are strong ought to bear the weakness of the weak, and not seek to please ourselves.

THEOLOGY WITHIN CHAPTER 16

17 Now I beseech you, my brethren, beware of those who cause divisions and offences contrary to the doctrine which you have been taught; keep away from them.

18 For those who are such do not serve our Lord, Yahshua the Christ, but serve their own belly; and by smooth words and fair speeches deceive the hearts of the simple people.

19 But your obedience is known to everyone. I rejoice therefore on your behalf, and I want you to be wise in regard to good things and pure concerning evil things.

20 The God of peace will soon crush Satan under your feet. The grace of our Lord Yahshua the Christ be with you.

The First Epistle of Sha'ul The Apostle To The Corinthians

Chapter 1

Sha'ul, called to be an apostle of Lord Yahshua the Christ through the will of Lord Yahweh, and brother Sosthenes,

2 To the Church of Yahweh which is at Corinth, the invited and holy ones who are sanctified by Yahshua the Christ, and to all of them in every place who invoke the name of our Lord Yahshua, both theirs and ours:

3 Grace be to you and peace from Lord Yahweh, our Father, and from our Lord Yahshua the Christ.

4 I thank my God always on your behalf, for the grace of Lord Yahweh that has been given to you by Yahshua the Christ;

5 For in everything you are enriched by him in all utterance and in all knowledge;

6 Because the testimony of Yahshua has been confirmed in you,

7 And you do not lack any of his gifts but wait for the manifestation of our Lord, Yahshua the Christ.

8 Who will also strengthen you to the end, so that you may be blameless in the day of our Lord Yahshua.

9 Lord Yahweh, by whom you have been called to the fellowship of his Son Yahshua the Christ our Lord, is trustworthy.

10 Now I beseech you, my brethren, in the name of our Lord Yahshua, to be of one accord, and let there be no divisions among you but be perfectly united in one mind and in one thought.

11 For I have been informed about you, my brethren, by the household of Chloe that there are disputes among you.

12 Now this I say because there are some among you who say, I am a follower of Sha'ul; and some who say, I am a follower of Apollos; and some who say, I am a follower of Kepa; and some who say, I am a follower of Yahshua the Christ.

13 Why? Is Yahshua divided? or was Sha'ul crucified for you? or were you baptized in the name of Sha'ul?

14 I confess to my God that I have baptized none of you except Crispus and Gaius;

15 So no man can say that I have baptized in my own name.

16 And I baptized also the household of Stephanas. I do not know whether I have baptized anyone else.

17 For Yahshua the Christ did not send me to baptize, but to preach the gospel; and not to rely on the wisdom of words, lest the cross of Yahshua the Christ should be in vain.

18 To those who have gone astray, the preaching of the cross is foolishness; but to us who are saved, it is the power of Lord Yahweh.

19 For it is written, I will destroy the wisdom of the "wise," and I will do away with the understanding of the "prudent."

20 Where is the wise? where is the scribe? where is the learned of this world? Has not Lord Yahweh made foolish the "wisdom" of this world?

21 Since all the wisdom which Lord Yahweh had given was not understood by the world to know Lord Yahweh, it pleased Lord Yahweh that those who believed by the simple gospel could be saved.

22 For the Jews demand signs, and the Greeks seek after wisdom;

23 But we preach Yahshua the Christ crucified, which is a stumbling block to the Jews and is foolishness to the Greeks;

24 But for those who are called, both Jews and Gentiles, Yahshua the Christ is the power of Lord Yahweh and the wisdom Lord Yahweh;

25 Because the "foolishness" of Lord Yahweh is wiser than men, and the "weakness" of Lord Yahweh is stronger than men.

26 For consider also your own calling, my brethren, not many among you are wise in terms of worldly things and not many among you are mighty and not many among you belong to nobility.

27 But Lord Yahweh has chosen the "foolish" ones of the world to put the wise to shame; and Lord Yahweh has chosen the "weak" ones of the world to embarrass the mighty;

28 And He has chosen those of humble families in the world, and the lowly and those who are "insignificant," in order to belittle those who consider themselves important,

29 So that no man should boast in his presence.

30 But you also belong to Lord Yahweh through Yahshua the Christ who, from Lord Yahweh, is wisdom and righteousness and sanctification and salvation to all of us.

31 As it is written, He who glories, let him glory in the Lord.

THEOLOGY WITHIN CHAPTER 2

2:9 But as it is written, The eye has not seen and the ear has not heard and the heart of man has not conceived the things which Lord Yahweh has prepared for those who love Him.

12 Now we have received not the spirit of the world, but the Spirit that is from Lord Yahweh, that we may understand the gifts that are given to us by Lord Yahweh.

13 For the things which we discuss are not dependent on the knowledge of words and man's wisdom, but on the teaching of the Spirit; thus explaining spiritual things to the spiritually minded.

14 For the material man rejects spiritual things; they are foolishness to him; neither can he know them, because they are spiritually discerned.

16 For who knows the mind of the Lord that he may teach it? But we have the mind of Yahshua the Christ.

CHAPTER 3

So I, my brethren, could not converse with you as with spiritual men, with you as with spiritual men, but as with worldly men and even as with little children in Yahshua the Christ.

2 I have fed you with milk (mild truth), and not with meat (strong truth); for hitherto you were unable to eat it, and even now you are not ready for it because you are still worldly;

3 For as long as there is among you envying and strife and divisions, are you not worldly and still following the material things?

4 For while one says, I am a follower of Sha'ul; and another, I am a follower of Apollos; are you not worldly?

5 Who then is Sha'ul and who is Apollos, but ministers through whom you were converted; each one is gifted according as the Lord gave to him.

6 I have planted, Apollos watered; but Lord Yahweh gave the increase.

7 So then neither he who plants, nor he who waters deserves the credit; but Lord Yahweh who gives the increase.

8 Thus the planter and the waterer are equal; and each one shall receive his own wages according to his own labor.

9 For we work together with Lord Yahweh; you are Lord Yahweh's work and Lord Yahweh's building.

10 According to the grace of Lord Yahweh which is given to me, as a wise master builder, I have laid the foundation, and another builds thereon.

11 For other foundation can no man lay then that which is already laid, which is Yahshua the Christ.

12 Now if any man build on this foundation gold, silver, precious stones, wood, hay, stubble;

13 Every man's work shall be plainly seen; for the light of the day shall expose it, because it shall be revealed by fire; and the fire shall test every man's work and show of what sort it is.

14 and the builder whose work survives shall receive his reward.

15 and the one whose work shall be burned, he shall suffer loss; but he himself shall be rescued, even as one who has been saved from the fire.

16 Do you not know that you are the temple of Lord Yahweh, and that the Spirit of Lord Yahweh dwells in you?

17 And whoever defiles the temple of Lord Yahweh, Lord Yahweh will destroy; for the temple of Lord Yahweh is holy, and that temple is you.

18 Let no man deceive himself. Whoever among you thinks he is wise in this world, let him consider himself a fool so that he may become wise.

19 For the wisdom of this world is foolishness before Lord Yahweh. For it is written, He catches the wise in their own craftiness.

20 And again, The Lord knows that the thoughts of the "wise" are vain.

21 Therefore, let no man boast about men. For all things are yours,

22 Whether Sha'ul or Apollos or Kepa or the world or life or death or things present or things to come; all things are yours;

23 And you are Yahshua's, and Yahshua is Lord Yahweh's.

CHAPTER 4

This is the way you should consider us: as the servants of Yahshua the Christ, and as stewards of the mysteries of Lord Yahweh.

2 Henceforth, it is required of stewards that every one of them must be faithful.

3 But as for me, it is of little importance that I am judged by you or by anyone else, because I do not judge myself.

4 For I know nothing of which I am guilty; yet I may not be right in this, for my judge is the Lord.

5 Therefore do not judge before the time, until the Lord comes and brings to light the hidden things of darkness and reveals the thoughts of the hearts; then shall every man have praise from Lord Yahweh.

6 These things concerning myself and Apollos, my brethren, I have pictured for your sakes, that in our example you may learn not to think beyond that which is written, and let no one exalt himself over his fellow man on account of any man.

7 For who has examined you? And what do you have which was not given to you? And if you did receive it, then why do you boast as if you had not received it?

8 For a long time you have been full and enriched, and you have waxed strong without our counsel. And I would to Lord Yahweh you were as kings, so that we also may reign with you.

9 For I think Lord Yahweh has placed us, the apostles, last as if we were condemned to death; for we have become a spectacle to the world and to angels and to men.

10 We are fools for the Christ's sake, but if you are wise in Yahshua the Christ; we are weak, but you are strong; you are praised, but we are despised.

11 Even to this very hour we both hunger and thirst, and are naked and mistreated and have no permanent home;

12 And labor, working with our own hands; being cursed we bless, being persecuted we endure;

13 Being reviled, we intreat; we are looked upon as the refuse of the world, and we are the revilement of every man to this day.

14 I do not write these things to make you feel ashamed, but to advise you as beloved children.

15 For though you have ten thousand instructors in Yahshua the Christ, yet you will not have many fathers; for in Yahshua the Christ, I have begotten you through the gospel.

16 I beseech you, therefore, to follow me.

17 This is why I have sent Timotheus to you, who is my beloved son and faithful in the Lord, who shall remind you of my manner of life in Yahshua the Christ, just I teach in all the churches.

18 There are some among you who are puffed up, thinking I am unwilling to come to you.

19 But I will come to you very soon, if the Lord wills, and then I shall find out not the words of these men who exalt themselves, but their power.

20 For the kingdom of Lord Yahweh is not in the word, but in power.

21 Now what do you desire? Shall I come to you with a rod or with love and in the spirit of meekness?

CHAPTERS 5

6 Your boasting is not good. Do you not know that a little leaven will leaven the whole lump?

7 Clean out therefore the old leaven, so that you may be a new lump, just as you are unleavened. For our Passover is Yahshua the Christ, who was sacrificed for our sake.

8 Therefore let us celebrate the festival, not with the old leaven, neither with the leaven of evil and bitterness, but with the leaven of purity and sanctity.

9 I wrote to you in an epistle not to associate with immoral persons.

10 I do not mean that you should separate completely from all the immoral people of this world or from the fraudulent and extortioners or from idolaters; otherwise you would be obliged to leave this world.

CHAPTERS 6

9 Do you not know that the wicked shall not inherit the kingdom of Lord Yahweh? Be not mislead; neither the immoral nor idolaters nor adulterers nor the corrupt nor men who lie with males,

10 Nor extortioners nor thieves nor drunkards nor defrauders shall inherit the kingdom of Lord Yahweh.

11 And some of these evils were to be found in some of you, but you have been cleansed and have been sanctified and made righteous in the name of our Lord Yahshua the Christ, and through the Spirit of our God.

14 And as Lord Yahweh has raised our Lord, so He will raise us also by his own power.

15 Do you not know that your bodies are the members of the Christ? How then can one take a member of the Christ and make it the member of a harlot? Far be it.

16 Or do you not know that he who joins his body to a harlot is one body with her? For it is said, The two shall become one body.

17 But he who unites himself with our Lord, becomes one with him in spirit.

18 Keep away from fornication. Every sin that a man commits is outside his body; but he who commits adultery, sins against his own body.

19 Or do you not know that your body is the temple of the Holy Spirit that dwells within you, which you have of Lord Yahweh, and you are not your own?

20 For you have been bought with a price; therefore glorify Lord Yahweh in your body and in your spirit, because they belong to Lord Yahweh.

CHAPTER 7

Now concerning the things which you wrote to me. It is proper for a husband not to have intimacy with his wife at times.

2 Nevertheless, because of the danger of immorality, let every man hold to his own wife, and let every woman hold to her own husband.

3 Let the husband give to his wife the love which he owes her; and likewise also the wife to her husband.

4 The wife has no authority over her own body, but her husband; and likewise also the husband has no authority over his own body, but his wife.

5 Therefore do not deprive one another except when both of you consent to do so, especially at the time when you devote yourselves to fasting and prayer; and then come together again, so that Satan may not tempt you because of your physical passion.

6 But I say this only to weak persons, for it is not part of the law.

7 For I would that all men were like myself in purity. But every man has his proper gift from Lord Yahweh, one after this manner and another after that.

8 I say this to those who have no wives, and to widows: It is better for them to be as I am;

9 But if they cannot endure it, let them marry; for it is better to marry than to burn with passion.

10 But those who have wives, I command {not I, but my Lord}, Let not the wife be separated from her husband;

11 But if she separate, let her remain single, or be reconciled to her husband; and let not the husband desert his wife.

12 But to the rest, I {not my Lord} say this: If any brother has a wife who is not a convert, and she wishes to live with him, let him not leave her.

13 And the woman who has a husband who is not a convert but is content to live with her, let her not leave him.

14 For the husband who is not a convert is sanctified through the wife who is a convert, and the wife who is not a convert is sanctified through the husband who is a convert; otherwise, their children would be impure, but in such cases they are pure.

15 But if the one who is not a convert wishes to separate, let him separate. In such cases, a convert {man or woman} is free; for Lord Yahweh has called us to live in peace.

16 For how do you know, O wife, that you shall save your husband? Or how do you know, O husband, that you shall save your wife?

17 But every man, according as the Lord has distributed to him, and every man, as Lord Yahweh has called him, so let him walk. And this I command also for all the churches.

18 If a man was circumcised when he was called, let him not adhere to the party of uncircumcision. And if he was uncircumcised, when he was called, let him not be circumcised.

19 For circumcision is nothing, and uncircumcision is nothing, but the keeping of the Lord's commandments is everything.

20 Let every man remain in the station of life in which he is called.

21 If you were a slave, care not for it; but if you can be made free, use it rather.

22 For a slave who is called by our Lord, is the Lord's freeman; likewise, a freeman who is called, is also the Christ's servant.

23 You have been bought (by the Lord) with a price; you must not therefore become slaves of men.

24 My brethren, let every man in whatever station of life he was called, remain therein, serving Lord Yahweh.

25 Now concerning virginity, I have no command from Lord Yahweh; yet I give my advice as one who has been favored by Lord Yahweh to be trustworthy.

26 And I suppose that this is good for the present necessity, therefore I say, It is better for a man to remain as he is.

27 If you are married, do not seek divorce. If you are divorced from a wife, do not seek a wife.

28 But if you (a virgin) marry, you do not sin; if she (a virgin) marry, she does not sin. Nevertheless, such shall have trouble in the flesh; but I would spare you.

29 But this I do say, my brethren: The time is short; let those who have wives be as though they had none;

30 And those who weep, as though they had not wept; and those who rejoice, as though they had not rejoiced; and those who buy, as though they did not possess anything;

31 And those who make use of this world should not abuse it, for the fashion of this world is passing away.

32 Therefore, I would that you were free from worldly cares. For he who is unmarried is concerned in the things of his master, so as to please his master.

33 And he who is married is concerned with worldly things, in order to please his wife.

34 So there is a difference between a married woman and a virgin. She who is unmarried is concerned about the welfare of her Lord, and to be pure both in body and spirit; but she who is married is concerned with worldly things, in order to please her husband.

35 I am saying this for your own benefit; I am not trying to snare or put a yoke on you, but I exhort you to be perfect before the Lord, and faithful without distraction.

36 If any man thinks that he behaves uncomely toward his virgin daughter because she has passed the bloom of youth, and also because he has not given her in marriage and that he should give her, let him strive to behave well toward her.

37 If he has sincerely decided that his daughter should remain single, he does well.

38 So then he who gives his virgin daughter in marriage does well; and he who does not give his daughter in marriage does even better.

39 A wife is bound by the law as long as her husband lives; but if her husband dies, she is free to marry whom she pleases, but only a Christian.

40 But, in my opinion, she is happier to remain as she is. And I think also that I have the Spirit of Lord Yahweh.

CHAPTER 8

Now concerning sacrifices offered to idols: We know well that we all have knowledge; knowledge makes for pride, but love ennobles.

2 And if any man thinks that he knows anything, he knows nothing yet as he ought to know.

3 But if any man loves Lord Yahweh, the same is known of him.

4 Concerning the eating of food offered to idols, we know that an idol is nothing, and that there is no other God except Lord Yahweh.

5 For though there are those that are called gods, whether in heaven or earth, just as there are many gods and many lords,

6 To us there is one God, the Father, from whom comes every thing and by whom we live; and one Lord Yahshua the Christ, by whom are all things, and we by him.

7 Howbeit, there is not in every man that knowledge; for some with clear conscience eat that which has been offered to idols as a sacrifice; and their conscience being weak, is defiled.

8 But meat does not bring us closer to Lord Yahweh; for neither if we eat, are we the better; neither if we do not eat, are we the worse.

9 But be careful lest this liberty of yours becomes a stumbling block to the weak.

10 For if anyone should see you, who has knowledge, at a table in the temple of idols, shall not the conscience of him who is weak embolden him to eat that which is sacrificed to idols?

11 So the one who is weak and for whom Yahshua the Christ died, will be lost through your indifference.

12 And if you offend your brothers, and so influence their weak consciences, you also offend the Christ.

13 Therefore, if meat which is sacrificed to idols causes my brother to stumble, I will eat no such meat so that I may not cause my brother to offend.

CHAPTER 9

Am I not a free man? Am I not an apostle? Have I not seen Yahshua the Christ our Lord? Are you not my work in my Lord?

2 If I am not an apostle to others, yet to you I am, then you are the seal confirming my apostleship.

3 So my answer to those who criticize me is this:

4 Have we not the right to eat and to drink?

5 And have we not the right to travel with a Christian wife, just as the rest of the apostles do, and as the brothers of our Lord, and as Kepa?

6 I and Bar-Nabba, have not we the right to live without working?

7 What officer commands an army at his own expense? Or who plants a vineyard and does not eat of its fruits? Or who feeds sheep, and does not eat of the produce of his flock?

8 I say these things as a man. Behold the law says them also.

9 For it is written in the law of Moshe, You shall not muzzle the ox that treads out the wheat. Why? Is Lord Yahweh concerned only for the ox?

10 No. It is known that he said it for our sakes, and it was written for our sakes because the plough-man must plough in hope, and he who threshes in hope of the crop.

11 Now if we have sown among you spiritual things, is it too much that we should reap material things from you?

12 If others have this authority over you, have we not the greater right? Nevertheless, we have not used this authority; but we have endured all things so that we would not hinder the gospel of Yahshua the Christ.

13 Do you not know that those who work in the holy place are maintained out of the temple? And those who minister at the altar share the offerings with the altar?

14 Even so has our Lord commanded that those who preach his (the Lord's) gospel should live by his gospel.

15 But I have used none of these privileges; neither have I written these things that it should be so done to me; for it were better for me to die than that any man should declare my glorying.

16 For though I preach the gospel, I have nothing to glory of; for I am under obligation; yea, woe to me if I preach not the gospel!

17 For if I do this thing willingly, I have my reward; but if against my will, I still have a stewardship entrusted to me.

18 What then is my wage? This is it. When I preach the gospel of Yahshua the Christ, I do it without thought of recompense, and I have not abused the power given to me in the gospel.

19 Even though I am free from all men, I have made myself a servant unto all, that I might gain the more.

20 So with the Jews I became as a Jew, that I might win the Jews; and with those who are under the law, I became as one who is under the law, that I may win those who are under the law.

21 To those who are without law; I became like one who is without law so that I may win them who are without law, even though I am not lawless before Lord Yahweh because I am under the law of Yahshua the Christ.

22 With the weak I became as weak, that I may win the weak. I became everything to every man so that I may by all means bring salvation to everyone.

23 And this I do for the gospel's sake, that I may be a partaker of the gospel.

24 Do you not know that the runners in a race all run, but only one is victorious? So you must run so that you may obtain victory.

25 And every man who battles in the contest frees his mind from everything else. And yet they run to win a garland which is perishable; but we strive to win that which is everlasting.

26 I therefore so "run", not for something that is uncertain; and so I fight, not as one who beats the air;

27 But I conquer and subdue my body so that, by no chance, when I preach to others, will I be a hypocrite.

CHAPTER 10

Moreover, brethren, I want you to know that our fathers were all under the cloud and all passed through the sea;

2 And all were baptized by Moshe, both in the cloud and in the sea;

3 And all ate the same spiritual food;

4 And all drank the same spiritual drink; for they drank of that spiritual Rock that followed them, and that Rock was Yahshua the Christ.

5 But with many of them, Lord Yahweh was not well pleased; for they were smitten in the wilderness.

6 But they became an example to us, so that we should not covet evil things as they did covet.

7 Neither should we become idolaters, as some of them; as it is written, The people sat down to eat and drink, and rose up to quarrel.

8 Neither should we commit adultery, as some of them have committed; for in one day, twenty-three thousand of them fell dead.

9 Neither should we tempt the Christ, as some of them tried to tempt him; for they were destroyed by snakes.

10 Neither should you murmur, as some of them murmured; for they were destroyed by the hand of the destroyer.

11 Now all of these things which happened to them are an example for us; and they are written to warn us, for the fulfillment of the ages has come in our time.

12 Therefore, let him who thinks he can stand, take heed so that he may not fall.

13 No other temptation has overtaken you but that which is common to man; but Lord Yahweh is faithful; He will not allow you to be tempted beyond your endurance; and He will make a way for you to escape your temptation, so that you may be able to bear it.

14 Therefore, my beloved, keep away from idolatry.

15 I speak as to wise men; you are able to judge what I say.

16 The cup of thanksgiving which we bless, is it not the communion of the blood of Yahshua the Christ? The bread which we break, is it not the communion of the body of Yahshua the Christ?

17 For just as the loaf of bread is one, so we are all one body; for we are all partakers of that one bread.

18 Behold Israel, whose observance is after the flesh; do not those who eat the sacrifices become partakers of the alter?

19 What do I say then? That the idol is anything, or that the sacrifice to idols is anything? No.

20 But what the pagans sacrifice, they sacrifice to devils and not to Lord Yahweh; and I would not have you in fellowship with devils.

21 You cannot drink the cup of our Lord and the cup of devils; you cannot be partakers of the table of our Lord and of the table of devils.

22 Are we trying to provoke our Lord to anger? Are we stronger than he?

23 Everything is lawful for me, but not everything is expedient; everything is lawful for me, but not everything improves morality.

24 But let no man seek for himself alone, but let every man seek for his neighbor also.

25 Anything for sale in the market place, you can eat without question for conscience sake;

26 For the earth, and the fullness thereof, is the Lord's.

27 If any pagan should invite you, and you wish to go, you may eat without question for conscience sake, whatever is set before you.

28 But if anyone say to you, This meat has been offered as a sacrifice, then do not eat it for the sake of him who told you, and for conscience sake.

29 But the conscience of which I speak is not yours, but the conscience of him who told you; for why is my liberty judged by another man's conscience?

30 For if I by grace am made worthy, why should I be reproached for that for which I give thanks?

31 Whether therefore you eat or drink, or whatsoever you do, do all to the glory of Lord Yahweh.

32 Give no offense, neither to the Jews nor to the Gentiles, nor to the Church of Lord YHWH;

33 Just as I please all men in all things, not seeking my own good, but the good of many, that they may be saved.

CHAPTER 11

Take example by me, even as I also follow Yahshua the Christ.

2 Now I praise you, my brethren, that you remember me in all things and keep the ordinances as I delivered them to you.

3 But I would have you know that the head of every man is Yahshua the Christ; and the head of the wife is her husband; and the head of Yahshua the Christ is Lord Yahweh.

4 Every man who prays or prophesies with his head covered, dishonors his head.

5 And every woman who prays or prophesies with her head uncovered, dishonors her head; for she is equal to her whose head is shaven.

6 For if a woman does not cover her head, let her also cut off her hair; but if it be a shame for a woman to be shorn or shaven, let her cover her head.

7 For a man indeed ought not cover his head, because he is the image and the glory of Lord Yahweh; but the woman is the glory of the man.

8 For the man was not created from the woman; but the woman was created from the man.

9 Neither was the man created for the woman; but the woman for the man.

10 For this reason, the woman ought to be modest and cover her head as a mark of respect to the angels.

11 Nevertheless, in our Lord there is no preference between man and woman, neither between woman and man.

12 For as the woman is of the man, even so is the man by the woman; but all things are of Lord Yahweh.

13 Judge for yourselves; is it comely for a woman to pray to Lord Yahweh with her head uncovered?

14 Does not even nature itself teach you that if a man have long hair, it is a disgrace to him?

15 But if a woman have long hair, it is a glory to her; for her hair is given her for a covering.

16 But if any man dispute these things, we have no precedent, neither has the Church of Lord YHWH.

17 Now I give you these commands, not to praise you, for you have not made progress but have become worse.

18 First of all, when you gather in the church, I hear that there are divisions among you; and I partly believe it.

19 For controversies are bound to be among you, that those who are approved may be made manifest among you.

20 When you gather together therefore, you do not eat and drink as is appropriate on the day of our Lord.

21 But some men eat their supper before others; and so it happens that one is hungry and another is drunken.

22 Why? Have you not houses to eat and drink in? Or do you not respect the Church of Lord YHWH, and want to shame those who have nothing? What shall I say to you? Shall I praise you? No, for this, I cannot praise you.

23 For I myself received from our Lord that which I also delivered to you, That our Lord, Yahshua, on that very night in which he was betrayed took bread;

24 And when he had given thanks, he broke it and said, Take and eat; this is my body which is broken for you; do this in remembrance of me.

25 Likewise after supper, he gave also the cup and said, This cup is the new testament in my blood; do this, as often as you drink it, in remembrance of me.

26 For whenever you eat this bread and drink from this cup, you commemorate our Lord's death until his coming.

27 Therefore whosoever shall eat of the Lord's bread and drink from his cup unworthily, shall be guilty of the blood and body of the Lord.

28 For this reason, let a man examine himself and eat of this bread and drink from this cup.

29 For he who eats and drinks unworthily, eats and drinks to his condemnation; for he does not discern the Lord's body.

30 This is the reason many are sick and weak among you, and many are dying.

(it seems that the bread and drink called "Eucharist", is more than a symbol)

31 For if we would judge ourselves, we would not be judged.

32 But when we (while still alive) are judged by our Lord, we are simply chastened, so that we may not be condemned with the world.

33 Hereafter, my brethren, when you come together to eat, wait for one another.

34 And if any man hunger, let him eat at home so that you may not come together unto condemnation. As to the rest of the things, I will instruct you when I come.

CHAPTER 12

Now concerning spiritual gifts, my brethren, I want to remind you;

2 That once you were pagans, and without exception you were carried away by dumb idols.

3 Therefore I want you to understand that no man speaking by the Spirit of Lord Yahweh, calls Lord Yahshua accursed; and that no man can say that Lord Yahshua is the Lord but by the Holy Spirit.

4 Now there are diversities of spiritual gifts, but the one Holy Spirit.

5 And there are diversities of ministries, but the same Lord.

6 And there are diversities of powers, but it is the one God who works all things in all men.

7 But the manifestation of the Holy Spirit is given to every man as help to every man.

8 For to one is given by the Holy Spirit, the word of wisdom; to another, the word of knowledge by the Holy Spirit.

9 To another, faith by the Holy Spirit; to another, gifts of healing by the Holy Spirit;

10 To another, the working of miracles; to another, prophecy; to another, the discerning of spirits; to another, different languages; and to another, the interpretation of languages.

11 But all of these gifts are wrought by the Holy Spirit, dividing to every one severally as he will.

12 For as the body is one and has many members, and all the members of the body, even though many, are one body, so also is the Christ.

13 For all of us are baptized by one Spirit into one body, whether Jews or Gentiles, whether bond or free; and we have all received through the one Holy Spirit.

14 The body of the Christ is not one member, but many.

15 For if the "foot" should say, Because I am not the "hand," I am not part of the body; is it therefore not a member of the body?

16 And if the "ear" should say, because I am not the "eye," I am not a member of the body; is it therefore not a member of the body?

17 If the whole body were "eyes," where would the "hearing" be? And if the whole were "hearing," where would "smelling" be?

18 But now Lord Yahweh has set every member in the body as it pleased Him.

19 If it were all one member, where would the body be?

20 But now they are many members, yet but one body.

21 The "eye" cannot say to the "hand," I have no need of you; nor can the "head" say to the "feet," I have no need of you.

22 But rather those members of the body which are considered to be delicate are necessary.

23 And on those members of the body which we think to be less honorable, we bestow more abundant honor; and the parts that are uncomely we dress with greater care;

24 For our comely parts have no need for attention. But Lord Yahweh has so tempered the body together, and has given greater honor to the member which is inferior,

25 That there may be no discord in the body, but that they may care one for another, all members should be equal.

26 So when one member is in pain, all the members suffer with it; and if one member is honored, all the members will glory with it.

27 Now you are the body of the Christ, and you are members in your respective places.

28 For Lord Yahweh has set in his church; first apostles, then prophets, then teachers, then performers of miracles, then those who have the gift of healing, then helpers, then leaders, and then speakers in diverse languages.

29 Are all apostles? Are all prophets? Are all teachers? Are all workers of miracles?

30 Do all have the gifts of healing? Do all speak in divers languages? Or do all interpret?

31 But if you are searching for the greater gifts, I will show you a more excellent way.

CHAPTER 13

Though I speak with the languages of men and of angels, and have not charity in my heart, I am become as sounding brass or a tinkling cymbal.

2 And though I have the gift of prophecy, and understand all mysteries and all knowledge; and though I have all faith, so that I could move mountains, and have not charity in my heart, I am nothing.

3 And though I bestow all my goods to feed the poor, and though I give my body to be burned, and have not charity in my heart, I gain nothing.

4 Charity is long-suffering and kind; charity does not envy; charity does not make a vain display of itself, and does not boast,

5 Charity does not behave unseemly nor seeks its own, is not easily provoked, thinks no evil;

6 Charity does not rejoice over iniquity, but does rejoice in the truth;

7 Charity bears all things, believes all things, hopes all things, endures all things.

8 Charity never fails; but whether there be prophecies, they shall fail; whether there be languages, they shall cease; whether there be knowledge, it shall vanish away.

9 For we know in part, and we prophesy in part.

10 But when that which is perfect is come, then that which is im-perfect shall come to an end.

11 When I was a child, I spoke and understood as a child, I also thought as a child; but when I became a man, I put away childish things.

12 For now we see though a mirror, darkly; but then face to face. Now I know in part; but then I shall know even as also I am known.

13 And now abide faith, hope, and charity, these three; but the greatest of these is charity.

Chapter 14

Follow after charity, and desire spiritual gifts, above all that you may prophesy.

2 For he who speaks in an unknown language speaks not to men, but to Lord Yahweh; for no man understands what he says; however through the Holy Spirit, he speaks mysteries.

3 But he who prophesies speaks to men for moral improvement, encouragement, and comfort.

4 He who speaks in an unknown language, edifies himself; but he who prophesies edifies the church.

5 I would that you all spoke various languages, but I would rather that you prophesied; for he who prophesies is greater than he who speaks various languages, unless he interprets; however, if he interprets, he edifies the church.

6 Now, my brethren, if I should come to you and speak in diverse languages, what would I profit you, except I speak to you either by means of revelation or by knowledge or by prophesying or by teaching?

7 For even when things without life give sound, whether flute or harp, except they make a distinction between one tone and another, how shall it be known what is sung or played?

8 For if the trumpet give an uncertain sound, who will prepare himself for the battle?

9 Even so you, except you utter by the language words easy to be understood, how shall it be known what you say? You shall speak as into the air.

10 For behold, there are many kinds of languages in the world, yet none of them without expression.

11 So if I do not understand the utterance, I shall be as a barbarian to the speaker, and the speaker shall be as a barbarian to me.

12 Likewise you, since you are zealous of spiritual gifts for the edification of the church, seek that you may excel in these gifts.

13 Thus, he who speaks in an unknown language prays that he may interpret it.

14 For if I pray in an unknown language, my spirit prays, but my understanding is unfruitful.

15 What then shall I do? I will pray with my spirit and I will pray with my understanding also; I will sing with my spirit, and I will sing with my understanding also.

16 Otherwise, if you say a blessing with the spirit, how can one who occupies the place of the unlearned say Amen to your thanksgiving, since he does not understand what you say?

17 For indeed you bless well, but your fellow man is not enlightened.

18 I thank Lord Yahweh that I speak with languages more than you all;

19 But in the church I would rather speak five words with my understanding, so that I may teach others also, rather than speak ten thousand words in an unknown language.

20 My brethren, be not like infants in your understanding; only to evil things be like innocent children, but in your understanding be mature.

21 In the law it is written, With a foreign speech and in another language, I will speak to this people; yet for all that, they will not listen to me, says the Lord.

22 Thus, the gift of languages is instituted as a sign, not for believers, but for unbelievers; but prophesying is not meant for those who do not believe, but for those who believe.

23 If therefore the whole church assembles together and all speak in different languages, and there enter unlearned people or unbelievers, will they not say, They are fanatical?

24 But if all prophesy, and an unlearned man or an unbeliever enter, he will be convinced by all, and he will be set right by all.

25 Thus the secrets of his heart will be revealed, and then he will fall on his face, and he will worship Lord Yahweh, and say, Truly, Lord Yahweh is among you.

26 Therefore I say to you, my brethren, when you gather together, whoever among you has a psalm to sing, has a doctrine, has a revelation, has the gift of languages, or the gift of interpretation, let everything be done for moral improvement.

27 And if any man should speak in an unknown language, let two or at most three speak, and speak one by one; and let one interpret.

28 But if there is no one to interpret, let him who speaks in an unknown language keep silence in the church; and let him speak to himself and to Lord Yahweh.

29 Let the prophets speak two or three in turn, and the others discern what is said.

30 And if anything is revealed to another who is seated, let the first speaker hold his peace.

31 For you may all prophesy one by one, so that every one may learn and be comforted.

32 For the spirits of the prophets are subject to the prophets.

33 For Lord Yahweh is not a God of confusion but of peace, and He is in all churches of the saints.

34 Let your women keep silent in the church, for they have no permission to speak; but they are to be under obedience as is said in the law.

35 And if they wish to learn anything, let them ask their husbands at home; for it is a shame for women to speak in the church.

36 What? Did the word of Lord Yahweh come from you? Or did it come for you only?

37 If any one among you thinks he is a prophet or that he is inspired by the Holy Spirit, let him acknowledge that these things that I write to you are the commandments of our Lord.

38 But if any man be ignorant, let him be ignorant.

39 Therefore, my brethren, desire earnestly to prophesy, and do not prohibit speaking in unknown languages.

40 Let all things be done decently and in order.

THEOLOGY WITHIN CHAPTER 15

3 For I delivered to you first of all that which I had received, that Yahshua the Christ died for our sins according to the scriptures;

4 And that he was buried, and that he rose again on the third day according to the scriptures;

42 So also is the resurrection of the dead. The human body is sown in corruption; the body is raised in incorruption:

43 The body is sown in dishonor; it is raised in glory: it is sown in weakness; it is raised in power:

44 It is sown a natural body; it is raised a spiritual body. There is a natural body and there is a spiritual body.

50 Now this I say, my brethren, that flesh and blood cannot inherit the kingdom of Lord Yahweh; neither does corruption inherit incorruption.

51 Behold, I tell you a mystery: We shall not all die, but we shall all be changed.

52 In a moment, in the twinkling of an eye, at the last trumpet; for the trumpet shall sound and the dead shall be raised incorruptible, and we shall be changed.

53 For this corruptible must put on incorruption, and this mortal must put on immortality.

56 The sting of death is sin; and the strength of sin is the law.

57 But thanks be to Lord Yahweh, who has given us the victory through our Lord: Yahshua the Christ.

58 Therefore, my beloved brethren, be steadfast, unmoveable, always abounding in the work of the Lord, for as much as you know that your labor is not in vain in the Lord.

THEOLOGY WITHIN CHAPTER 16

16:13 Watch, stand firm in the faith, be valiant, be strong.

14 Let all your deeds be done with charity.

22 Whoever does not love our Lord, Yahshua the Christ, let him be accursed.

23 The grace of our Lord, Yahshua the Christ, be with you.

24 My love be with you all in Yahshua the Christ. Amen.

The Second Epistle of Sha'ul The Apostle

To The Corinthians

THEOLOGY WITHIN CHAPTER 2

14 Now thanks be to Lord Yahweh, who has made us in the pattern of the Christ, and makes manifest the savior of his knowledge through us in every place.

17 For we are not like those who corrupt the word of Lord Yahweh; but according to the truth, and as men of Lord Yahweh, we speak through Yahshua the Christ in the sight of Lord Yahweh.

THEOLOGY WITHIN CHAPTER 3

3 For you are known to be the epistle of Yahshua the Christ ministered by us, written not with ink, but with the Spirit of the living God; not on tablets of stone, but on tablets of the living heart.

4 Such is the trust that we have through Yahshua the Christ toward Lord Yahweh.

5 Not that we are sufficient of ourselves to think anything as of ourselves; but our strength comes from Lord Yahweh,

6 Who has made us worthy to be ministers of the new covenant; not of the letter, but of the Spirit; for the letter of the law punishes with death, but the Spirit gives life.

CHAPTER 4

For this reason, we are not weary of the ministry in which we are engaged, just as we are not weary of the mercies that have been upon us;

2 But we have renounced the hidden things of shame, and we do not practice cunning nor do we handle the word of Lord Yahweh deceitfully; but by manifestation of the truth, we commend ourselves to every man's conscience before Lord Yahweh.

3 If our gospel is hidden, it is hidden to those who are lost,

4 To those in this world whose minds have been blinded by the "god" (Satan) of this system of things, because they did not believe, lest the light of the glorious gospel of Yahshua the Christ, who, is the likeness of Lord Yahweh, should not shine on them.

5 For we do not preach about ourselves, but about Yahshua the Christ, our Lord; and as to ourselves, we are your servants for Yahshua's sake.

6 For Lord Yahweh, who said, Let light shine out of darkness, has shone in our hearts so that we may be enlightened with the knowledge of the glory of Lord Yahweh in the person of his Son Yahshua the Christ.

7 But we have this treasure in earthen vessels, that the excellency of power may be from Lord Yahweh, and not from us.

8 We are distressed in every way, but not overwhelmed; we are harassed on all sides, but not conquered;

9 Persecuted, but not forsaken; cast down, but not destroyed;

10 For we always bear in our bodies, the death of Yahshua, so that the life of Yahshua may also be made manifest in our bodies.

11 For if we who live, are delivered to death for Lord Yahshua's sake, so also will the life of Lord Yahshua be made manifest in our mortal bodies.

12 Thus death is close to us, but life is near to you.

13 We have the same spirit of faith; as it is written, I believed, and therefore we also speak,

14 Knowing that He who raised our Lord, Yahshua the Christ, shall raise us also by Yahshua the Christ, and shall present us with you.

15 For all things are for your sakes so that the abundant grace may, through the thanksgiving of many, be added to the glory of Lord Yahweh.

16 For this reason, we do not grow weary; for though the outer man perish, yet the inner man is renewed day by day.

17 For while the troubles of the present time are little and light, a great and limitless glory for ever and ever is prepared for us.

18 We do not rejoice in the things which are seen, but we rejoice in the things which are not seen; for the things which are seen are temporal, but the things which are not seen are eternal.

CHAPTER 5

For we know that if our earthly house were destroyed, we still have a building made by Lord Yahweh, a house not made with human hands, eternal in heaven.

2 We also weary over this earthly house, earnestly longing to be clothed upon with our house which is in heaven.

3 If so, be that being clothed, we shall not be found naked.

4 While we are in this earthly house, we groan because of its weight; yet we are unwilling to leave it, but rather wish to add to it, so that death will be overcome by life.

5 Now He who has prepared us for this very thing is Lord Yahweh, who also has given to us the pledge of his Spirit.

6 Therefore we know and are convinced that so long as we dwell in the body, we are absent from our Lord.

7 For we walk by faith, and not by sight.

8 This is why we are confident, and anxious to be absent from the body, and to be present with our Lord.

9 Wherefore we endeavor, that whether present or absent, we may be pleasing to Lord Yahweh.

10 For we must all stand before the judgment seat of the Yahshua the Christ, that everyone may be rewarded according to that which he has done, whether it be good or bad.

11 Knowing therefore the fear of our Lord, we try in a persuasive way to win men; so we are very well understood by Lord Yahweh; and I trust we are also understood by you.

12 We are not boasting of ourselves to you, but we give you occasion to glory on our behalf before those who glory as hypocrites but who are not sincere in heart.

13 For if we go wrong, we answer to Lord Yahweh, and if we go right, it is for you.

14 For the love of Yahshua the Christ compels us to reason thus: that if one died for all, then all were dead;

15 And that he died for all, that those who live may not henceforth live for themselves, but for him who died and rose for them.

16 And now from henceforth, we do not know any one in the body; even though once we had known Yahshua the Christ in the body, we no longer know him now.

17 Whoever from now on is a follower of Yahshua the Christ is a new creature; old things have passed away.

18 And all remaining things have become new through Lord Yahweh who has reconciled us to Himself by Yahshua the Christ, and He has given to us the ministry of reconciliation;

19 For Lord Yahweh was in Yahshua the Christ, who has reconciled the world with his majesty, not counting their sins against them; and has committed to us the word of reconciliation.

20 Now then we are ambassadors for Yahshua the Christ, as though Lord Yahweh did beseech you by us; we beseech you for Yahshua the Christ, be reconciled to Lord Yahweh.

21 For Yahshua, who did not know sin, made himself sin for your (and our) sakes, that we may, through Yahshua, be made the righteousness of Lord Yahweh.

CHAPTER 6

So we, as helpers, beseech you that the grace of Lord Yahweh, which you have received, may not be in vain among you.

2 For He said, I have answered you in an acceptable time, and I have helped you on the day of salvation; behold, now is the acceptable time; and behold, now is the day of salvation.

3 Give no occasion for offense to anyone or in anything, so that there be no blemish in our ministry;

4 But in all things, let us show ourselves to be the ministers of Lord Yahweh in much patience, in tribulations, in necessities, in imprisonment,

5 In scourgings, in bonds, in tumults, in toilings, in vigils, in fastings;

6 By purity, by knowledge, by long-suffering, by kindness, by the Holy Spirit, by sincere love,

7 By the word of truth, by the power of Lord Yahweh, by the armor of righteousness on the right hand and on the left,

8 By honor and dishonor, by praise and reproach, as deceivers, and yet true;

9 As unknown, and yet well known; as dying, and behold, we live; as chastened, and not dying;

10 As sorrowful, yet always rejoicing; as poor, yet enriching many; as having nothing, and yet possessing all things.

11 O Corinthians, we have told you everything, and our hearts are relieved.

12 You are not constrained by us, but are urged by you affections.

13 I speak as to my children, render me my reward which is with you, increase your love toward me.

14 Do not unite in marriage with unbelievers, for what fellowship has righteousness with iniquity? Or what mingling has light with darkness?

15 Or what accord has Yahshua the Christ with Satan? Or what portion has a believer with an unbeliever?

16 Or what harmony has the temple of Lord Yahweh with idols? For you are the temple of the living God; as it is said, I will dwell in them and walk in them; and I will be their God, and they shall be my people.

17 Wherefore come out from among them, and be separate, says the Lord, and touch not the unclean thing; and I will receive you,

18 And I will be a Father to you, and you shall be my sons and daughters, said the Almighty Lord Yahweh.

CHAPTER 7

Having therefore these promises, my beloved, let us cleanse ourselves from all filthiness of the flesh and spirit, and let us serve in holiness in the reverence of Lord Yahweh.

2 Be patient; my brethren, we have wronged no man, we have corrupted no man, we have defrauded no man.

3 I do not say this to condemn you; for I have said before that you are in our hearts, to die and live with you.

4 I am familiar enough to speak boldly with you, great is my glorying of you; I am filled with satisfaction, and I am overwhelmed with joy in all our troubles.

5 For ever since we came to Macedonia, our bodies have had no rest and have been troubled by everything, war without and fears within.

6 Nevertheless Lord Yahweh, who comforts the meek, comforted us by the coming of Titus;

7 And not by his coming only, but also by the comfort with which he was comforted in you, for he brought us the good news concerning your love toward us, your mourning and your zeal on our behalf; and when I heard it, I rejoiced exceedingly.

8 For even though I made you feel sorry with the epistle, I do not regret, even though it has caused sorrow; for I can see that though that very epistle has made you feel sorry, the sorrow was only for an hour.

9 But it has made me exceedingly happy, not because you were sorry, but because your sorrow led to repentance; for you were sorry over the things of Lord Yahweh, so that you lack nothing from us.

10 For sorrow over the things of Lord Yahweh causes enduring repentance of the soul, and brings one to life; but sorrow over the things of the world causes death.

11 For behold, that very thing which distressed you on account of Lord Yahweh has resulted much more in painstaking effort, in apology, anger, fear, love, zeal, and vengeance. In all things you have proved yourselves clear in this matter.

12 Be that as it may, though I wrote to you, I did not do it for the one who had done the wrong nor for the one who had suffered the wrong, but that your painstaking care for us may be known before Lord Yahweh.

13 Therefore we were comforted, and with our consolation we rejoiced exceedingly in the joy of Titus, for his spirit was refreshed by you all.

14 For I was not ashamed in the things which I have boasted to him about you; but just as all the things about which we have spoken to you are true, even so our boasting to Titus is found to be true.

15 And his affections have increased more toward you, as he remembers the obedience of you all, how you received him in fear and trembling.

16 I rejoice therefore that I have confidence in you in all things.

CHAPTER 8

Moreover, our brethren, we want you to know that the grace of Lord Yahweh has been bestowed on the churches of Macedonia;

2 How that in a great trial of affliction, the abundance of their joy and their deep-rooted poverty abounded to the riches of their liberality.

3 For to their power, I can testify, yes, and beyond their power they have shared of their own accord,

4 And besought us most earnestly that they may be partakers in the gift for the ministration to the saints.

5 And this they did, not only as we expected, but first they gave themselves to our Lord, and then to us by the will of Lord Yahweh.

6 Inasmuch as we desired Titus, that as he had begun, so he would also finish this same gift among you.

7 Therefore, as you abound in every thing, in faith, in the word of Lord Yahweh, in knowledge, in all perseverance, and by our love toward you, you should likewise excel in this gracious favor also.

8 I am not making a demand on you, but I am prompted by the devotion of your fellow believers to test the sincerity of your love.

9 For you know the gracious gift of our Lord Yahshua the Christ, that though he was rich, yet for your sakes he became poor, so that you, through his poverty, may be rich.

10 Herein I give you my advice, that it may help you to go forward and accomplish what you, of your own accord, began to do last year.

11 Now therefore perform by works that which you wished to do; and as you were eager to promise it, so fulfill from that which you have.

12 For if there is a willingness to give, every man can give according to that which he has, and not according to that which he has not, and his gift will be acceptable.

13 This is not intended to relieve other men and add a burden to you;

14 But that there may be an equality at this particular time, that your abundance may be a supply for their want, that their abundance also may be a supply for your want, that there may be equality.

15 As it is written, He who had gathered much, had nothing over; and he who had gathered little, had no lack.

16 But thanks be to Lord Yahweh, who put the same vigorous care into the heart of Titus for you.

17 For indeed he has accepted our appeal; and because he was very desirous, he went to you of his own accord.

18 And we have also sent with him our brother, who has received praise throughout all the churches for his preaching of the gospel;

19 So that he also has been chosen by the churches to travel with us for this relief which is administered by us to the very glory of Lord Yahweh, and for our own encouragement;

20 But we are careful in this, lest any one should blame us in connection with this generous help which is administered by us.

21 For we are very careful to do the right thing, not only in the presence of Lord Yahweh, but also in the presence of men.

22 And we have also sent our brother with them, who has often been proved by us in many things, that he is earnest, and now is more earnest because of the abundant trust he has in you.

23 And as to Titus, he is my partner and helper among you; and as to our other brethren, they are the apostles of the churches to the glory of Yahshua the Christ.

24 Henceforth, you can show the proof of your love and of our boasting on your behalf to them before all the churches.

THE ONLY THEOLOGY WITHIN CHAPTER 9

6 But remember this: He who sows sparingly shall also reap sparingly; and he who sows generously shall also reap generously.

7 So let every man give according to what he has decided in his mind, not grudgingly or of necessity; for Lord Yahweh loves a cheerful giver.

8 Lord Yahweh is able to make all goodness abound to you, and may you always have enough of everything for yourselves, and may you abound in every good work.

9 As it is written, He has distributed liberally, and given to the poor; and his righteousness endures for ever.

10 Now he who gives seed to the sower and bread for food, will supply and multiply your seed and cause the fruits of your righteousness to grow,

11 That you may be enriched in everything, in all liberality; for such generosity enables us to perfect thanksgiving to Lord Yahweh.

12 For the administration of this service not only supplies the wants of the saints, but it also is made abundant by many thanksgivings to Lord Yahweh.

13 By this experiment of charitable service, they glorify Lord Yahweh in that you have subjected yourselves to the faith of the gospel of Yahshua the Christ, and through your generosity you have become partakers with them and with all men,

14 And they offer prayer on your behalf with greater love, because of the abundance of the grace of Lord Yahweh which has been on you.

15 Thanks be to Lord Yahweh for his incomparable gift.

CHAPTER 10

Now I, Shaul, beseech you by the gentleness and meekness of Yahshua the Christ; even though I am humble when present among you, I have the confidence when I am far away,

2 I beseech you not to be troubled when I arrive, by the things which I hope to carry out; for it is my purpose to put to scorn those men who regard us as if we lived after the flesh.

3 For though we do live an earthly life, we do not serve worldly things.

4 For the weapons which we use are not earthly weapons, but are of the might of Lord Yahweh by which we conquer rebellious strongholds,

5 Casting down imaginations, and every false thing that exalts itself against the knowledge of Lord Yahweh, and capturing every thought to the obedience of Yahshua the Christ;

6 And we are prepared to seek vengeance on those who are disobedient, when your obedience is fulfilled.

7 Do you judge by outward appearance? If any man thinks that he himself belongs to Yahshua the Christ, let him know this of himself: that just as he belongs to Lord Yahshua, so we also belong.

8 For though I should boast somewhat more of our authority, which the Lord has given us for edification, and not for your destruction, I should not be ashamed.

9 But I am hesitant, lest I seem as if I were trying to frighten you with my letter.

10 For there are men who say that his epistles are weighty and powerful; but his bodily appearance is weak, and his speech foolish.

11 But let him who supposes so consider this: that just as we express ourselves in our epistles when we are away, so are we also in deed when we are present.

12 For we dare not count or compare ourselves with those who are proud of themselves; for it is because they measure themselves by themselves that they do not understand.

13 We do not boast beyond our measure, but according to the measure of the rule which Lord Yahweh has distributed to us, a measure to reach even to you.

14 It is not because we are unable to climb where you are, nor are we trying to misrepresent ourselves; for we have climbed where we are preaching the gospel of Yahshua the Christ;

15 And we do not boast of things beyond our measure; that is, by other men's labor, but we have the hope, that when your faith grows, we shall be enlarged according to our measure.

16 And we shall become strengthened so that we may preach the gospel in the regions beyond you, and not boast of the things already done by others.

17 But he who glorifies, let him glorify in the Lord.

18 For it is not the one who praises himself who is approved, but the one whom the Lord praises.

CHAPTER 11

I wish you to be patient with me for a while, so that I may speak plainly, and I am sure you will be patient.

2 For I am zealous for you with the zealousness of Lord Yahweh, for I have espoused you to one husband, that I may present you as a pure virgin to Yahshua the Christ.

3 But I am afraid that just as the serpent through his deceitfulness misled Eve, so your minds should be corrupted away from the sincerity that is in that is in Yahshua the Christ.

4 For if he who has come to you and preaches another Christ, whom we have not preached, or if you have received another spirit which you had not received, or another gospel which you had not accepted, you may have listened to him.

5 For I think that I am not, in the least, inferior to the most distinguished apostles.

6 But though I am a poor speaker, I am not poor in knowledge; but we have been thoroughly made manifest among you in all things.

7 I probably have acted foolishly in humbling myself, that you may be exalted, because I preached the gospel of Lord Yahweh to you freely.

8 I deprived other churches, taking supplies from them, in order to minister to you.

9 And when I came to you and was in need, I did not burden any of you because my wants were supplied by the brethren who came from Macedonia; I have taken care of myself in every way, and I will so continue to keep myself so that I will not be a burden to you.

10 As the truth of Yahshua the Christ is in me, no man shall stop me of this glorifying in the regions of Achaia.

11 Why? Because I do not love you? Lord Yahweh knows that I do love you.

12 But what I do, I will continue to do, so as to give no occasion to those who seek an occasion; and that, in whatever they boast, they may not be found equal to us;

13 For they are false apostles and deceitful workers, posing as apostles of Yahshua the Christ.

14 There is no marvel in this; for Satan disguises himself as an angel of light,

15 It is no great thing if his ministers also pose as the ministers of righteousness, whose end shall be according to their works.

16 I say again, let no man think me a fool; if otherwise, yet as a fool receive me, that I may glorify myself a little.

17 What I now say, I speak not after our Lord, but as it were foolishly, on this occasion of glorifying.

18 Because many glorify on the things of the flesh, I glorify also.

19 For you endure fools readily, knowing that you yourselves are wise.

20 For you endure the man who dominates you, the man who lives at your expense, the man who takes from you, the man who exalts himself over you, and the man who smites you on the face.

21 I speak this as a reproach, as though we were weak. Now I speak foolishly; in whatsoever other men are bold, I venture also.

22 Now if the Hebrews, so am I. If they are descendants of Avraham, so am I.

23 If they are ministers of Yahshua the Christ {I speak as a fool}, I am greater than they; in labor more than they, in wounds more than they, in imprisonments more than they, and in danger of death many times.

24 By the Jews I was scourged five times, each time forty stripes less one.

25 Three times I was beaten with rods, once I was stoned, three times I was in shipwreck, a day and a night I have been adrift in the sea in shipwreck.

26 On many journeys I have been in perils from rivers, in perils of robbers, in perils from my own kinsmen, in perils in the city, in perils in the wilderness, in perils in the sea, in perils from false brethren;

27 In toil and weariness, in sleepless nights, in hunger and thirst, through much fasting, in cold and nakedness.

28 Besides other things and the many calling on me everyday, I have also the care of all the churches.

29 Who is sick That I do not feel the pain? Who stumbles that does not have my heartfelt sympathy?

30 If I must needs glory, I will glory of my sufferings.

31 The God and Father of our Lord Yahshua the Christ, who is blessed forever and ever, Knows that I do not lie.

32 At Damascus the general of the army of King Aretas placed the city of the Damascenes under guard in order to seize me;

33 And I was lowered in a basket from a window over the city wall, and thus I escaped from his hands.

CHAPTER 12

Glorifying is proper, but there is no advantage in it, and I prefer to relate the visions and revelations of our Lord.

2 I know a man in Yahshua the Christ more than fourteen years ago, but whether I know him in the body or out of the body, I do not know; Lord Yahweh knows; this very one was caught up to the third heaven.

3 And I still know this man, but whether in the body or whether out of the body, I cannot tell; Lord Yahweh knows;

4 How that he was caught up to paradise (the third heaven) and heard unspeakable words, which it is not lawful for a man to utter.

5 Of such a person, I will glorify; but of myself, I will not glorify, except in my weakness.

6 But even if I should desire to glorify, I will not be a fool; for I will tell the truth; but now I refrain, lest anyone should think more of me than what he sees me to be and what he hears from me.

7 And lest I should be exalted through the abundance of the revelations, there was delivered to me a thorn in my flesh, an angel of Satan to buffet me, lest I should be exalted.

8 Three times I besought my Lord concerning this thing, that it may depart from me.

9 And the Lord said to me, My grace is sufficient for you; for my (Sha'ul's) strength is made perfect in weakness. Most gladly therefore I would rather glory in my infirmities, that the power of Yahshua the Christ may rest upon me.

10 Therefore I am content with infirmities, insults, hardships, persecutions, and imprisonments for Yahshua the Christ's sake; for when I am physically weak, then I am spiritually strong.

11 Behold, I am foolish to glorify but you have forced me; for you ought to have testified concerning me: for in no way am I less than those apostles who are highly honored, though I am nothing.

12 The miracles which the apostles have wrought, I have wrought among you also in all patience, in signs, in wonders, and mighty deeds.

13 For what do you lack that other churches have, except it be that I myself was not burdensome to you? Forgive me this fault!

14 Behold, this is the third time I am prepared to come to you; and I will not burden you; for I seek nothing from you but yourselves; for children are not under obligation to lay up treasure for the parents, but the parents for the children.

15 I will gladly pay my expenses, and I will even give myself for the sake of your souls; though the more I love you, the less you love me.

16 But be it so, I did not burden you; nevertheless as a shrewd man, I caught you with guile.

17 Why? Did I extort anything from you by any of the men whom I sent to you?

18 I requested Titus to visit you, and I sent brethren with him. Did Titus extort anything from you? Did we not walk in the same spirit, and did we not walk in the same steps?

19 Why? Do you still think we are apologizing? No! We speak before Lord Yahweh in Yahshua the Christ; and we do all these things, my beloved, for your moral improvement.

20 For I fear, lest when I come to you, I shall not find you such as I wish to find you, and that you also will not find me as you wish to find me, lest there be controversies, envyings, angers, stubbornness, accusations, slanderings, boastings, and disorders.

21 Perhaps when I come to you, my God (Lord Yahweh) will humble me, and I will mourn over many who have sinned and who have not repented of the impurity, immorality, and lasciviousness which they have committed.

Chapter 13

This is the third time I am ready to come to you, for by the mouth of two or three witnesses every charge is sustained.

2 I have told you before, and again I tell you in advance, just as I have told you on my two previous visits; and now even while I am far away, I write to those who have sinned and to all others, that if I come again, I will not spare anyone;

3 Since you seek a proof of Yahshua the Christ speaking in me, he has never been weak among you, but is mighty in you.

4 For though Lord Yahshua was crucified through weakness, yet he lives by the power of Lord Yahweh. As we are weak with him, so we are alive with him by the power of Lord Yahweh who is within you.

5 Examine yourselves, whether you are in the same faith; heal your souls. Do you not realize that Yahshua the Christ is in you? If this is not so, then you are rejected.

6 But I trust that you shall know that we are not rejected.

7 And I pray to Lord Yahweh that our testing will find nothing wrong with you; but that you may be found doing good things, even though we may appear as though we were rejected.

8 For we cannot do anything against the truth, but for the truth.

9 For we are glad when we are weak and you are strong; and this also we pray for, that you may be perfected.

10 Therefore I write these things while I am far away, so that when I come, I need not deal harshly with you, according to the authority which my Lord has given me, which is for your edification and not for your destruction.

11 Henceforth, my brethren, rejoice, be perfect, be of good comfort, be of one mind, live in peace; and the God of love and peace, shall be with you.

12 Greet one another with a holy kiss.

13 All the saints salute you.

14 The peace of our Lord Yahshua the Christ, the love of Lord Yahweh, and the fellowship of the Holy Spirit, be with you all. Amen.

The Epistle of Sha'ul The Apostle To The Galatians

Chapter 1

Sha'ul, an apostle, not sent by men nor appointed by man, but by Yahshua the Christ and by Lord Yahweh the Father, who raised Yahshua from the dead,

2 And all the brethren who are with me, to the churches of Galatia:

3 Grace be to you, and peace from Lord Yahweh the Father and from our Lord Yahshua the Christ,

4 Who gave himself for our sins that he may deliver us from this present evil world, according to the will of Lord Yahweh our Father;

5 To whom be glory for ever and ever. Amen.

6 I am surprised how soon you have turned to another gospel, away from Yahshua the Christ who has called you by his grace,

7 A gospel which does not even exist; howbeit, there are men who have stirred you up and want to pervert the gospel of Yahshua the Christ.

8 But though we, or an angel from heaven, preach any other gospel to you than that which we have preached to you, let him be accursed.

9 As I have said before, so say I now again, If anyone preaches any other gospel to you than that which we have preached to you, let him be accursed.

10 Do I now persuade men of Lord Yahweh? Or do I seek to please men? For if I tried to please men, I should not be a servant of Yahshua the Christ.

11 But I want you to know, my brethren, that the gospel which I preached was not from men.

12 For I did not receive or learn it from man, but through the revelation of Yahshua the Christ.

13 You have heard of the manner of my life in time past in the Jews' religion, how beyond measure I persecuted the Church of Lord Yahweh and tried to destroy it.

14 And how that I was far more advanced in the Jews' religion than many of my age among the people of my race; for above all, I was especially zealous for the doctrines of my forefathers.

15 But when it pleased Lord Yahweh, who had chosen me from my birth and called me by his grace,

16 To reveal his Son to me, that I may preach him among the Gentiles, I did not immediately disclose it to any human being;

17 Neither did I go up to Jerusalem to them who had been apostles before me; but instead I went to Arabia and returned again to Damascus.

18 Then after three years, I went up to Jerusalem to see Kepa, and stayed with him fifteen days.

19 But I did not see any one of the other apostles except Ya'akov, the brother of our Lord.

20 Now the things which I write to you, behold, I confess before Lord Yahweh, I do not lie.

21 After that, I went to the regions of Syria and Cilicia;

22 And by face, I was unknown to the churches of Yahshua the Christ in Judea.

23 For they had heard only this much; that he who had persecuted us before now, preached the faith which previously he tried to destroy.

24 And they praised Lord Yahweh because of me.

CHAPTER 2

2:16 Know that a man is not justified by the works of the law but by the faith in

Yahshua the Christ, even we have believed in Yahshua the Christ, that we may be justified by the faith in Yahshua the Christ but not by the works of the law; for by the works of the law shall no human being be justified.

17 But if, while we seek to be justified by Yahshua, is therefore our Lord Yahshua a minister of sin? Far be it!!

20 I am crucified with Yahshua the Christ; nevertheless I live; yet not I, but Yahshua the Christ lives in me; and the life which I now live in the flesh, I live by the faith of the Son of Lord Yahweh, who loved me and gave himself for me.

21 I do not frustrate the grace of Lord Yahweh; for if righteousness comes by means of the law, then Yahshua the Christ died in vain.

CHAPTER 3

O foolish Galatians, who has bewitched you from your faith after Yahshua the Christ, crucified, has been pictured before your eyes?

2 I only want to know this from you, Did you receive the Spirit through the works of the law or through obedience to faith?

3 Are you so foolish, after having begun with spiritual things, to end now with things of the flesh?

4 Have you believed all these things in vain? If that is how you think, your suffering will have been for nothing.

5 Does he who gives you the Spirit and works miracles among you, do these things by the works of the law or by obedience to faith?

6 Just as Avraham believed Lord Yahweh, and it was accounted to him for righteousness,

7 Therefore, you must know that those who trust in faith are the children of Avraham.

8 Because Lord Yahweh knew in advance that the Gentiles would be declared righteous through faith, he first preached to Avraham, as it is said in the Holy Scripture, In you shall all the Gentiles be blessed.

9 So then, it is the believers who are blessed through Avraham the faithful.

10 For those who rely on the works of the law are still under the curse; for as it is written, Cursed is everyone who does not practice everything which is written in the book of the law.

11 But that no man is justified by the law before Lord Yahweh, is evident; for as it is written, The righteous shall live by faith.

12 Thus, the law is not made by faith, but, whosoever shall do the things which are written in it shall live in it.

13 Yahshua the Christ has redeemed us from the curse of the law by becoming accursed for our sakes: for it is written, Cursed is everyone who hangs on a cross,

14 That the blessing of Avraham may come on the Gentiles through Yahshua the Christ, that we may receive the promise of the Spirit through faith.

15 My brethren, I speak as I would to an assembly of men: Though it be but a man's covenant, yet if it be confirmed, no man can reject it or change anything in it.

16 Now the promises were made to Avraham and to his descendants as a covenant. He did not say, To your descendants, as of many, but, To your descendants, as one, that is Yahshua the Christ.

17 And this I say, That the covenant which was previously confirmed of Lord Yahweh in Yahshua the Christ, cannot be repudiated and the promise nullified by the law which came four hundred and thirty years later.

18 For if the inheritance is by the law, then it would not be as the fulfillment of promise; but Lord Yahweh gave it to Avraham by promise.

19 Then what is the use of the law? It was added because of your transgression, till the coming of the heir to whom the promise was made; and the law was given by angels by the hand of a mediator.

20 Now a mediator does not represent one alone, but Lord Yahweh is one.

21 Is the law then against the promises of Lord Yahweh? Far be it; for if a law had been given which could have wrought salvation, righteousness would truly have come as the result of the law.

22 But the scripture has included everything under sin, that the promise by the faith of Yahshua the Christ may be given to those who believe.

23 But before faith came, we were guided by the law while we were waiting for the faith which was to be revealed.

24 The law then was our pathfinder to bring us to Yahshua the Christ, that we may be justified by faith.

25 But since faith has come, we no longer are in need of the pathfinder.

26 For you are all the children of Lord Yahweh by faith in Yahshua the Christ.

27 For those who have been baptized in the name of Yahshua the Christ, have put on Yahshua the Christ.

28 There is neither Jew nor Gentile, there is neither slave nor free, there is neither male nor female; for you are all one in Yahshua the Christ.

29 So if you belong to Yahshua the Christ, then you are descendants of Avraham, and his heirs according to the promise.

Chapter 4

Now this I say; That the heir, as long as he is young, cannot be distinguished from the servants even though he is the lord of them all.

2 But he is under guardians and stewards until the time appointed by his father.

3 Even so we, when we were young, were subject to the principles of this world;

4 But when the fulness of the time was come, Lord Yahweh sent forth his Son who, born of a woman, became subject to the law,

5 To redeem them who were under the law, that we may receive the adoption of sons.

6 And because you are sons, Lord Yahweh has sent forth the Spirit of his Son into your hearts crying, Abba, Abon, O Father, our Father.

7 From now on you are not servants, but sons; and if sons, then heirs of Lord Yahweh through Yahshua the Christ.

8 Howbeit then, when you did not know Lord Yahweh, you served those things which, from their nature, were not gods.

9 But now after you have known Lord Yahweh, and above all, are known of Lord Yahweh, you turn again to those weak and poor principles, and you wish again to come under their bondage.

10 You still observe days and months, and times and years.

11 I am afraid that perhaps I have labored among you in vain.

12 My brethren, I beseech you, put yourself in my place; just as once I put myself in your place. You have not offended me at all.

13 You know that I was weak in the flesh when I preached the gospel to you at first.

14 And yet, you did not despise me nor reject me on account of my weakness; but you received me as an angel of Lord Yahweh, even as Yahshua the Christ.

15 Where is then the blessedness you had? For I can testify concerning you that, if it had been possible, you would have plucked out your own eyes and given them to me.

16 Am I therefore become your enemy because I tell you the truth?

17 These men do not envy you for good, but they would dominate you so that you may envy them.

18 But it is good to be zealously affected in a good thing, and not only when I am present with you.

19 My little children, for whom I am in travail again until Yahshua the Christ be a reality in you,

20 I wish I could be with you now, and could change the tone of my voice, because I am deeply concerned about you.

21 Tell me, you who desire to be under the law, do you not hear the law?

22 For it is written that Avraham had two sons, one by a bondmaid and one by a freewoman.

23 He who was born of the bondmaid was born after the flesh; but he who was born of the freewoman was born by promise.

24 Now these things are symbolic of the two covenants, the one from Mount Sinai giving birth to bondage, which is Hagar.

25 For this Hagar is Mount Sinai in Arabia, and surrenders to Jerusalem which now is, and is in bondage with her children.

26 But the Jerusalem which is above is free, and is the mother of us all.

27 For as it is written, Make merry, O you barren who bear not; rejoice and cry, O you who travail not; for the children of the one in disfavor are more numerous than the children of the one who is favored.

28 Now we, my brethren, are the children of promise, as was Yitz'chak.

29 But as then, he who was born after the flesh persecuted him who was born after the Spirit, even so it is now.

30 Nevertheless, what does the scripture say? Cast out the bondmaid and her son; for the son of the maidservant shall not inherit with the son of the freewoman.

31 So then, my brethren, we are not children of the maidservant but we are children of the freewoman.

CHAPTER 5

Stand firm, therefore, in the liberty with which Yahshua the Christ has made us free, and not be harnessed again under the yoke of servitude.

2 Behold, I, Sha'ul, tell you that if you are merely physically circumcised in the Jewish law of the b'rit-milah, and not spiritually circumcised in your heart, then Yahshua is of no benefit to you.

3 For I testify again to every man who merely is physically circumcised, that he is under obligation to fulfill the whole law.

4 You, who seek justification by the law; have ceased to adhere to Yahshua the Christ, and you are fallen from grace.

5 For we through the Spirit, wait for the hope of righteousness by faith.

6 For in Yahshua the Christ, neither is circumcision nor uncircumcision anything, but faith which is accomplished by love, is.

7 You were progressing well; who confused you that you should not obey the truth?

8 Your persuasion comes from him who called you.

9 A little leaven, leavens the whole lump.

10 I have confidence in you through our Lord, that you will consider no other beliefs, and that he who troubles you shall bear his judgment, whoever he is.

11 And I, my brethren, if I still preach the physical circumcision, why should I be persecuted? Why? Has the cross ceased to be a stumbling block?

12 I wish those who are troubling you, would be expelled.

13 For, my brethren, you have been called to liberty; only do not use your liberty for an occasion to the things of the flesh, but by love serve one another.

14 For the whole law is fulfilled in one saying, that is, You shall love your neighbor as yourself.

15 But if you harm and plunder one another, take heed lest you be consumed one by another.

16 This I say then: Lead a spiritual life, and you shall never commit the lust of the flesh.

17 For the flesh craves that which is harmful to the spirit, and the spirit opposes the things of the flesh; and the two are contrary to one another, so that you are unable to do whatever you please.

18 If you are led by the Holy Spirit, you are not under the law.

19 For the works of the flesh are well known, which are these: adultery, impurity, lasciviousness,

20 Idolatry, witchcraft, enmity, strife, jealousy, anger, stubbornness, seditions, heresies,

21 Envyings, murders, drunkenness, revelings, and all such things; as I have told you before and as I say to you now, those who practice such things shall not inherit the kingdom of Lord Yahweh.

22 But the fruits of the Spirit are love, joy, peace, patience, gentleness, goodness, faith,

23 Meekness, and self-control; there is no law against these.

24 And those who belong to Yahshua the Christ, have controlled their weaknesses and passions.

25 Let us therefore live in the Spirit, and surrender to the Spirit.

26 Let us not be desirous of vain glory, provoking one another, envying one another.

CHAPTER 6

My brethren, if any one be found at fault, you who are spiritual must restore him in a spirit of meekness; and be careful lest you also be tempted.

2 Bear one another's burdens, and so fulfill the law of Yahshua the Christ.

3 For if man thinks himself to be something, when he is nothing, he deceived himself.

4 But let every man examine his own work; and then may he glory within himself, alone and not among others.

5 For every man shall bear his own burden.

6 Let him who is taught the word, become a partaker with him who teaches all good things.

7 Do not be deceived; Lord Yahweh is not mocked; for whatever a man sows, that shall he also reap.

8 He who sows things of the flesh, from the flesh he shall reap corruption; he who sows things of the Spirit, from the Spirit he shall reap life everlasting.

9 Let us not be weary in well-doing; for in due season we shall reap, if we faint not.

10 Therefore, as we have opportunity, let us do good to all men, especially to those who belong to the household of faith.

11 You can see how long a letter which I have written to you with my own hand.

12 Those who desire to glory in the things of the flesh, are the ones who compel you to be physically circumcised only, lest they should suffer persecution for the cross of Yahshua the Christ.

13 For not even they who are only physically circumcised obey the law; but they want you to be physically circumcised so that they may glorify over your flesh.

14 But as for me, I have nothing of which to glorify except the cross of our Lord Yahshua the Christ by whom the world is crucified to me, and I am crucified to the world.

15 For in Yahshua the Christ, neither circumcision nor uncircumcision is anything, but it is a new creation that counts.

16 And upon those who follow this path be peace and mercy; and upon the Israel of Lord Yahweh be peace and mercy.

17 From henceforth let no man trouble me, for I bear in my body the marks of our Lord Yahshua the Christ.

18 My brethren, the grace of our Lord Yahshua the Christ be with your spirit. Amen.

The Epistle of Sha'ul The Apostle To The Ephesians

Chapter 1

Sha'ul, an apostle of Yahshua the Christ by the will of Lord Yahweh, to those who are in Ephesus, saints and believers in Yahshua the Christ:

2 Peace be with you and grace from Lord Yahweh our Father, and from our Lord Yahshua the Christ:

3 Blessed be the God and Father of our Lord Yahshua the Christ, who has blessed us with all spiritual blessings in heaven through Yahshua the Christ;

4 Just as from the beginning He has chosen us through him before the foundation of the world, that we may become holy and without blemish before Him.

5 And He marked us with his love to be his from the beginning, and adopted us to be sons through Yahshua the Christ, as it pleased his will,

6 To the praise of the glory of his grace that He has poured upon us by his beloved one.

7 In him we have salvation, and in his blood we have forgiveness of sins, according to the richness of his grace,

8 That grace which has abounded in us, in all wisdom and spiritual understanding,

9 And made known to us the mystery of his will that he has ordained from the very beginning, to work through it;

10 As a dispensation of the fulness of times, that all things may be made new in heaven and on earth through Yahshua the Christ,

11 By whom we have been chosen, and he had marked us from the beginning so he wanted to carry out everything according to the good judgment of his will,

12 That we should become the first to trust in Yahshua the Christ, to his honor and his glory,

13 In whom, you also have heard the word of truth, which is the gospel for your salvation; in him you have believed, so you are sealed with the Holy Spirit which was promised,

14 Which is the pledge of our inheritance, for the salvation of those who are saved and for the glory of his honor.

15 Wherefore I also, since I heard of your faith in our Lord Yahshua the Christ and your love toward all the saints,

16 Never cease to give thanks for your sakes, and to mention you in my prayers.

17 So that the God of our Lord Yahshua the Christ, the Father of glory, may give you the spirit of wisdom and revelation in the knowledge of Him,

18 And so that the eyes of your understanding may be enlightened, that you may know what is the hope of his calling and what are the glorious riches of his inheritance in the saints,

19 And what is the exceeding greatness of his power in us as the result of the things we believe, according to the skill of his mighty power,

20 Which He wrought through Yahshua the Christ when He raised him from the dead and set him at his own right in heaven,

21 Far above all angels, power, might, dominion, and every name that is named, not only in this world but also in the world which is to come,

22 And has put all things under his feet, and made him, who is above all things, the head of the church,

23 Which is his body and confirmation of him who fulfills all things and every thing.

CHAPTER 2

And he has quickened you also who were dead because of your sins and offenses;

2 In which you previously walked according to the course of this world, and according to the will of the supreme ruler (Satan) of the air, the spirit which is active in the children of disobedience.

3 In those very deeds in which we were also corrupted from the very beginning through the lusts of the flesh, fulfilling the desires of the flesh and of the mind, thereby we became the children of wrath, even as others.

4 But Lord Yahweh, who is rich in mercy, for his great love with which He loved us,

5 Even when we were dead in our sins, has made of live together with Yahshua the Christ, by whose grace we are saved;

6 And He has raised us up with Him, and seated us with Him in heaven through Yahshua the Christ.

7 In the ages to come, He may show the exceeding riches of his grace in his kindness toward us through Yahshua the Christ.

8 For it is by his grace that you are saved through faith; not of your doing; it is the gift of Lord Yahweh:

9 Not of works, lest any man should boast.

10 For we are his creations, created through Yahshua the Christ ultimately for good works, and Lord Yahweh has before ordained that we should live in them.

11 Wherefore, remember that you were Gentiles in the flesh from the beginning, and you were called uncircumcision, differing from that which is called circumcision, which is the work of the hands of the flesh.

12 At that time you were without Yahshua, beings aliens to the customs of Israel and strangers to the covenants of the promise, without hope and without Lord Yahweh in the world.

13 But now, through Yahshua the Christ, you who sometimes were far off are brought near by the blood of Yahshua the Christ.

14 For he is our peace, who has made both one, and has broken down the wall of separation between them;

15 And he has abolished, by his precious body, the enmity between them, and he has abolished the ordinances of the law by his commandments, that he may create in his person, from the two, a new man, thus making peace;

16 And he reconciled both in one body with Lord Yahweh, and he destroyed the enmity with his cross;

17 And he came and preached peace to you who are far away and to those who are near.

18 Through him we both are able to draw near by one Spirit to the Father.

19 Thus from henceforth you are neither strangers nor foreigners, you are fellow citizens with the saints and children of the household of Lord Yahweh;

20 And you are built upon the foundation of the apostles and prophets, Yahshua the Christ himself being the cornerstone of the building:

21 And through him the whole building is fashioned and grows into a holy temple through the help of the Lord;

22 You are also built by him for a habitation of Lord Yahweh through the Spirit.

CHAPTER 3

For this cause I, Sha'ul, am a servant of Yahshua the Christ for the sake of you Gentiles.

2 Have you ever heard of the dispensation of the grace of Lord Yahweh which was given to me for you?

3 For the mystery was made known to me by a revelation, as I have briefly written you before,

4 So that when you read it, you can understand my knowledge of the mystery of Yahshua the Christ,

5 Which was not made known to the sons of men in ages past, as it is now revealed to his holy apostles and prophets by the Spirit,

6 That the Gentiles should be fellow heirs and partakers of his body, and of the promise which is given through him by the gospel.

7 Of that very gospel, I have been a minister, according to the gift of the grace of Lord Yahweh which was given to me by the effectual working of his power.

8 Even to me, who is less than the least of all the saints, this grace was given, that I should preach among the Gentiles about the unsearchable riches of Yahshua the Christ,

9 And that I may enlighten all men that they may see what is the dispensation of the mystery which, for ages, had been hidden from the world by Lord Yahweh who created all things by Yahshua the Christ;

10 To the intent that now unto the angels and powers which are in heaven, the manifold wisdom of Lord Yahweh may be made known by the church,

11 Which is the wisdom He prepared, in ages past, and has carried out in Lord Yahshua the Christ;

12 In whom we have freedom of access with confidence in his faith.

13 Therefore, I ask that I may not grow weary in my afflictions for your sakes, which is for your happiness.

14 For this cause, I bow my knees to the Father of our Lord Yahshua the Christ,

15 For Whom all Fatherhood in heaven and in earth is named,

16 To grant you, according to the riches of his glory, to be strengthened with might by his Spirit,

17 That Yahshua the Christ may dwell in your inner man by faith, and in your hearts by love, strengthening your understanding and your foundation,

18 So that you may be able to comprehend with all the saints what is the height, depth, length, and breadth,

19 And to know the love of Yahshua the Christ which surpasses all knowledge, that you may be filled with all the fulness of Lord Yahweh.

20 Now to Him who is able, by power, to do for us more than anyone else, and to do for us more than we ask or think, according to his mighty power that works in us,

21 Unto Him be glory in his church by Yahshua the Christ throughout all ages, world without end. Amen.

CHAPTER 4

I therefore, a servant of our Lord, beseech you to live as is worthy of the rank to which you are called,

2 With all humility and gentleness and with patience, forbearing one another in love,

3 Endeavoring to preserve the harmony of the Spirit in the bond of peace,

4 That you may become one body and one Spirit, even as you are called in one hope of your calling;

5 There is one Lord, one faith, and one baptism;

6 One God and Father of all, who is above all and through all, and in all of us.

7 But to every one of us is given grace according to the measure of the gift of Yahshua the Christ.

8 Wherefore it is said, He ascended on high, and took possession of heaven and gave good gifts to men.

9 Now that he ascended, what is it but that he also descended first into the inner parts of the earth?

10 So he that descended is the same also that ascended far above all heavens, that he may fulfill all things.

11 And he has assigned some as apostles, some as prophets, some as evangelists, some as pastors, and some as teachers;

12 For the perfecting of the saints, for the work of the ministry, for the edifying of the body of Yahshua the Christ,

13 Until we all become one in faith and in the knowledge of the Son of Lord Yahweh, and become a perfect man according to the measure of the stature of the fullness of Yahshua the Christ,

14 That we henceforth be not as children easily stirred and carried away by every wind of false doctrines of men, who through their craftiness, are artful in deceiving the people;

15 But that we be sincere in our love, so that in everything we may progress through Yahshua the Christ who is the head.

16 It is through him that the whole body is closely and firmly united at all joints, according to the measure of the gift which is given to every member, for the guidance and control of the body, in order to complete the edifying of the body in love.

17 This I say therefore and testify in the Lord, that you henceforth live not as other Gentiles who live in the vanity of their minds.

18 And whose understanding is dark, and who are alienated from the life of Lord Yahweh, because they have no knowledge, and because of the blindness of their hearts;

19 And who have given up their hope, and have surrendered themselves to wantonness and to the practice of all uncleanness in their covetousness.

20 But that is not what you have been taught about Yahshua the Christ;

21 If you have truly heard him and have been taught by him, as the truth is found in Yahshua,

22 Lay aside all your former practices, that is to say, the old man, which is degenerated with deceitful lusts,

23 And be renewed in the spirit of your mind,

24 And put on the new man, who is created by Lord Yahweh in righteousness and true holiness.

25 Therefore you must put lying away from you and speak the truth, every man with his neighbor; for we are members, one of another.

26 Be angry, but sin not; and let not the sun go down upon your anger:

27 And do not give the devil a chance.

28 From henceforth let him that stole, steal no more; but rather, let him labor with his hands and do good deeds, that he may have something to give to him who is in need.

29 Let no evil word proceed from your mouth, but words that are good and useful for edification, that they will impart blessing to those who hear them.

30 And do not grieve the Holy Spirit of Lord Yahweh, whereby you are sealed to the day of salvation.

31 Let all bitterness, wrath, anger, clamoring, and blasphemy be put away from you, together with all malice;

32 And be kind and tenderhearted one to another, forgiving one another, even as Lord Yahweh has forgiven us through Yahshua the Christ.

CHAPTER 5

Be therefore followers of Lord Yahweh, as beloved children.

2 And walk in love, as Yahshua the Christ also has loved us and has given himself for us, as an offering and a sacrifice to Lord Yahweh for a sweet savor.

3 But let not immorality or any uncleanness or covetousness be heard of among you, as becomes saints;

4 Neither cursing nor foolish words, nor insults, nor words of flattery, none of which are necessary; but instead of these, let thanks be offered.

5 You should know this, that no one guilty of fornication, no unclean person, and no covetous man who serves idols, has any inheritance in the kingdom of Yahshua the Christ and of Lord Yahweh.

6 Let no man deceive you with vain words; for because of these things, the anger of Lord Yahweh comes onto the children of disobedience.

7 Therefore, do not be partakers with them.

8 For previously you were ignorant, but now you have been enlightened by our Lord, and should therefore live like children of light.

9 For the fruits of light are found in all goodness, righteousness, and truth,

10 And so you must discern that which is acceptable before our Lord.

11 Have no part in the unfruitful works of darkness; bur rather, condemn them.

12 For it is a shame even to speak of the things that are done by them in secret.

13 For all things that are condemned are exposed by the light; and anything that is made manifest is light.

14 Therefore it is said, Awake, O sleeper and rise from the dead, and Yahshua the Christ shall give you light.

15 Watch therefore, that you live a glorious life, not as foolish men but as wise,

16 Who take advantage of their opportunity; for these are difficult days.

17 Therefore, do not lack wisdom, but understand what the will of Lord Yahweh is.

18 And do not become drunk with wine, wherein is intemperance; but be filled with the Spirit,

19 Speaking to you souls in psalms, hymns, and spiritual songs, sing with your heart to the Lord,

20 Giving thanks always for all men to Lord Yahweh, the Father, in the name of our Lord Yahshua the Christ.

21 Submit yourselves to one another in the love of Yahshua the Christ.

22 Wives, submit yourselves to your husbands as to your Lord.

23 For the husband is the head of the wife, even as Christ is the head of the church, and he is the savior of the body.

24 Therefore as the church is subject to Yahshua the Christ, so let the wives be to their own husbands in every thing.

25 Husbands, love your wives, even as Yahshua the Christ loves his church and gave himself for it,

26 That he may cleanse and sanctify by the washing of water and by the word,

27 In order to build for himself a glorious church, without stain or wrinkle, or any such thing; but that it should be holy and without blemish.

28 So should men love their wives as their own bodies. He who loves his wife, loves himself.

29 For no man ever yet hated his own body, but nourishes it and cherishes it, even as Yahshua the Christ does for his church.

30 For we are members of his body, of his flesh, and of his bones.

31 For this reason shall a man leave his father and mother, and shall be joined to his wife, and they two shall be one flesh.

32 This is a great mystery; but I speak concerning Yahshua the Christ and his church.

33 Nevertheless, let every one of you so love his wife as himself, and the wife see that she reverence her husband.

CHAPTER 6

Children, obey your parents in our Lord, for this is right.

2 This is the first commandment with promise: Honor your father and your mother,

3 That it may be well with you, and you may live long on the earth.

4 And parents, do not provoke your children to anger; but bring them up in the discipline and teaching of our Lord.

5 Servants, be obedient to your masters according to the flesh, with reverence, trembling, and with a sincere heart, as to Yahshua the Christ;

6 Not with eye service, as hypocrites, but as the servants of Yahshua the Christ, doing the will of Lord Yahweh from the heart.

7 And serve well with your whole self; with love, as to our Lord, and not to men,

8 Knowing that whatever good thing any man does, the same shall he receive from our Lord, whether he be a servant or a freeman.

9 Also, masters, do the same things for your servants, forgiving their faults, because you also have your own Master in heaven; and there is no partiality with Him.

10 From henceforth, my brethren, be strong in our Lord, and in the power of his might.

11 Put on the whole armor of Lord Yahweh, that you may be able to stand against the wiles of the devil.

12 For your conflict is not only with flesh and blood, but also with the fallen angels, with powers, with the rulers of this world of darkness, and with the evil spirits under the heavens.

13 Therefore put on the whole armor of Lord Yahweh, that you may be able to meet the evil one. And being prepared, you shall prevail.

14 Arise, therefore, gird your loins with truth and put on the breastplate of righteousness;

15 And have your feet shod with the preparation of the gospel of peace;

16 Together with these, take for yourselves the shield of faith, for with it you shall be able to quench all the flaming darts of the wicked.

17 Put on the helmet of salvation, and take the sword of the Spirit, which is the word of Lord Yahweh;

18 And pray always, with all prayer and supplication in the Spirit; and in that prayer be watchful at all times, praying constantly and supplicating for all the saints,

19 And for me also, that words may be given to me as soon as I open my mouth, so that I may boldly preach the mystery of the gospel,

20 For which I am a messenger in chains, that I may speak openly about it, as I ought to speak.

21 In order that you also may know my affairs and what I do, Tychicus, a beloved brother and a faithful minister in our Lord, shall make known to you all things;

22 I have sent him to you for the same purpose; that you may know how I am, and that he may comfort your hearts.

23 Peace be to our brethren, and love with faith from Lord Yahweh the father, and from our Lord Yahshua the Christ.

24 Grace be with all them that love our Lord Yahshua the Christ in sincerity. Amen.

The Epistle of Sha'ul The Apostle To The Philippians

CHAPTER 1

Sha'ul and Timotheus, servants of Yahshua the Christ, to all the saints in Yahshua the Christ who are at Philippi, together with the elders and deacons:

2 Grace be to you, and peace from our Father Lord Yahweh, and from Lord Yahshua the Christ.

3 I give thanks to my God for your steady remembrance of me.

4 In all my prayers for you, I make supplication with joy,

5 For your fellowship in the gospel from the very first day until now,

6 Being confident of this very thing, that he who has begun the good work among you, the same will continue it until the day of our Lord Yahshua the Christ;

7 And this is the right way for me to think of you all, for I have you in my heart because through all my imprisonment and my defense and confirmation of the truth of the gospel, you have been partakers with me of grace.

8 For Lord Yahweh is my witness of how much I love you through the love of Yahshua the Christ.

9 And for this I pray, that your love may abound yet more and more in knowledge and in all spiritual understanding,

10 So that you may choose the things that are excellent and that you may be pure and without offense in the day of the Christ.

11 And be filled with the fruits of righteousness which are by Yahshua the Christ, to the glory and the praise of Lord Yahweh.

12 Now I would have you know this, my brethren, that my work has been greatly furthered by the gospel;

13 And the reasons for my imprisonments have been made manifest by Yahshua the Christ to all Caesar's court and to all men.

14 And many of the brethren in our Lord have grown confident by my imprisonment and, with increasing boldness, speak the word of Lord Yahweh without fear.

15 While some of them preach only because of envy and strife, others preach Yahshua the Christ in good will and love;

16 For they know that I am appointed for the defense of the gospel;

17 But those who preach Yahshua the Christ out of contention, do it not sincerely, but do it expecting to increase the hardship of my imprisonment.

18 And I have rejoiced and still do rejoice in this, that in every way, whether in pretense or in truth, Yahshua the Christ is preached.

19 For I know that through your prayers and the gift of the Spirit of Yahshua the Christ, all these things will ultimately turn out for my salvation,

20 Just as it is my earnest hope and expectation that in nothing shall I be ashamed, but that openly as always, so also now will Yahshua the Christ be magnified through my body, whether in life or death.

21 For to live in Yahshua the Christ is life, and to die in Yahshua the Christ is gain.

22 Even if my labors bear fruits in this life of the flesh, I do not know what to choose.

23 For I am torn between two desires; the desire to depart so that I may be with Yahshua the Christ which is much better,

24 And the desire to remain in the flesh which is more needful for you.

25 And this I surely know, that I shall be spared and remain for your joy and for the furtherance of your faith,

26 So that when I come again to you, your rejoicing in Yahshua the Christ will abound by my coming to you again.

27 Only conduct yourselves as becomes the gospel of Yahshua the Christ, so that whether I come and see you or whether I am far away, I may hear of your good conduct, that you are standing firm in one spirit and in one mind, and triumphing together through the faith of the gospel,

28 And that in nothing are you terrified by our adversaries whose conduct is the sign of their own destruction, and this is from Lord Yahweh.

29 For it has been given to you not only to believe in Yahshua the Christ, but also to suffer for his sake,

30 And that you may endure such trials as those which you have seen me in, and such as you now hear that I am in.

CHAPTER 2

If therefore, you have found consolation in Yahshua the Christ, wholehearted love, fellowship of the Spirit, or compassion and mercies,

2 Complete my joy by being in one accord, one love, and one mind.

3 Do nothing through strife or vain glory; but in humility let each regard his neighbor better than himself.

4 Let no one be mindful only of his own things, but let everyone be mindful of the things of his neighbor also.

5 Reason this within you, which Yahshua the Christ also reasoned,

6 Who, being in the form of Lord Yahweh, did not consider it robbery to be equal with Lord Yahweh; (Yahshua the Christ participated in creation so he shares Lord Yahweh's diety; <u>also:</u> see verses **9** and **10** below. But, the Father still outranks the Son)

7 And took upon himself the form of a servant, and was in the likeness of men;

8 And, being found in the form of a man, he humbled himself and became obedient to death, even the death of the cross;

9 Therefore, Lord Yahweh also has highly exalted Yahshua and gave him a name which is above every other name,

10 That at the name of Yahshua, every knee should bow, of those in heaven, of those on earth, and those under the earth,

11 And every tongue shall confess that Yahshua the Christ is the Lord, to the glory of Lord Yahweh who is his Father.

12 From now on, my beloved, just as you have always been obedient, not only in my presence, but much more in my absence, work out your own salvation with reverence and trembling.

13 For it is Lord Yahweh who inspires you with the will to do the good things which you desire to do.

14 Do all things without disputing and doubting,

15 That you may be sincere and blameless, like the innocent children of Lord Yahweh, in the midst of a crooked and perverse generation, among whom you shine as lights in the world;

16 For to them you are the light of life; that I may rejoice in the day of Yahshua the Christ, for I have not run in vain nor labored in vain.

17 Yes, even if my blood be offered upon the sacrifice and the service of your faith, I am happy and rejoice with you all.

18 Likewise, you also must be happy and rejoice with me.

19 But I trust in our Lord Yahshua the Christ to send Timotheus to you soon, that I also may be at ease when I learn of your well-being.

20 For I have no one here as interested as I am, who will sincerely care for your welfare;

21 For all seek their own, not the things which are Yahshua the Christ's.

22 But you know the proof of him, that as a son with the Father, he has served with me in the gospel.

23 I hope to send him to you presently, as soon as I see how it will go with me.

24 But I trust in my Lord that I myself shall also come shortly.

25 But right now I am forced through circumstances to send to you Epaphroditus, who is a brother, an assistant, and co-worker with me. He is also your apostle and one who ministers to my wants.

26 For he has been longing to see you all, and has been depressed because he knew you had heard that he had been sick.

27 For indeed he was sick to the point of death, but Lord Yahweh had mercy on him; and not on him only, but on me also, lest I should have sorrow upon sorrow.

28 I have therefore sent him quickly, so that when you see him again, you may rejoice and that I may be relieved from anxiety.

29 Welcome him, therefore, in the Lord with all joy; and honor those who are like him,

30 Because, for the work of Yahshua the Christ, he came near to death; and by his self-denial, he made good your lack of service to me.

CHAPTER 3

Henceforth, my brethren, rejoice in our Lord. It does not bother me to write the same things to you, because they enlighten you.

2 Beware of vicious men, beware of evil workers, and beware of circumcising.

3 For we who are the true people of circumcision, who worship Lord Yahweh in Spirit (the Holy Spirit) and glory in Yahshua the Christ, and yet do not rely of things of the flesh.

4 As for me, I once relied on things of the flesh. However, if a man thinks his hope is on things of the flesh, I have more hope than he has;

5 For I was circumcised when I was eight days old, being an Israelite by race, of the tribe of Binyamin, a Hebrew son of Hebrews, and a Pharisee according to the law;

6 And concerning zeal, I was a persecutor of the church; and according to the standards of righteousness of the law, I was blameless.

7 But these things which once were a gain to me, I counted a loss for the sake of Yahshua the Christ.

8 And I still count them all a loss for the sake of abundant knowledge of Yahshua the Christ, my Lord, for whom I have lost everything, and I have considered all those things as refuse, so that I may abound in Yahshua the Christ,

9 And be found in him, since I have no righteousness of my own gained from the law, but the righteousness which comes through the faith of Yahshua the Christ; that is, the righteousness which comes from Lord Yahweh,

10 So that through this righteousness, I may know Lord Yahshua and the power of his resurrection, and be a partaker of his sufferings, even to a death like his,

11 That I may by any means attain the resurrection from the dead.

12 Not as though I had already attained or were already perfect; but I am striving so that I may reach that for which Yahshua the Christ appointed me.

13 My brethren, I do not consider that I have reached the goal; but this on thing I do know, forgetting those things which are behind, I strive for those things which are before me;

14 I press toward the goal to receive the prize of victory of Lord Yahweh's highest calling through Yahshua the Christ.

15 Therefore, let those of you who are perfect think about these things; and if you reason in any other way, Lord Yahweh will reveal even that to you.

16 Nevertheless, whereto we have already attained, let us walk by the same path and with one accord.

17 My brethren, be followers like me, and observe those who walk such a path, and then you will be examples as we are.

18 For there are many who live otherwise, of whom I have often told you, and now I tell you with tears that they are the enemies of the cross of Yahshua the Christ,

19 Whose end is destruction, whose "god" is their belly, and whose glory is in their shame; whose thought is on earthly things.

20 But our labors are in heavenly things, from whence we look for our Savior who is our Lord Yahshua the Christ,

21 Who shall transform our poor body to the likeness of his glorious body, according to his mighty power, whereby he is able even to subdue all things to himself.

CHAPTER 4

Henceforth, my dearly beloved brethren, my joy and crown, in this manner stand firm in our Lord, my beloved.

2 I beseech Euodias and I beseech Syntyche to be of one accord in our Lord.

3 I beseech you also, my true yoke-fellow, help those women who labored with me in the gospel, together with Clement and with the rest of my fellow laborers whose names are written in the book of life.

4 Rejoice in our Lord always; and again I say, Rejoice.

5 Let your humility be know to all men. Our Lord is at hand.

6 Do not worry over things, but always by prayer and supplication with thanksgiving let your requests be made known to Lord Yahweh.

7 And the peace of Lord Yahweh, which passes all understanding, shall keep your hearts and minds through Yahshua the Christ.

8 Finally, my brethren, whatever is true, whatever is honest, whatever is just, whatever is pure, whatever is lovely, whatever is of good report: if there is any virtue and if there is any praise, think about these things.

9 Those things which you have learned, received, heard, seen in me, and do; and the God of peace shall be with you.

10 But I rejoiced in our Lord greatly, that you have continued to care for me, just as you have always cared, even though you yourselves have not had sufficient to meet your needs.

11 Nor am I saying this simply because I am in want; for I have learned to make what I have, sufficient to meet my needs.

12 I know what it is to be poor, and I know what it is to be rich; I have gone through many things, both to be full and to be hungry, both to have plenty and to be in want.

13 I can do all things through Yahshua the Christ who strengthens me.

14 But you have done well to share my difficulties.

15 Now you Philippians know also that in the beginning of the gospel, when I departed from Macedonia, no church shared with me as concerning giving and receiving, but you only.

16 For even at Thessalonica, you sent more than once to meet my needs.

17 I do not say this because I want a gift, but because I want to see the fruits of the gospel increased to you.

18 I have received everything I need, and it is more than enough; I am satisfied, having received everything you sent me by Epaphroditus, and it was welcome as a fragrant perfume and a sacrifice acceptable and well pleasing to Lord Yahweh.

19 But my God will supply all your needs according to his riches in the glory of Yahshua the Christ.

20 Now to Lord Yahweh, our Father, be glory and honor for ever and ever. Amen.

21 Salute every saint in Yahshua the Christ. The brethren who are with me, greet you.

22 All the saints salute you, especially those who are of Caesar's household.

23 The grace of our Lord, Yahshua the Christ, be with you all. Amen.

The Epistle of Sha'ul The Apostle To The Colossians

CHAPTER 1

Sha'ul, an apostle of Yahshua the Christ by the will of Lord Yahweh, and Timotheus our brother,

2 To those who are at Colosse, holy brethren and believers in Yahshua the Christ: Peace be with you, and grace from Lord Yahweh our Father, and grace from Lord Yahshua the Christ.

3 Always we give thanks to Lord Yahweh, The Father of our Lord Yahshua the Christ, and always we pray for you,

4 Since we heard of your faith in Yahshua the Christ and of your love for all the saints,

5 For the hope which is preserved for you in heaven, of which you heard before in the true word of the gospel,

6 Which has been preached to you, just as it has been preached throughout the world, growing and bringing forth fruits, as it does also in you, since the day you heard of it and knew the grace of Yahshua in truth,

7 Just as you have learned it from Epaphras our beloved fellow servant, who is for your sakes a faithful minister of Yahshua the Christ,

8 And who has made known to us your love for spiritual things.

9 For this cause we also, since the day we heard it, do not cease to pray for you and to ask that you may be filled with the knowledge of the will of Lord Yahweh in all wisdom and in all spiritual understanding,

10 That you may live a righteous life, please Lord Yahweh with all good works, and bring forth good fruits and grow in the knowledge of Lord Yahweh;

11 And be strengthened with all might, according to the greatness of his glory, in all patience and long-suffering,

12 So that you may joyfully give thanks to Lord Yahweh the Father, who has enlightened us and made us worthy partakers of the inheritance of the saints,

13 And has delivered us from the power of darkness, and has brought us to the kingdom of his beloved Son,

14 By whom we have obtained forgiveness of sins and salvation.

15 He (Yahshua the Christ) is the image of the invisible God, and is the first-born of every creature:

16 And through him were created all things that are in heaven and on earth, visible and invisible; whether imperial thrones, lordships, angelic orders, or dominions, all things were in his hand and were created by him;

17 And he is before all things, and by him all things are sustained.

18 And Yahshua the Christ is the head of the body, the church; for he is the beginning, the first-fruits of the resurrection from the dead, that in all things he may be the first;

19 For it pleased Lord Yahweh to complete all things in Yahshua;

20 And by his hand to reconcile everything to himself; and through his blood shed on the cross to make peace both for those who dwell on earth and those who dwell in heaven.

21 Even to you, who in times past, were alienated and hostile in your minds because of your evil works, peace has now been given,

22 Through the sacrifice of his body and his death, so that he may raise you before him, holy and without reproach, and blameless,

23 If you continue in your faith and if your foundation is firm, and if you are not moved from the hope of the gospel which you have heard and which has been preached to every creature under heaven, and for which I, Sha'ul, have become a minister;

24 And now rejoice in my sufferings for you, and make up that which is lacking of the sufferings of Yahshua the Christ in my flesh for his body's sake, which is the church;

25 For which I became a minister, according to the dispensation of Lord Yahweh which has been given to me for you, fully to preach the word of Lord Yahweh everywhere,

26 Even the mystery which has been hidden from ages and from generations, but now is revealed to his saints;

27 To whom Lord Yahweh wanted to make known the riches of the glory of this mystery among the Gentiles; which is Yahshua the Christ in you, the hope of our glory.

28 Him we preach, teach, and make known to every man in all wisdom, that we may cause every man to become perfect through Yahshua the Christ;

29 And to this end, I labor and strive through the help of the power which is given to me.

CHAPTER 2

I would that you knew how I struggled for your sakes and for the sake of those who are at Laodicea, and for the rest who have not seen me personally,

2 That their hearts may be comforted, and that they may be brought near by love to all the riches of the full assurance of understanding of the knowledge of the mystery of Lord Yahweh the Father and of Yahshua the Christ,

3 In whom are hidden all the treasures of wisdom and knowledge.

4 And I say this so that no man may beguile you with enticing words.

5 For though I am far away from you in the flesh, yet I am with you in spirit, and I rejoice to see your orderliness and the sincerity of your faith in Yahshua the Christ.

6 Just as you have therefore accepted our Lord Yahshua the Christ, so you must be led by him,

7 Rooted and built up in him, and established in the faith as you have been taught, abounding therein with thanksgiving.

8 Beware, lest any man mislead you through philosophy and vain deceit after the teaching of men, after the principles of the world, and not after Yahshua the Christ.

9 For in him is embodied all the fullness of the divine quality.

10 And it is through him that you also have been made complete, for he is the head of all angelic orders and powers,

11 In whom also you are circumcised with a circumcision made without hands, in putting off the sinful body by the circumcision of Yahshua the Christ;

12 And you were buried with Yahshua the Christ in baptism, and by him you were raised with him, for you believed in the power of Lord Yahweh who raised him from the dead.

13 And you, who once were dead in your sins and the uncircumcision of your flesh, he has granted to live with him, and he has forgiven you all your sins;

14 And by his commandments, he canceled the written bond of our sins, which stood against us; and he took it out of the way, nailing it to his cross;

15 And by putting off his mortal body, he exposed the powers of evil, and through his person he put them openly to shame.

16 Let no man therefore create a disturbance among you about eating and drinking, or about the division of the feast days, the beginning of the months and the day of the Sabbath.

17 These are shadows of things to come; but the main objective is Yahshua the Christ.

18 Let no man, by pretense of sincerity, doom you so that you worship angels; for he is bold about the things he has not seen, and foolishly he is proud of his intellectual powers;

19 That very person does not uphold the Head by whom the whole body is constructed and stands with the joints and members, and grows through the discipline of Lord Yahweh.

20 Therefore, if you have died with Yahshua the Christ, and are apart from the principles of the world, why then should you be doomed as though living in the world?

21 Do not touch; do not taste; do not follow;

22 For these things are customs which are changeable, and they are the commandments and doctrines of men.

23 And it appears that there is some word of wisdom in these things when presented by the humble person in reverence for Lord Yahweh, provided they disregard the things of the flesh, not those things which are honorable but only those things which satisfy the pleasure of the flesh.

CHAPTER 3

If you then are risen with Yahshua the Christ, seek those things which are above, where Yahshua the Christ sits on the right hand of Lord Yahweh.

2 Set your mind on things above, not on things on the earth,

3 For you are dead, and your life is hidden with Yahshua the Christ in Lord Yahweh.

4 When Yahshua the Christ, who is our life, shall appear, then shall you also appear with him in glory.

5 Mortify therefore your earthly members: Immorality, uncleanness, intemperate desires, evil lusts, and covetousness; for these are idolatry,

6 And it is because of these things that the wrath of Lord Yahweh comes on the children of disobedience.

7 In the past you also lived among these things, and you were perverted by them.

8 But now put off from you all these: anger, wrath, malice, blasphemy, foul conversation.

9 Do not lie one to another, but put away the old life with all its practices;

10 And put on the new life which is renewed in knowledge after the pattern in which it was originally created,

11 Where there is neither Jew nor Gentile, circumcision nor uncircumcision, Greek nor barbarian, slave nor freeman; but Yahshua the Christ is all and in all men.

12 Therefore as the elect of Lord Yahweh, holy and beloved, put on mercy, kindness, gentleness, humbleness of mind, meekness, patience;

13 Forbearing one another, and if anyone has a complaint against his fellow man, just as Yahshua the Christ forgave you, so should you also forgive.

14 And with all these things have love, which is the bond of perfection.

15 And let the peace of Yahshua the Christ govern your hearts; for that end, you are called in one body; and be thankful to Yahshua the Christ;

16 And let his word dwell in you abundantly in all wisdom, teaching and admonishing one another in psalms, hymns, and spiritual songs, singing with grace in your hearts to Lord Yahweh.

17 And whatever you do in word or deed, do it in the name of our Lord Yahshua the Christ, giving thanks through him to Lord Yahweh the Father.

18 Wives, submit yourselves to your own husbands, as it is appropriate in Yahshua the Christ.

19 Husbands, love your wives, and be not bitter toward them.

20 Children, obey your parents in all things, for this is well pleasing to our Lord.

21 Parents, do not provoke your children, that they may not be discouraged.

22 Servants, obey your human masters in all things, not with eye-service, hypocrites; but with a sincere heart, in reverence for the Lord.

23 And whatever you do, do it heartily as to our Lord but not to men,

24 Knowing that from the Lord you shall receive the reward of the inheritance; for you serve the Lord Yahshua the Christ.

25 But the wrongdoer shall be rewarded according to the wrong which he has done; and there is no respect of persons.

CHAPTER 4

Masters, do to your servants that which is just and fair, knowing that you also have a Master in heaven.

2 Continue in prayer, and watch in the same with thanksgiving;

3 And pray for us also, that Lord Yahweh may open to us a door for preaching, to speak the mystery of Yahshua the Christ for whose sake I am imprisoned,

4 So that I may make it manifest and speak about it as I should.

5 Live wisely in peace with those who are outside the church, and avoid offending.

6 Let your conversation be gracious, seasoned with salt, and you should know how to answer every man.

7 All things concerning me will be made known to you by Tychicus, who is a beloved brother and a faithful minister and fellow servant in the Lord,

8 Whom I send to you for this very purpose, that he may know the state of your affairs and comfort your hearts,

9 Together with Onesimus, a faithful and beloved brother, who is one of you. They shall make known to you all the things which have happened to us.

10 Aristarchus, my fellow prisoner, salutes you, together with Mark who is cousin to Barnabba, concerning whom you have been instructed; and if he comes, receive him,

11 And receive Yahshua the Christ. These are of the circumcision, and the only ones who have helped me toward the kingdom of Lord Yahweh; and they have been a comfort to me.

12 Epaphras, who is one of you, a servant of Yahshua the Christ, salutes you, always laboring for you in prayer, that you may stand perfect and complete in all the will of Lord Yahweh.

13 For I can testify concerning Him that He has a great zeal for you and for those who are in Laodicea and Hierapolis.

14 Luke, the beloved physician and Demas greet you.

15 Salute the brethren in Laodicea, and salute Nymphas and his family and the congregation that meets at his house.

16 And when this epistle has been read to you, see that it is read also in the church of the Laodiceans; and likewise you read the epistle written from Laodicea.

17 And say to Archippus, Take heed to the ministry which you have received in our Lord, and that you fulfill it.

18 This salutation is by the hand of me, Sha'ul. Remember my imprisonment. Grace be with you. Amen.

The First Epistle of Sha'ul The Apostle To Timothy

THE BIBLICAL TEACHING STARTS IN CHAPTER 2

5 For there is one God, and one mediator between Lord Yahweh and men, the man Yahshua the Christ,

6 Who gave himself as a ransom for all mankind, a testimony which came in due time.

7 For that testimony, I was appointed a preacher and an apostle; I tell the truth and I lie not; and I became the teacher of the Gentiles in a true faith.

8 I wish, therefore, that men pray everywhere, lifting up their holy hands without anger and doubting thoughts.

9 In like manner also, let the apparel of women be simple and their adornment be modest and refined; not with braided hair or gold, pearls, or other costly array;

10 But let them be engaged in good works, as is becoming women who profess reverence for Lord Yahweh.

CHAPTER 3

This is a true saying: If a man desires the office of a church elder, he aspires to a good work.

2 He who becomes an elder must be blameless; the husband of one wife, mentally alert, sober, of good behavior, given to hospitality, and apt at teaching;

3 Not given to wine, not hasty to strike, not quarrelsome, but meek, not greedy of filthy lucre;

4 One who rules well his own household and keeps his children under submission to bring them up with all purity.

5 For if a man does not know how to rule well his own household, how shall he take care of the Church of Lord Yahweh?

6 He should not be a recent convert, lest he become proud and fall into the condemnation of the devil.

7 Moreover, he must have a good report from outsiders, lest he fall into reproach and the snares of the devil.

8 Likewise, deacons must be pure, not double-tongued, not given to much wine, not greedy of filthy lucre;

9 But they must uphold the divine mystery of faith with a pure conscience.

10 Let these first be examined, and then let them minister after they have been found blameless.

11 Likewise, their wives must be chaste, mentally alert, faithful in all things, and not slanderers.

12 Let the deacons be appointed from those who have not been polygamous, ruling their children and their own households well.

13 For those who minister well earn good recognition for themselves and grow more familiar with the faith of Yahshua the Christ.

14 These things I write to you, although hoping to come to you soon,

15 So that if I am delayed, you may know how you ought to conduct yourself in the house of Lord Yahweh which is the church of the living God, the pillar and foundation of the truth.

16 Truly great is this divine mystery of righteousness; it is revealed in the flesh, justified in the Spirit, seen by angels, preached to the Gentiles, believed on in the world, and received up into glory.

CHAPTER 4

Now the Spirit says expressly that in the latter times some shall depart from the faith, following after misleading spirits and doctrines of devils,

2 Who with false appearance mislead and speak lies, and are seared in their own conscience,

3 Who prohibit marriage, and demand abstinence from foods which Lord Yahweh has created for use and thanksgiving of those who believe and know the truth.

4 For all things created by Lord Yahweh are good; nothing is to be rejected if it is received with thanksgiving.

5 For it is sanctified by the word of Lord Yahweh and prayer.

6 If you teach these things to the brethren, you will be a good minister of Yahshua the Christ, brought up by the words of faith and in the good doctrine which you have been taught.

7 Refuse foolish and old wives' fables, and train yourself in righteousness.

8 For physical training profits only for a little while; but righteousness is profitable in all things, having promise of the life that now is and of that which is to come.

9 This is a true saying and worthy to be accepted.

10 Because of this, we both toil and suffer reproach, because we trust in the living God, who is the savior of all men, especially of those who believe.

11 These things command and teach.

12 Let no man despise your youth; but be ab example to believers, in word, behavior, love, faith, and in purity.

13 And until I come, strive to study, and continue in prayer and teaching.

14 Do not neglect the gift that you have, which was given to you by prophecy and by virtue of the laying on of the hands of the presbytery.

15 Meditate upon these things; give yourself wholly to them, so that it may be known to all that you are progressing.

16 Take heed to yourself and to your teachings; and be firm in them; for in doing this, you shall both save yourself and those who hear you.

Chapter 5

Do not rebuke an elder, but treat him as a father, and the younger men as your brothers;

2 And the elder women treat as mothers, and the younger women as your sisters, with all purity.

3 Honor widows who are widows indeed.

4 And if any of the widows have children or grandchildren, let them know that aid should be first sought from those of their own household so that the children have the opportunity to repay their obligations to their parents; for this is acceptable before Lord Yahweh.

5 Now she who indeed is a widow and destitute trusts in Lord Yahweh and is constant in prayers and supplications both night and day.

6 But she who lives wholly for pleasure is dead while she lives.

7 Continually charge them with these things, so that they may be blameless.

8 But if any man does not provide for his own, and especially for those who are of his own household who are of the faith, he has denied the faith and is worse than an unbeliever.

9 When you select a worthy widow to help, select one who is not less than the age of threescore (sixty) years, who has been the wife of one man only,

10 And is well spoken of for good works. If she has raised children, if she has lodged strangers, if she has washed the feet of the saints, if she has comforted the distressed, if she has been diligent in every good work.

11 But refuse the younger widows when they begin to feel natural passion which alienates them from Yahshua the Christ, they will marry.

12 Their judgments await them (if they stray from the Christ and do not marry) because they have become untrue to their first faith.

13 And with it all, they learn to be idle, wandering about from house to house; and not only to be idle, but tattlers also and busybodies, speaking things which they ought not.

14 I would, therefore, that the younger widows (maintain their first faith) marry, bear children, manage their own households, and give no occasion to the adversary for disdain.

15 For, as conditions are now, some have already strayed after Satan.

16 If any believers, either man or woman, have widows in their families, let them feed the widows, and do not let them be a burden on the congregation, so that the church may have enough for those who are widows indeed.

17 Let the elders who minister well be esteemed worthy of double honor, especially those who labor in the word and doctrine.

18 For the scripture says, You shall not muzzle the ox that threshes. And again, The laborer is worthy of his hire.

19 Do not accept an accusation against an elder unless it is supported by the testimony of two or three witnesses.

20 Those who sin, rebuke in the presence of all men so that others may fear.

21 I adjure you before Lord Yahweh and our Lord Yahshua the Christ, and before his elect angels that you observe these things without prejudice, doing nothing by partiality.

22 Do not lay hands hastily on any man, neither be a partaker of other men's sins; keep yourself pure.

23 Do not drink water in excess, but use a little wine for your stomach's sake and because of your frequent illnesses.

24 There are men whose crimes are well known and the notoriety of them precedes them to the house of judgment, and there are others, the notoriety of whose crimes follows after them;

25 Likewise also the fame of the good works of some is well known beforehand; and if their acts are otherwise, they cannot be hidden either.

Chapter 6

Let all of those who are servants, honor and respect their masters in every way, so that the name of Lord Yahweh and his doctrines may not be blasphemed.

2 Those who have masters who are believers, let them not despise them because they are brethren; but rather, serve them more zealously because they are believers and beloved in whose service they find rest. These things, teach and exhort.

3 If there is any man who teaches a different doctrine, and does not offer the wholesome words of our Lord Yahshua the Christ and the doctrine of reverence to Lord Yahweh,

4 He is proud, knowing nothing, and dotes on an argument and quarrels on the use of a word and this is the cause of envy, controversy, blasphemy, and evil premeditation.

5 And strife among men whose minds are corrupt and who are cut off from the truth and who think worshipping Lord Yahweh is for worldly gain; keep away from such people.

6 But our gain is greater contentment, for it is the worship of Lord Yahweh.

7 For we brought nothing into this world, and it is certain that we can carry nothing out.

8 Therefore, let us be satisfied with food and clothing;

9 For those who desire to be rich fall into temptation and snares, and into many foolish and hurtful lusts which drown men in degeneration and destruction.

10 For the love of money is the root of all evil; and there are some men who have coveted it and have thereby erred from the faith, and have brought to themselves many sorrows.

11 But you, O man of Lord Yahweh, flee these things; and follow after righteousness, piety, faith, love, patience, and meekness.

12 Fight the good fight of faith, lay hold upon eternal life to which you are called, having made a true profession before many witnesses.

13 I charge you in the presence of Lord Yahweh, the giver of life to all; and I charge you before Yahshua the Christ, who gave a good testimony before Pontius Pilate,

14 That you obey this charge without spot and without stain until the appearing of our Lord Yahshua the Christ,

15 Who is to be revealed in his due time, blessed and almighty God, the King of kings and Lord of lords,

16 Who alone has immortality, dwelling in the light which no man can approach, and whom no man has seen, nor can see; to him be honor and dominion for ever and ever, Amen.

17 Charge those who are rich in this world that they be not proud, nor trust in the uncertainty of riches, but in the living God who gives us all things so abundantly for our comfort,

18 That they do good works, and become rich in good deeds, and be ready to give and willing to share,

19 Laying up in store for themselves a good foundation against the time to come, that they may lay hold upon the true life.

20 O Timothy, be careful of that which is entrusted to you; flee from empty echoes and from the perversion of false science;

21 For those professing this have strayed from the faith. Grace be with you. Amen.

The Second Epistle of Sha'ul The Apostle To Timothy

CHAPTER 1

Sha'ul, an apostle of Yahshua the Christ by the will of Lord Yahweh, and by the promise of life which is in Yahshua the Christ,

2 To Timotheus, a dearly beloved son: Grace, mercy, and peace from Lord Yahweh who is the Father, and from Yahshua the Christ who is our Lord.

3 I thank Lord Yahweh whom I have served from boyhood with a pure conscience, that I have always remembered you in my prayers night and day.

4 I am anxious to see you and I still remember your tears; I am filled with joy,

5 Especially when I am reminded of your true faith, which dwelt first in your grandmother Lois and your mother Eunice, and I am sure now in you also.

6 For this reason, I remind you to stir up the gift of Lord Yahweh, the gift which is in you by the laying on of my hand.

7 For Lord Yahweh has not given us the spirit of fear but of power, of love, and of good discipline.

8 Be not, therefore, ashamed of the testimony of our Lord, nor of me his servant; but bear the hardships that go along with the preaching of the gospel through the power of Lord Yahweh,

9 Who has saved us and called us with a holy calling, not according to our works, but according to his own will and his grace, which was given to us in Yahshua the Christ before the world began,

10 And is now made manifest by the appearing of our Savior Yahshua the Christ, who has abolished death, and has revealed life and immortality through the gospel,

11 To which I am appointed a preacher, and an apostle, and a teacher of the Gentiles.

12 For this cause, I suffer these things; nevertheless I am not ashamed; for I know whom I have trusted, and I am sure he will take care of me until that day.

13 Let this example of sound words which you have heard from me, abide with you in the faith and love which is in Yahshua the Christ.

14 That good thing which was committed to you, keep by the help of the Holy Spirit which dwells in us.

15 This you know, that all those in Asia Minor have turned away from me, of whom are Phygellus and Hermogenes.

16 Let our Lord grant mercy to the house of Onesiphorus; for he has often refreshed me, and he was not ashamed of the chains of my imprisonment;

17 But when he was in Rome, he searched for me diligently and found me.

18 Let our Lord grant to him that he may find mercy in heaven, where our Lord is, in that day; and of how he ministered to me at Ephesus, you know very well.

CHAPTER 2

You, therefore, my son, be strong in the grace that is in Yahshua the Christ.

2 And the things which you have heard from me by many witnesses, entrust these to faithful men, who shall be able to teach others also.

3 Therefore, endure hardships as a good soldier of Yahshua the Christ.

4 No man can be a soldier and also entangle himself with the things of this life, if he would please him who has chosen him to be a soldier.

5 And if a man also strive for mastery in contest, he is not crowned except he compete lawfully.

6 The husbandman who labors should be the first to be sustained by the fruits.

7 Perceive these things: and may our Lord give you wisdom in all things.

8 Remember Yahshua the Christ who rose from the dead, he who was a descendant from David according to my gospel;

9 Because of him I suffer hardships, even to bonds like a malefactor; but the word of Lord Yahweh is not restricted.

10 Therefore I endure all things for the sake of the elect, that they may also obtain the salvation which is in Yahshua the Christ, with eternal glory.

11 This is a true saying: For if we die with him (Yahshua the Christ), we shall also live with him:

12 If we suffer, we shall also reign with him; if we deny him, he will also deny us;

13 But if we believe not in him, yet he will still remain faithful; for he cannot deny himself.

14 You should keep these things in remembrance as a testimony before our Lord, that the faithful should not argue over words in which there is no profit but which are destruction to those who listen to them.

15 Strive to conduct yourself perfectly before Lord Yahweh as a soldier without reproach and as one who preaches straight-forwardly the word of truth.

16 Shun empty and worthless words, for they only increase the ungodliness of those who argue over them.

17 And their word will be like a canker eating in many; such as Hymenaeus, and Philetus,

18 Who have strayed from the truth, saying that the resurrection of the dead is already passed, thus destroying the faith of some.

19 Nevertheless the foundation of Lord Yahweh stands firm, having this seal: The Lord knows those who are his, and He will save from iniquity every one who calls upon the name of the Lord.

20 But in a great house there are not only vessels of gold and of silver, but also of wood and of earth; some for formal use on occasions of honor, and others for service.

21 If therefore a man purifies himself from these things, he will become like a vessel pure for honor, worthy of the master's use, and ready for every good work.

22 Keep away from all the lusts of youth, and follow after righteousness, faith, love, and peace with those who call on our Lord with a pure heart.

23 Keep away from foolish disputes which do not educate; you know they cause strife.

24 A servant of our Lord must not quarrel, but be gentle to all men, apt at teaching and patient,

25 So that he may discipline gently those who argue against him; and perhaps Lord Yahweh will grant them repentance and they will know the truth,

26 And that they may recover themselves out of the trap of Satan, who, had drawn them to his will.

CHAPTER 3

Know this; that in the last days, disastrous times will come.

2 And men shall be lovers of themselves and lovers of money, covetous, boasters, proud, conceited, blasphemers, disobedient to parents, ungrateful, wicked,

3 Without natural affection, truce breakers, false accusers, addicts to lust, brutal, despisers of those that are good,

4 Traitors, hasty, high-minded, lovers of pleasures more than lovers of Lord Yahweh;

5 Having a form of "godliness," but far from the power of Lord Yahweh; turn away from such people.

6 For of this sort, are those who creep into houses and captivate women who are sunken in sin, led away with divers lusts,

7 Ever striving to learn, and never able to come to the knowledge of the truth.

8 Now just as Jannes and Jambres stood up against Moshe, so do these also resist the truth, men of corrupt minds and far off from the faith.

9 But they shall not progress, for their folly is well known to every man, even as that of the others also was.

10 But you have been a follower of my teaching, manner of life, purpose, faith, patience, charity, love, steadfastness,

11 Persecution, and sorrows; you know the things which I endured at Antioch, at Iconium, and at Lystra; how I was persecuted, and yet my Lord delivered me from all these.

12 Likewise, all those who wish to live a godly life in Yahshua the Christ shall suffer persecution.

13 But bad and deceptive men shall grow worse and worse, deceiving and being deceived.

14 But hold fast to the things which you have learned and have been assured of, knowing from whom you have learned them,

15 And knowing that, from your childhood, you have learned the holy scriptures which are able to make you wise to salvation through faith in Yahshua the Christ.

16 All scripture written by the inspiration of the Holy Spirit is profitable for doctrine, for reproof, for correction, and for instruction in righteousness;

17 So that Lord Yahweh's people may become complete, thoroughly perfected for every good work.

CHAPTER 4

I solemnly charge you before Lord Yahweh and our Lord Yahshua the Christ, who shall judge the quick and the dead when his kingdom is come,

2 Preach the word; and stand by it zealously in season and out of season; rebuke, and reprove, through all patience and teaching.

3 For the time will come when men will not listen to sound doctrine; but they will add for themselves extra teachers according to their desires, being lured by enticing words;

4 And they will turn away their ears from the truth, and they will turn to fables.

5 But you must be awake to all things, endure hardships, do the work of a preacher, and fulfill your ministry.

6 From henceforth I am ready to die, and the time of my departure is at hand.

7 I have fought a good fight, I have finished my race, I have kept my faith:

8 Henceforth, there is preserved for me a crown of righteousness, which my Lord who is the righteous judge, will give me at that day; and not to me only but also to all those who have loved his appearing.

9 Make every effort to come to me soon;

10 For Demas has forsaken me, having loved this world, and has gone, to Thessalonica; Crespos to Galatia, and Titus to Dalmatia.

11 Only Luke is with me. Take Mark and bring him with you; for he is useful to me for the ministry.

12 I have sent Tychicus to Ephesus.

13 The book-carrier which I left at Troas with Carpus, bring it with you when you come, and the books, especially the parchment scrolls.

14 Alexander, the blacksmith, has done me much evil; our Lord reward him according to his works;

15 You beware of him also; for he has greatly opposed our words.

16 When I first wrote to you, there was no one with me, for all had forsaken me; do not hold this against them.

17 Nevertheless, my Lord stood by me and strengthened me, that by me the preaching may be fulfilled and that all the Gentiles may hear; and I was delivered out of the lion's mouth.

18 And my Lord shall deliver me from every evil work, and he will give me life in his heavenly kingdom. To Him be glory for ever and ever. Amen.

19 Salute Priscilla, Aquila, and their household; and Onesiphorus.

20 Erastus has remained at Corinth; but I left Trophimus sick at the city of miletus.

21 To make every effort to come before winter. Eubulus greets you, and Pudens, Linus, Claudia, and all the brethren.

22 Our Lord Yahshua the Christ be with your spirit. Grace be with all of us. Amen.

The Epistle of Sha'ul to Titus

Chapter 1

Sha'ul, who is a servant of Lord Yahweh, who is an apostle of Yahshua the Christ in the faith of Lord Yahweh's elect, and who is in the knowledge of true godliness;

2 In the hope of eternal life, which the true God promised ages ago;

3 And has in due time revealed his word by our preaching, which preaching has been entrusted to me by the command of Lord Yahweh our Savior;

4 To Titus, a true son in the common faith: Grace and peace from Lord Yahweh the Father and from our Lord Yahshua the Christ our Savior.

5 For this cause I left you in Crete, that you should set in order the things that are wanting, and ordain elders in every city where there is a need as I had commanded you.

6 Appoint only an elder who is balmeless and the husband of one wife, and one who has faithful children, who do not curse and who are not intemperate.

7 For an elder must be blameless, and a steward of Lord Yahweh; and he must not be self-willed, not quick tempered, not excessive in the use of wine, not too ready to strike with his hand, not a lover of filthy lucre;

8 But a lover of hospitality, a lover of good things, sober, just, pious, and temperate of worldly desires;

9 Holding fast the doctrine of faith, so that he may be able to comfort by his sound doctrine, and to rebuke those who are proud.

10 For there are many unruly, vain talkers, and deceivers of the people, especially those who belong to the circumcision,

11 Whose mouths must be stopped, for they corrupt many families, teaching things which they ought not, for the sake of filthy lucre.

12 One of them, even a prophet of their own, said, The Cretians are always liars, vicious beasts with empty bellies.

13 This testimony is true. Therefore rebuke them sharply, that they may be sound in the faith,

14 And not give heed to Jewish fables (but give heed to Jewish truth) and do not give heed to commandments of men who hate the truth.

15 To be pure, all things are pure; but nothing is pure to those who are defiled and faithless; even their mind and conscience is defiled.

16 They profess to know Lord Yahweh, but in works they deny Him, and they are abominable and disobedient, condemning every kind of good work.

Chapter 2

But you must preach the things which are proper to sound doctrine.

2 Teach the older men to be vigilant, sober, pure, sound in faith, sound in love, sound in charity, and sound in patience.

3 Teach the older women likewise, to behave as becomes the worship of Lord Yahweh, not false accusers, not enslaved to much wine; but to become teachers of good things,

4 That they may teach the young women to be modest, to love their husbands and their children,

5 To be discreet, chaste, good homemakers, obedient to their own husbands, so that no one can reproach the word of Lord Yahweh.

6 Likewise, exhort the children to be modest.

7 In everything show yourself an example in all good works, and in your teaching let your word be sound.

8 Choose sound words which are instructive so that no man can point the finger of scorn at us, and so that he who is against us may be shamed when he can find nothing evil to say about us.

9 Exhort servants to be obedient to their own masters, and to please them well in all things; not contentious,

10 Not stealing, but manifesting true sincerity that they may adorn the doctrine of Lord Yahweh our Savior in all things.

11 For the grace of Lord Yahweh which brings salvation, has been revealed to all men.

12 It teaches us to renounce ungodliness and worldly lusts, and to live in this world soberly, righteously, and in godliness,

13 Looking for that blessed hope and the glorious appearing of the great God and our Savior Yahshua the Christ,

14 Who gave himself for us, that he may save us from all iniquity, and may purify us to be his own, a new people, zealous of good works.

15 Speak these things, and exhort and rebuke with all authority. Let no man despise you.

CHAPTER 3

Remind all to be obedient and submissive to princes and governors, and to be ready for every good work,

2 And not to speak evil against any man, and not to be quarrelsome; but to be meek, in every respect showing gentleness to all men.

3 For we ourselves also were sometimes foolish, disobedient, misled, and serving various lusts and passions, living in malice and envy, hated and also hating one another.

4 But after the goodness and kindness of Lord Yahweh our Savior was manifested,

5 Not by works of righteousness which we have done, but according to his mercy, He saved us by the washing of regeneration and renewing of the Holy Spirit,

6 Which He shed on us abundantly, through Yahshua the Christ our Savior,

7 That being justified by his grace, we should be made heirs to the hope of eternal life.

8 This is a true saying, and these things I want you to constantly affirm, so that those who believe in Lord Yahweh may be careful to do good works continually. These things are good and profitable to men.

9 But avoid foolish questions, genealogies, contentions, and the theological arguments of the scribes, for they are unprofitable and vain.

10 After you have admonished the heretic once or twice, shun him,

11 Knowing that he who is such, is corrupt; he sins and condemns himself.

12 When I send Artemas or Tychicus to you; endeavor to come to me at Nicopolis; for I have decided to winter there.

13 See that Zenas, the scribe, and Apollos are given a good farewell on their journey, that they lack nothing.

14 And let our people be taught to do good works in times of emergency, that they be not unfruitful.

15 All who are with me salute you. Greet those who love us in the faith. Grace be with you all. Amen.

The Epistle of Sha'ul to
Philemon

CHAPTER 1

Sha'ul, a prisoner for the sake of Yahshua the Christ, and brothe Timotheus, to Philemon our dearly beloved and our fellow worker,

2 And to our beloved Apphia and Archippus our fellow laborer, and to the congregation in your house:

3 Grace be with you and peace from Lord Yahweh our Father, and from our Lord Yahshua the Christ.

4 I thank my God and I always make mention of you in my prayers,

5 Since I have heard of your faith and love, which you have toward our Lord Yahshua and toward all the saints,

6 That the participation of your faith may bear fruits in works by the acknowledging of everything that is good which you have in Yahshua the Christ.

7 For we have great joy and consolation in your love, and the hearts of the saints are refreshed.

8 For this reason, I have great boldness in Yahshua the Christ, to command to you those things which are right,

9 And for love's sake I earnestly beseech you; even I, Sha'ul, an old man as you know, and now also a prisoner for the sake of Yahshua the Christ.

10 I beseech you on behalf of my son Onesimus, whom I converted during my imprisonment:

11 But of whom in the past you could not make use, but now he is very useful both to you and to me.

12 I send him to you again; welcome him as my own child;

13 For I would have kept him with m to minister to me in your place during my imprisonment for the gospel;

14 But I did not wish to do anything without consulting you, that your goods deeds may not be done as though by compulsion, but of your own desire.

15 Perhaps this was the reason why he left you for a while, that you can now have him for ever;

16 Henceforth not as a servant, but as more than a servant, a brother beloved, specially to me, and much more to you, both in the flesh and in our Lord.

17 Now, therefore, if you still count me as a partner, welcome him as you would me.

18 And if he has caused you any loss or if he owes you anything, put it on my account.

19 I, Sha'ul, have written this with my own hand; I will repay it, not reminding you that you owe to me even your own life.

20 Indeed, my brother, let me have comfort through you in our Lord; refresh my heart in Yahshua the Christ.

21 Because I have confidence in your obedience, I wrote to you knowing that you will also do more than I ask.

22 In addition to all this, prepare me a lodging; for I hope that through your prayers, I shall be spared to come to you.

23 Epaphras, my fellow prisoner in Yahshua the Christ, salutes you;

24 So do Mark, Aristarchus, Demas, and Luke, my fellow workers.

25 The grace of our Lord Yahshua the Christ be with your spirit. Amen.

The Epistle of Sha'ul the Apostle to the Hebrews

CHAPTER 1

From of old, Lord Yahweh spoke to our fathers by the prophets in every manner and in all ways; and in these latter days He has spoken to us by his Son,

2 Whom He has appointed heir to all things, and by whom also He made the worlds;

3 For he is the brightness of his glory and the express image of his being, upholding all things by the power of his word; and when he had {through himself} cleansed our sins, then he sat down on the right hand of the Majesty on high;

4 And he (Yahshua the Christ) is greater than the angels, just as the name he has inherited is a more excellent name than any of theirs.

5 For to which of the angels has Lord Yahweh at any time said: You are my (THE) Son, this day have I begotten you? And again, I will be to him a Father, and he shall be to me a Son?

6 And again, when He brought the first-begotten into the world, He said, Let all the angels of Lord Yahweh worship him.

7 And of the angels He said thus: Who makes his angels spirits; his ministers a flaming fire.

8 But unto the Son He said: Lord Yahweh is your throne, for ever and ever; the scepter of thy kingdom is a righteous scepter.

9 Thou hast loved righteousness and hated iniquity; therefore, your God has anointed you with the oil of gladness more than thy fellows.

10 And from the very beginning thou hast laid the foundations of the earth; and the heavens are the works of thy hands;

11 They shall pass away; but thou shall endure; and they all shall wear out like a garment;

12 And as a cloak thou shall fold them up, and they shall be changed; but thou are the same, and thy years shall never end.

13 For to which of the angels has He at any time said, Sit thou at my right hand until I make thine enemies thy footstool?

14 Are they not all ministering spirits sent forth in the service for those who shall inherit life everlasting?

CHAPTER 2

Therefore we should give earnest heed to the things which we have heard, lest at any time they be lost.

2 For if the word spoken by angels has been affirmed, and every one who has heard it and transgressed it has received a just reward,

3 How shall we escape, if we neglect the very things which are our salvation and which were first spoken by our Lord and were proved to us by those who had heard him,

4 And to which Lord Yahweh testified with signs and wonders, and with various miracles, and with the gift of the Holy Spirit given according to his will?

5 For unto the angels has He not put in subjection the world to come, whereof we speak.

6 But as the scripture testifies, saying, What is man that thou are mindful of him? and the Son of man, that thou visit him?

7 For Thou has made man a little lower than the angels; and has crowned him with glory and honor, and has set him as ruler over the works of thy hands;

8 Thou has put all things in subjection under his feet. By putting all things under his control, He left nothing that He did not put under subjection to him. But now we do see yet that all things are in subjection to him.

9 We see that he is Yahshua the Christ, who humbled himself to become a little lower than the angels through the suffering and his death, but now he is crowned with glory and honor; for he tasted death for the sake of every human.

10 And it was proper for him to pay fully, in whose hand is everything and for whom are all things, to bring many sons to glory so that from the very beginning of their salvation, they are made perfect through sufferings.

11 For both he who sanctifies and those who are sanctified are all of one origin; for this reason, he is not ashamed to call them brethren,

12 Saying, I will declare thy name to my brethren; in the midst of the congregation will I praise thee.

13 And again, I will put my trust in him. And again, Behold me and the children which Lord Yahweh has given me.

14 Forasmuch then as the children are partakers of flesh and blood, Yahshua the Christ also likewise partook of the same; and by his death, he has destroyed him who had the power of death, that is, the devil.

15 And Lord Yahshua has released them who, through fear of death all their lives, were subject to slavery.

16 For he did not take on him the likeness of angels; but he did take on him the offspring of Avraham.

17 Therefore, it behooved him that he should resemble his brethren, that he may be a merciful and faithful high priest in the things of Yahshua the Christ, to make reconciliation for the sins of the people.

18 For since he himself has suffered, being tempted, he is able to help others who are tempted.

CHAPTER 3

From henceforth, O my holy brethren, called by a call from heaven, look to this Apostle and high Priest of our faith, Yahshua the Christ,

2 Who was faithful to Him who appointed him, as also Moshe was faithful to all his house.

3 The glory of Yahshua the Christ is much greater than that of Moshe, just as the honor of the builder of the house is greater than the house itself.

4 For every house is built by some man; but He who builds all things is Lord Yahweh.

5 And Moshe as a servant was faithful to all his house, and was a testimony of those things which were to be spoken after;

6 But Yahshua the Christ as a son over his own house, whose house we are, if to the end we hold fast with confidence to the glory of his hope.

7 Therefore, as the Holy Spirit said: Today if you will hear his voice,

8 Harden not your hearts to provoke Him, as the murmurers did in the day of temptation in the wilderness.

9 Your fathers tempted Me even though they examined and saw my works for forty years;

10 Therefore I was not pleased with that generation, and said, These are a people whose hearts have been misled and they have not known my ways.

11 So I swore in my anger, They shall not enter into my rest.

12 Take heed therefore, my brethren, lest perhaps there is a man among you who has an evil heart and is not a believer, and you will be cut off from the living God.

13 But search your hearts daily, until the day which is called The day, to the end that no man among you be hardened through the deceitfulness of sin.

14 For we are made partakers of Yahshua the Christ, if from the beginning to the very end we hold steadfast to this true covenant,

15 As it is said, Today, if you hear even the echoes of his voice, do not harden your hearts to anger Him.

16 Who are those who have heard and provoked Him? Were they not those who came out of Egypt under Moshe, although not all of them?

17 But with whom was He displeased for forty years? Was it not especially with those who had sinned and whose bones lay in the wilderness?

18 And against whom did He swear that they should not enter into his rest, except against those who did not listen?

19 So we see that they could not enter in because they did not believe.

CHAPTER 4

Let us therefore fear, while the promise of entering his rest remains, lest some among you find that they are prevented from entering.

2 For the gospel was preached to us as it was preached to them also, but the word they heard did not benefit them, because it was not mixed with faith in those who heard it.

3 But we who have believed will enter into rest, as He said: As I have sworn in my wrath, they shall not enter into my rest; for behold, the works of Lord Yahweh were from the very foundation of the world.

4 For it is said concerning the Sabbath, Lord Yahweh rested on the seventh day from all his works.

5 And here again He said, they shall not enter into my rest.

6 There was a chance for some to enter therein, but they to whom the gospel was first preached did not enter because they would not listen;

7 And again, after a long time He appointed another day, as it is written above; for David said, Today if you hear his voice, harden not your hearts.

8 For if Y'hoshua, the son of Nun, had given them rest, he would not afterward have spoken of another day.

9 It is therefore the duty of the people of Lord Yahweh to keep the Sabbath.

10 For he who has entered into his rest also has ceased from his own works, as Lord Yahweh did from his.

11 Let us strive therefore to enter into that rest, lest any man fall like those who were disobedient.

12 For the word of Lord Yahweh is living, powerful, and sharper than any two-edged sword, piercing even to the point of division between soul and spirit, and between the joints, marrow, and bones, and is a discerner of the thoughts and intents of the heart.

13 And there is no creature hidden from his sight; but all things are naked and open before the eyes of Him to Whom we are to answer.

14 We have, therefore, a great high priest who has ascended into heaven, Yahshua the Christ, the Son of Lord Yahweh; let us remain firm in his faith.

15 For we do not have a high priest who cannot share our infirmities, but we have one who was tempted with everything as we are, and yet without sin.

16 Let us, therefore, come openly to the throne of his grace, that we may obtain mercy and find grace to help in time of need.

Chapter 5

For every high priest chosen from among men is ordained on behalf of men about things pertaining to Lord Yahweh, that he may offer both gifts and non-payment sacrifices for sins;

2 He is one who can humble himself and have compassion on those who are ignorant and go astray; for he himself also is subject to weaknesses.

3 Because of these, he is obliged, just as he offers sacrifices for the people, likewise to offer for himself on account of his own sins.

4 And no man takes this honor to himself, but only he who is called of Lord Yahweh, as was Aharon.

5 So also Yahshua the Christ did not glorify himself by becoming a high priest, but Lord Yahweh glorified him and said to him, Thou art my Son; today have I begotten thee.

6 And He said also in another place, Thou art a priest for ever after the order of Melchisedec.

7 Even when Lord Yahshua was clothed in the flesh, he offered prayers and supplications, with vehement cries and tears to Him who was able to save him from death; and verily he was heard.

8 And though he was a good Son, because of fear and suffering which he endured, he learned obedience.

9 And he grew to be perfect and became the author of life everlasting to all who obey him;

10 So by Lord Yahweh, he was called a high priest after the order of Melchisedec.

11 Now concerning this very Melchisedec we have much to say, but it is difficult to explain because you are dull of comprehension.

12 By now you should be teachers because you have been a long time in training; but even now you need to be taught the primary writings of the word of Lord Yahweh; but you are still in need of "milk," and not strong "meat."

13 For every man whose spiritual food is "milk" (elementary spiritual truth) is unfamiliar with the word of righteousness; for he is a "babe" ("baby" of a Christian).

14 But strong "meat" (advanced spiritual truth) belongs to those who are of full age, even those who by reason of use have their senses exercised to discern both good and evil.

CHAPTER 6

Therefore, let us leave the elementary word of Yahshua the Christ, and let us go on to perfection. Why do you again lay another foundation for the repentance from past deeds and for faith in Lord Yahweh?

2 And for the doctrine of baptisms, for the laying on of hands, for the resurrection of the dead, and for eternal judgment?

3 If the Lord permits, this we will do.

4 But this is impossible for those who have been baptized, have tasted the gift from heaven, and have received the Holy Spirit,

5 And have tasted the good word of Lord Yahweh and the powers of the world to come,

6 For them to sin again and be renewed again by repentance, they crucify the Son of Lord Yahweh a second time and put him to open shame.

7 For the earth, which drinks in the rain that falls abundantly on it, and brings forth herbs useful to those for whom it is cultivated, receives blessing from Lord Yahweh;

8 But if it should produce thorns and briers it is rejected and not far from being condemned; and at the end this crop will be burned up.

9 But beloved brethren, we expect from you the things that are good and that pertain to salvation, even though we speak in this manner.

10 For Lord Yahweh is not unjust to forget your works and your labor of love which you have made known in his name, for you have ministered to the saints and still do minister.

11 We desire that every one of you show the same diligence toward the fulfillment of your hope, even to the end,

12 And that you be not slothful, but be followers of those who through faith and patience have become heirs of the promise.

13 For when Lord Yahweh made a promise to Avraham, because there was none greater than Himself by whom He could swear, He swore by Himself,

14 Saying, Blessing, I will bless you, and multiplying, I will multiply you.

15 And so he was patient and obtained the promise.

16 For men swear by one who is greater than themselves; and in every dispute among them, the true settlement is by oaths.

17 Therefore, because Lord Yahweh wanted more abundantly to show to the heirs of promise that his agreement was unchangeable, He sealed it by an oath.

18 Thus, by the promise and by the, both of which is unchangeable, and neither of which could Lord Yahweh lie, we find courage to hold fast to the hope that has been promised by Him in Whom we have taken refuge.

19 That promise is like an anchor to us; it upholds the soul so that it may not be shaken, and it penetrates beyond the veil of the temple;

20 Therein Lord Yahshua has previously entered into the temple for our sakes, and become the high priest for ever after the order of Melchisedec.

Chapter 7

For this Melchisedec was king of Salem, the priest of the most high God, Lord Yahweh, who met Avraham returning from the slaughter of the kings and blessed him,

19 For the law made nothing perfect, but there is come in its place a better hope, by which we draw near to Lord Yahweh.

24 But this one (Yahshua the Christ), because he is immortal, has a priesthood which remains for ever.

25 Therefore he is able to save forever those who come to Lord Yahweh by him because he lives forever to make intercession for them.

26 For this is the kind of high priest which is proper for us: pure, without evil, undefiled, far away from sin, and made higher than the heavens;

27 And who needs not daily, as do those high priests, to offer up sacrifices, first for their own sins and then for the peoples sins; for this he did once when he offered up himself.

28 For the law appoints imperfect men to be priests; but the word of the oath which came after the law appoints the Son (Yahshua the Christ) who is perfect for evermore.

Chapter 8

Now above all we have a high priest who (Yahshua the Christ) is seated at the right hand of the throne of the Majesty in heaven;

2 And he (Yahshua the Christ) has become the minister of the sanctuary and of the true tabernacle which Lord Yahweh, not men, pitched.

3 For every high priest is appointed to offer gifts and sacrifices, therefore it is necessary that this man has something to offer also.

4 For if he were on earth, he would not be a priest, because there are priests who offer gifts according to the law,

5 Who serve the semblance and shadow of heavenly things, just as it was commanded to Moshe when he was about to make the tabernacle: See that you make all things according to the pattern showed to you in the mount.

6 But now Yahshua the Christ has received a ministry which is greater than that; just as the covenant in which he was made a mediator is greater, so are the promises greater than those given in the old covenant.

7 For if the first covenant had been faultless, then there would have been no need for the second.

8 For he found fault with them and said: Behold, the day is coming, says the Lord, when I will perfect a new covenant with the house of Israel and with the house of Judah;

9 Not according to the covenant that I made with their fathers int the day when I took them by the hand and led them out of the land of Egypt; and because they abode not in my covenant, I rejected them, says the Lord.

10 For this shall be the covenant that I will make with the house of Israel after those days, says the Lord: I will put my law into their minds and I will write my law in their hearts; and I will be their God and they shall be my people.

11 And no man shall teach his neighbor, neither his brother, saying, Know the Lord; for all shall know Me, from the youngest to the oldest.

12 And I will forgive their wickedness and I will no longer remember their sins;

13 For He has spoken of a new covenant; the first covenant has become old, and that which is old and obsolete is near destruction.

CHAPTER 9

Then verily the first covenant had also ordinances of divine service and a worldly sanctuary.

2 For the first tabernacle which was made had in it the candlestick, the table, and the shewbread; and it was called the sanctuary.

3 But the inner tabernacle, which is within the veil of the second door, was called the Holy of Holies.

4 And their was in it the golden censer and the ark of the covenant all overlaid with gold, and in it was the golden pot containing the manna, and Aharon's rod which budded, and the tablets of the covenant;

5 And over it the cherubim of glory, overshadowing the mercy seat; now is not the time to describe how these things were made.

6 The priests always entered into the outer tabernacle and performed their service of worship;

7 But into the inner tabernacle, the high priest entered alone, once every year, with the blood which he offered for himself and for the faults of the people.

8 By this, the Holy Spirit revealed that the way of the saints would not yet be made known so long as the old tabernacle remained,

9 Which was the symbol for that time, now past, in which were offered both gifts and sacrifices which could not make perfect the conscience of him who offered them,

10 But which served only for food and drink, and in various ablutions which are ordinances of the flesh and were imposed until the time of reformation.

11 But Yahshua the Christ, who had come, became the high priest of the good things which he wrought; and he entered into a greater and more perfect tabernacle which was not made by hands, and was not of this world;

12 And he did not enter with the blood of goats and calves, but by his own blood he entered in once into the holy place, and obtained for us everlasting salvation.

13 For if the blood of goats, calves, and the ashes of a heifer were sprinkled on those who were defiled, sanctified them even to the cleansing of their flesh,

14 How much more will the blood of Yahshua the Christ, who through the eternal Spirit offered himself without blemish to Lord Yahweh, purify our conscience from dead works so that we may serve the living God?

15 For this cause he became the mediator of the new covenant, and by his death he became salvation for those who transgressed the old covenant, that those who are called may receive the promise of eternal inheritance.

16 For where a testament is presented, it shows the death of its maker.

17 For a testament is of force after men are dead, otherwise it is of no strength so long as its maker lives.

18 For this reason, not even the first covenant was confirmed without blood.

19 For when Moshe had given every precept to all the people according to the law, Moshe took the blood of a heifer with water, scarlet wool, and hyssop, and he sprinkled it on the books and on all the people,

20 Saying, This is the blood of the covenant which has been ordained for you by Lord Yahweh.

21 That very blood he also sprinkled on the tabernacle and on all the vessels used for worship,

22 Because nearly everything, according to the law, is purified with the blood; and without shedding of blood there is no forgiveness.

23 It is necessary, therefore, that the patterns of things which are heavenly should be purified with these; but the heavenly things themselves, with sacrifices better than these.

24 For Yahshua the Christ has not entered into the holy place made with hands, which is the symbol of the true one; but he entered into heaven itself to appear before the presence of Lord Yahweh for our sakes.

25 Not so that he should offer himself many times, as does the high priest who enters into the holy place every year with blood which is not his own;

26 And if not so, then he would have been obliged to suffer many times from the very beginning of the world; but now at the end of the world, only once by his sacrifice did he offer himself to abolish sin.

27 And just as it is appointed for men to die once, and after their death, the judgment;

28 So Yahshua the Christ was once offered to bear the sins of many; so that at his second coming he shall appear without our sins for the salvation of those who look for him.

CHAPTER 10

For the law had in it a shadow of the good things to come, but was not the essence of the things themselves; hence, although the same sacrifices were offered every year, they could not perfect those who offered them.

2 For if they had once been perfected, they would have ceased from their offerings; for, from henceforth their minds would not have driven them into the sins from which they had once been cleansed.

3 But in those sacrifices, they remembered their sins every year.

4 For it is not possible that the blood of bulls and of goats could take away sins.

5 Therefore, when he entered into the world, he said, Sacrifices and offerings Thou (Lord Yahweh) did not desire, but Thou has prepared me a body;

6 Burnt offering and sin offering Thou has not required.

7 Then said I: Lo, I come; in the beginning of the books, it is written of me, I delight to do thy will, O Lord Yahweh.

8 Above when he said: Sacrifices, burnt offerings, and offerings for sins, Thou would not have, the very ones which were offered according to the law;

9 And after that he said: Lo, I come to do thy will, O Lord Yahweh. Thus He put an end to the first in order to establish the second.

10 By this very will, we are sanctified through the offering of the body of Yahshua the Christ once for all.

11 For every high priest appointed, ministered daily, offering the same sacrifices, which had never been able to cleanse sins;

12 But this one, after he (Yahshua the Christ) had offered one sacrifice for sins, sat down at the right hand of Lord Yahweh for ever.

13 From henceforth, there he will remain until his enemies are placed as a footstool under his feet.

14 For by one offering, he has perfected for ever those who are sanctified.

15 The Holy Spirit is also a witness to us; for he had said before,

16 This is the covenant that I will make with them after those days, says the Lord, I will put my law in their minds and I will write my law in their hearts.

17 And their iniquities and sins will I remember no more.

18 For where there is forgiveness of sins, there is no need for offering for sins.

19 Having therefore, my brethren, boldness to enter into the holiest by the blood of Yahshua.

20 By a new and living way which he has made new for us through the veil, that is to say, his flesh,

21 And having a great high priest over the house of Lord Yahweh,

22 Let us draw near with a true heart in full assurance of faith, having our hearts sprinkled and cleansed of evil thought, and our bodies washed with pure water.

23 Let us remain firm in the profession of our faith without wavering, for he who has promised us is faithful.

24 And let us consider one another to arouse love and good works,

25 Not forsaking the assembling of ourselves together, as is customary for some; but exhorting one another, and so much the more when you see that day approaching.

26 For if any man sin willfully after he has received the knowledge of the truth, then there is no more sacrifices to be offered for sins.

27 But he is ready for the fearful judgment and the fiery indignation which shall consume the adversaries.

28 He who transgressed the law of Moshe, on the word of two or three witnesses, died without mercy:

29 How much more punishment do you think he will receive who has trodden underfoot the Son of Lord Yahweh, and has considered the blood of his covenant, through which he had been sanctified, as ordinary blood and has blasphemed the Spirit of Grace?

30 For we know Him who said: Vengeance is mine, I will repay, says the Lord. And again, The Lord shall judge his people.

31 It is a fearful to fall into the hands of an angry God.

32 Remember therefore, the former days in which, after you received baptism, you endured many tribulations.

33 By reproach and trouble, you were made an object of ridicule; and you have also become companions of those men who have also endured these things.

34 And you had pity on those who were prisoners, and you took the seizure of your property cheerfully, for you know in yourselves that you have a better and a more enduring possession in heaven.

35 Do not lose, therefore, the confidence that you have, for it has a great reward.

36 For you have need of patience in order that you may do the will of Lord Yahweh and receive the promise.

37 For the time is all too short, and he who is to come will come and will not delay.

38 But the righteous shall live by my faith; and if any draw back, the soul which I am shall have no pleasure in him.

39 But we do not belong to those who draw back to perdition, but to the faith which restores the souls whom we are.

CHAPTER 11

Now faith is the substance of things hoped for, as it was the substance of things which have come to pass; and it is the evidence of things not seen,

2 And in this way, it became a testimony concerning the elders.

3 For it is through faith that we understand that the worlds were framed by the word of Lord Yahweh, so that the things which are seen came to be from those which are not seen.

4 It was by faith that Hevel (Abel) offered a more excellent sacrifice to Lord Yahweh than Kayin (Cain), and because of this, Hevel received a testimony that he was righteous, and Lord Yahweh testified to his offering; therefore, even though he is dead, he speaks.

5 By faith, Hanokh (Enoch) departed and did not taste death, and he was not found because Lord Yahweh took him; but before He took him away, there was a testimonial about Hanokh, that he pleased Lord Yahweh.

6 Without faith, man cannot please Lord Yahweh; for he who comes near to Lord Yahweh must believe that He is, and that He is a rewarder of those who seek Him.

7 By faith, Noach (Noah), when he was warned concerning the things not seen, became fearful and made an ark to save his household; and by it he condemned the world and became heir of righteousness which is by faith.

8 By faith, Avraham, when he was called to depart for the land which he was to receive for an inheritance, obeyed; and he went out without knowing where he was going.

9 By faith, Avraham became a sojourner in the land which was promised him as in a strange country, and he dwelt in tents with Yitz'chak and Ya'akov who are the heirs with him of the same promise;

10 For he looked for a city which has foundations, whose builder and maker is Lord Yahweh.

11 Through faith also, Sarah who was barren, received strength to conceive an offspring, and was delivered of a child when she was past age, because she was sure that he who had promised her was faithful.

12 Therefore, there sprang from one who was as good as dead, as many as the stars of the sky in number and as the grains of sand which is on the seashore, innumerable.

13 These all died in faith, not having received the promised land, but they saw it from afar, and rejoiced in it; and they acknowledged that they were strangers and pilgrims on earth.

14 For they who speak so, declare plainly that they seek a country for themselves.

15 And if they had a desire for that very country from which they went out, they had time to return to it again.

16 But now it is evident that they desire a better city, that city which is in heaven; therefore, Lord Yahweh is not ashamed to be called their God; for He has prepared for them a city.

17 By faith, Avraham, when he was tested, offered up Yitz'chak; he lifted upon the altar his only begotten son, even that very one who had been received in the promise,

18 Of whom it was said, In Yitz'chak shall your descendants be called;

19 And he reasoned within himself, It is possible for Lord Yahweh even to raise the dead; and because of this, Yitz'chak was given to him as a parable.

20 By faith in the things to come, Yitz'chak blessed Ya'akov and Esav (Esau).

21 By faith, Ya'akov, when he was dying, blessed both of the sons of Yosef, and he worshipped, leaning upon the head of his staff.

22 By faith, Yosef, when he died, made mention of the departure of the children of Israel and gave commandment concerning his bones.

23 By faith, the parents of Moshe, hid Moshe for three months after his birth because they saw that the infant boy was fair; and they were not afraid of the king's commandment.

24 By faith, Moshe, when he came to manhood, refused to be called the son of Pharaoh's daughter,

25 Choosing rather to suffer affliction with the people of Lord Yahweh than to enjoy the pleasures of sin for a short while.

26 And Moshe reasoned that the reproach of Yahshua the Christ was greater riches than the treasures of Egypt; for he looked forward to receive a reward.

27 By faith, Moshe forsook Egypt, not fearing the wrath of the king; and he survived after he had seen Lord Yahweh, who is invisible.

28 Through faith, Moshe instituted the Passover and sprinkled the blood, lest he who destroyed the first-born should touch them.

29 By faith, they passed through the Red Sea as by dry land; but in it the Egyptians were drowned when they made the attempt.

30 By faith, the walls of Jericho fell down after they had been encompassed seven days.

31 By faith, Rahab the harlot did not perish with those who were disobedient, for she had received the spies in peace.

32 And what more shall I say? For time would fail me to tell of Gid'on (Gideon), Barak, Shimshon (Samson), Jephthah, David, Sh'mu'el (Samuel), and the rest of the prophets,

33 Who through faith, conquered kingdoms, worked righteousness, obtained promises, stopped the mouths of lions,

34 Quenched the violence of fire, escaped the edge of the sword, out of weakness were made strong, became valiant in battle, routed the camps of enemies,

35 Restored to women their sons, raised people from the dead; while others died through tortures, not hoping for deliverance, that they may have a better resurrection;

36 Others endured mocking and scourging; still others were delivered to bonds and imprisonment;

37 Some were stoned, some were sawn apart, some died by the edge of the sword; others wearing sheepskins and goatskins wandered about as destitute, afflicted, and tormented,

38 Of whom the world was not worthy; they were like those who are lost in the desert, and in mountains, and in dens and caves of the earth.

39 Thus these all, having obtained a testimonial through the faith, did not receive the promise,

40 Because Lord Yahweh from the beginning provided for our help, lest without us they should not be made perfect.

CHAPTER 12

Therefore, seeing we also are surrounded with so great a cloud of witnesses, let us lay aside every weight and the sin which does so easily beset us, and let us run with patience the race that is set before us,

2 And let us look to Yahshua, who was the author and perfecter of our faith, and who, instead of the joy which he could have had, endured the cross, suffered shame, and is now seated at the right hand of the throne of Lord Yahweh.

3 See, therefore, how much he has suffered from the hands of sinners, from those who were a contradiction to themselves, lest you become weary and faint in your minds.

4 You have not yet come to the point of bloodshed in your striving against sin.

5 And you have forgotten the teaching which has been told to you as to children, My son, despise not the chastening of the Lord, do not let yourself faint when you are rebuked of him,

6 For whom the Lord loves, He chastens, and He disciplines the son with whom He is pleased.

7 Now, therefore, endure discipline, because Lord Yahweh acts toward you as toward sons; for where is the son whom the father does not discipline?

8 But if you are without discipline, that very discipline by which every man is trained, then you are strangers and not sons.

9 Furthermore, if our fathers of the flesh corrected us and we respected them, how much more then should we willingly be under subjection to our Spiritual Father, and live?

10 For they, only for a short while, disciplined us as seemed good to them; but Lord Yahweh corrects us for our advantage, that we may become partakers of his holiness.

11 No discipline, at the time, is expected to be a thing of joy, but of sorrow; but in the end it produces the fruits of peace and righteousness to those who are trained by it.

12 Therefore, be courageous and strong,

13 And make straight the paths for your feet, so that the member which is lame may not suffer but be healed.

14 Follow peace with all men, and holiness, without which no man shall see our Lord.

15 Take heed lest any man among you be found short of the grace of Lord Yahweh, or lest any root of bitterness spring forth and harm you, and thereby many be defiled,

16 Or lest any man among you be found immoral and weak like Esav, who sold his birthright for a morsel of meat.

17 For you know that afterward when he wished to inherit the blessing, he was rejected, and he had no chance of recovery, even though he sought it with tears.

18 For you have yet neither come near the roaring fire nor the darkness nor the storm nor the tempest,

19 Nor to the sound of the trumpet and the voice of the word; which voice they heard but refused so that the word will not be spoken to them anymore.

20 For they could not survive that which was commanded; for if even a beast drew near the mountain, the beast would be stoned.

21 And so terrible was the sight, that Moshe said: I fear and quake.

22 But you have come near to Mount Zion and to the city of the living God, the heavenly Jerusalem, and to the innumerable multitude of angels,

23 And to the congregation of the first converts who were enrolled in heaven and to Lord Yahweh, the Judge of all, and to the spirits of pious men made perfect,

24 And to Yahshua the Christ, the mediator of the new covenant, and to the sprinkling of his blood, which speaks a better message than Hevel (Abel) did.

25 Beware, therefore, lest you refuse him who speaks to you. For if they who refused him who had spoken with them on earth were not delivered, much more can we not escape if we refuse Him who speaks to us from heaven.

26 He is the one whose voice shook the earth; but now He has promised, saying, Once more I will shake not only the earth, but also heaven.

27 And these words, "Once more," signify the change of things which will be shaken, because they are made in order that the things which cannot be shaken may remain.

28 Therefore, receiving a kingdom which cannot be shaken, let us hold fast that grace whereby we may serve and please Lord Yahweh with reverence and godly fear;

29 For our God is a consuming fire.

CHAPTER 13

Let brotherly love remain in you.

2 And forget not hospitality toward strangers; for thereby some were worthy to entertain angels unawares.

3 Remember those who are in prison, as though you were a prisoner with them; remember those who suffer adversity, for you are human also.

4 Marriage is honorable in all, and the bed undefiled; but Lord Yahweh will judge those who practice vice and adultery;

5 Do not be carried away by the love of money; but be content with what you have; for the Lord Himself has said: I will never leave you nor forsake you.

6 So that we may boldly say: The Lord is my helper, and I will not fear what man may do to me.

7 Remember those who are your leaders, those who have spoken the word of Lord Yahweh to you; mark the completeness of their works, and imitate their faith.

8 Yahshua the Christ is the same yesterday, today, and forever.

9 Do not be carried away by strange doctrines. For it is a good thing to strengthen our hearts with grace; not with food because it did not help those who greatly sought after it.

10 We have an altar from which those who minister in the tabernacle have no right to eat.

11 For the flesh of the beasts, whose blood is brought into the sanctuary by the high priest for sin, is burned outside the camp.

12 Wherefore Yahshua also, that he may sanctify his people with his own blood, suffered outside the city.

13 Let us go forth therefore to him outside the camp, bearing his reproach.

14 For here we have not a permanent city, but we seek one to come.

15 By him, therefore, let us always offer the sacrifice of praise to Lord Yahweh, that is, the fruit of the lips giving thanks to his name.

16 And do not forget kindness and fellowship with the poor; for with such sacrifices, Lord Yahweh is well pleased.

17 Listen to your spiritual leaders and obey them; for they are watchful guardians of you souls, as one who must give account, that they may do it with joy and not with grief, for to do it with grief is unprofitable for you.

18 Pray for us; for we trust that we have a good conscience, being in all things willing to live honestly.

19 But above all, I beseech you to do this that I may return to you sooner.

20 Now the God of peace who brought again from the dead our Lord Yahshua the Christ, that great shepherd of the "sheep," through the blood of the everlasting covenant,

21 Make you perfect in every good work to do his will, working in us that which is well pleasing in his sight, through Yahshua the Christ; to whom be glory forever and ever. Amen.

22 And I beseech you, my brethren, to be patient in the word of comfort; for I have written you very briefly.

23 You should know that our brother Timotheus has been set at liberty; and if he should come soon, I will see you together with him.

24 Salute all your spiritual leaders and all the saints. All of the brethren of Italy salute you.

25 Grace be with you all. Amen.

The General Epistle of
Ya'akov (James)

CHAPTER 1

Ya'akov, a servant of Lord Yahweh and a servant of our Lord Yahshua the Christ, to the twelve tribes which are scattered among the Gentiles, greeting.

2 My brethren, take it as a joy to you when you enter into many and varied temptations;

3 For you know that the trial of faith will increase your patience.

4 And let patience be a perfect work, that you may be perfect and entire, lacking nothing.

5 If any of you lack wisdom, let him ask of Lord Yahweh who gives to all men liberally and with grace, and it will be given to him.

6 But let him ask of faith, not doubting. For he who doubts is like the waves of the sea driven by the wind and tossed.

7 Thus, let not that man suppose that he will receive anything of the Lord.

8 A double-minded man is unstable in all his ways.

9 Let the brother who is humble rejoice because he is exalted.

10 Let the rich man rejoice in his humbleness, because as the flower of the grass, so shall he pass away.

11 For as the sun rises with its burning heat and causes the grass to wither, the flower to fall and its beauty to perish, so also shall the rich man fade away in the course of his life.

12 Blessed is the man who endures temptations; for when he is tested, he shall receive the crown of life which Lord Yahweh has promised to those who love Him.

13 Let no man say when he is tempted: "I am tempted of Lord Yahweh"; for Lord Yahweh cannot be tempted with evil, neither does He tempt any man;

14 But every man is tempted by his own lust; he covets and is enticed.

15 Then when lust has conceived, it brings forth sin; and sin when it has matured, it brings forth death.

16 Do not err, my beloved brethren.

17 Every good and perfect gift is from above, and comes down from the Father of lights, with Whom there is no variableness nor shadow of change.

18 It is He who begot us of his own will with the word of truth, that we should be the first-fruits of his creatures.

19 Therefore, my beloved brethren, let every man be swift to hear, slow to speak, and slow to anger;

20 For the wrath of man does not bring about the righteousness of Lord Yahweh.

21 Therefore, cast away all filthiness and all the multitude of evil things; and receive with meekness, the engrafted word which is able to save you souls.

22 But be doers of the word, and not hearers only, deceiving yourselves.

23 For if any be a hearer of the word and not a doer, he is like a man who sees his face in a mirror;

24 For he sees himself and goes his way and forgets how he looked.

25 But whoever looks into the perfect law of liberty and abides in it is not merely a hearer of the word which can be forgotten but a doer of the work, and this man shall be blessed in his labor.

26 If any man thinks that he ministers to Lord Yahweh, and does not control his tongue, he deceives his own heart, and this man's ministry is in vain.

27 For a pure and holy ministry before Lord Yahweh the Father, is this: To visit the fatherless and widows in their affliction, and to keep himself unspotted from the world.

Chapter 2

My brethren, do not with hypocrisy uphold the glorious faith of our Lord Yahshua the Christ.

2 For if there should enter into your synagogue a man with gold rings and costly garments, and there should also enter a poor man in soiled clothing,

3 And you should attend to the one who wears the beautiful clothing and say to him, Sit here in a good place, and say to the poor man, Stand up there, or sit here before our footstool,

4 Are you not then showing partiality and thereby giving preference to evil thoughts?

5 Hear this, my beloved brethren: Has not Lord Yahweh chosen the poor of the world who are rich in faith to be heirs of the kingdom which Lord Yahweh has promised to those who love Him?

6 But you have despised the poor. Do not some rich men exalt themselves over you and drag you before the judgment seat?

7 Don't they blaspheme against that good name by which you are called?

8 If you fulfill the law of Lord Yahweh by this, as it is written, You shall love your neighbor as yourself, you do well;

9 But if you discriminate among men, you commit sin and you will be condemned by the law as transgressors of the law.

10 For whoever shall keep the whole law, even though he fail in but one statute, he is guilty as to the whole law.

11 For He who said: You shall not commit adultery, said also: You shall not murder. Now if you do not commit adultery but you murder, you have become a transgressor of the law.

12 So speak and so act as men who are to be judged by the law of liberty.

13 For a judgment without mercy will be on him who does not show mercy; for you exalt yourselves by having mercy over judgment.

14 Though a man say he has faith, what profit is it, my brethren, if he does not have works? Can faith save him?

15 If a brother or sister be naked and lacking of daily food,

16 And one of you says to him or her, Depart in peace, be warmed and be filled; yet you do not give to him or her those things which are needed for the body, what does it profit?

17 Even so, by itself, faith without works is dead.

18 For a man may say, You have faith and I have works; show me your faith without your works, and I will show you my faith by my works.

19 You believe that there is one God; you do well. The devils also believe, and they tremble.

20 Would you know, O weak man, that faith without works is dead?

21 Was not our father Avraham justified by works, when he raised Yitz'chak his son upon the altar?

22 You can see how his faith helped his works, and how by works his faith was made perfect.

23 And the scripture was fulfilled which said, Avraham believed Lord Yahweh, and it was accounted to him for righteousness; and he was called the Friend of Lord Yahweh.

24 You see then how a man by works becomes righteous, and not by faith only.

25 Likewise also was not Rahab the harlot justified by works when she welcomed the spies and sent them out another way?

26 For as the body without the spirit is dead, so also faith without works is dead.

CHAPTER 3

My brethren, let not many teachers be among you; but know that we are under a great judgment.

2 For in many things we all stumble. Anyone who does not offend in word, this one is a perfect man and able also to subdue his whole body.

3 Behold, we put bits into the mouths of horses, that they may obey us, and we turn about their whole bodies.

4 Behold also the ships; great as they are, when driven by severe winds, the ships are turned about with a very small rudder wherever the pilot wishes.

5 Even so the tongue is a little member and boasts great things. Likewise, a small fire sets ablaze large forests.

6 The tongue is a fire, and the sinful world is a forest; that very tongue while it is among our members, can defile our whole body and set on fire the course of nature which has rolled down from the beginning; and in the end it is consumed by fire.

7 For all kinds of beasts, birds, creatures of the sea, and of the land are under the subjugation of the will of man.

8 But the tongue, no man can tame; it is an unruly evil, full of deadly poison.

9 By the tongue, we bless the Lord (Yahshua) and the Father (Lord Yahweh); and by the tongue, we curse men who are made in the image of Lord Yahweh;

10 Out of the same mouth proceed curses and blessings. My brethren, these things ought not so to be.

11 Can there spring forth from the same fountain both sweet water and bitter water?

12 Can the fig tree, my brethren, bear olives? or the vine, figs? Likewise also, salt water cannot be made sweet.

13 Who is wise among you and has training? Let him prove his words by his good deeds in the humbleness of wisdom.

14 But if you have bitter envying among you or strife in your hearts, do not boast and do not lie against the truth.

15 This wisdom does not come from above, but it is earthly, sensual, and devilish.

16 For wherever envy and strife are, there is confusion and every sort of evil.

17 But the wisdom that is from above is first pure, then full of peace, and is gentle, obedient, full of mercy, full of good fruits, and is without partiality and is without hypocrisy.

18 And the fruit of righteousness is sown in peace by the peacemakers.

CHAPTER 4

From whence come conflicts and quarrels among you? Is it not from the lusts that war in your members?

2 You covet and do not obtain; you kill and envy, but you cannot possess; you strive and fight, yet you have nothing, because you do not ask.

3 You ask and you do not receive because you do not ask sincerely, you ask that you may satisfy your lusts.

4 O you adulterers! Do you not know that the love for worldly things is enmity with Lord Yahweh? Whoever, therefore, esteems worldly things is the enemy of Lord Yahweh.

5 Or do you think that the scripture said in vain: The pride that dwells in us is provoked by jealousy?

6 But our Lord has given us abundant grace. Therefore he said: Lord Yahweh humbles the proud, but gives grace to the humble.

7 Submit yourselves therefore to Lord Yahweh. Resist Satan, and Satan will flee from you.

8 Draw near to Lord Yahweh, and He will draw near to you. Cleanse your hands, O you sinners! And purify your hearts, O you of doubtful mind!

9 Humble yourselves and mourn; let your laughter be changed into weeping, and let your joy be changed into sorrow.

10 Humble yourselves before the Lord, and He will lift you up.

11 Do not speak against one another, my brethren, for he who speaks against his brother and judges his brother, is he who also speaks against the law and judges the law; but if you judge the law, you are not a doer of the law, but a judge of the law.

12 For there is one Lawgiver and Judge, who is able to save and able to destroy. Who are you to judge your neighbor?

13 What then shall we say of those who say, Today or tomorrow we will go to a certain city and will work there for a year and will trade and prosper?

14 They do not know what will happen tomorrow! For what is our life? It is but a vapor which appears for a little while and then vanishes away.

15 Instead of saying: Today or tomorrow we will go to a certain city and will work there for a year and will trade and prosper, they should say: If the Lord will, we shall live and do this or that.

16 But now they are proud in their boasting; all such pride is evil.

17 Therefore, he who knows to do good and does not do it, to him it is sin.

Chapter 5

O you rich men, weep and howl for the miseries which shall come upon you!

2 Your riches are destroyed and rotted, and your garments are moth-eaten.

3 Your gold and silver are tarnished, and the rust of them will be a testimony against you and will eat your flesh. The treasures which you have heaped together, will be as fire to you for the last days.

4 Behold, the wage of the laborers who have reaped your fields, that which you have fraudulently kept back, cries; and the cry of the reapers has already entered into the ears of the Lord of Sabaoth.

5 For you have had your luxuries on earth and you have been greedy; you have fed your bodies as for the day of slaughter.

6 You have condemned and murdered the righteous; and yet he does not resist you.

7 But, my brethren, be patient until the coming of the Lord Yahshua the Christ, just as the husbandman waits for the precious crop of his field, and has long patience for it, until he receives the early and the latter rain.

8 You be patient also; strengthen your hearts, for the coming of our Lord is at hand.

9 Complain not one against another, my brethren, lest you be condemned; for behold, judgment is at hand.

10 My brethren, take the prophets who have spoken in the name of the Lord for an example of patience in your suffering.

11 Behold, we count them happy who endure. You have heard of the patience of Iyov (Job), and you have seen what the Lord did for him at the end; for the Lord is very merciful and compassionate.

12 But above all things, my brethren, do not swear, neither by heaven, neither by the earth, and neither by any other oath; but let your words be yes, yes, and no, no, lest you fall under condemnation.

13 If any among you be afflicted, let him pray. If any be merry, let him sing psalms.

14 And if any be sick, let him call for the elders of the church, and let them pray over him, anointing him with oil in the name of our Lord:

15 And the prayer of faith shall heal the sick, and our Lord shall raise him up; and if he has committed sins, they shall be forgiven.

16 Confess your faults one to another, that you may be healed. The effectual fervent prayer of a righteous man is powerful.

17 Even Eliyahu, who was a weak man like ourselves, prayed earnestly that it may not rain upon the land, and it did not rain for three years and six months.

18 And he prayed again, and the heaven gave rain and the earth brought forth her fruits.

19 My brethren, if any of you do err from the way of the truth, and someone converts him from his error,

20 Let him know that he who converts a sinner from the error of his way, shall save that soul from death and shall wipe out a multitude of sins.

The First Epistle of Kefa
(Peter)

Chapter 1

Kefa, an apostle of Yahshua the Christ, to the chosen ones and pilgrims, scattered throughout Pontus, Galatia, Cappadocia, Asia Minor, and Bithynia,

2 Who have been chosen by the foreknowledge of Lord Yahweh the Father, through sanctification of the Spirit, to be obedient and to sprinkle the blood of our Lord Yahshua the Christ: Grace to you and peace be multiplied.

3 Blessed be Lord Yahweh, the Father of our Lord Yahshua the Christ, who by his abundant mercy has again renewed us spiritually to a lively hope by the resurrection of Yahshua the Christ from the dead,

4 To an inheritance incorruptible and undefiled, that does not fade away and is prepared in heaven for you,

5 While you are kept by the power of Lord Yahweh through faith for the life eternal which is ready to be revealed at the last time.

6 Wherein you will rejoice forever, though at present you are sorrowful for a while, through diverse trials which have come upon you,

7 So that the proof of your faith, being much more precious than refined gold which has been purified by fire, may be made manifest for the glory, honor, and praise at the appearing of Yahshua the Christ,

8 Whom you have not seen, but whom you yet love, and in whose faith rejoice with exceeding joy that cannot be described;

9 And you will receive the reward for your faith, even the salvation of you souls.

10 For which very salvation the prophets searched diligently when they prophesied concerning the grace which was to be given to you.

11 They searched to find out at what time it would be revealed, and the Spirit of Yahshua the Christ which dwelt in them testified beforehand the sufferings of Yahshua the Christ and the glory that should follow.

12 And everything they were searching for was revealed to them because they did not seek for their own benefit, but they prophesied the things which concerned us, the things which now have been revealed to you by those who have preached the gospel to you through the Holy Spirit sent from heaven; which things the angels also desire to look into.

13 Therefore gird up the loins of your mind, be wide awake and hope for the joy that is coming to you at the revelation of our Lord Yahshua the Christ;

14 Like obedient children, not partakers again in those sinful desires for which you once lusted in your ignorance;

15 But be you holy in all your conduct, just as he who has called you is holy;

16 Because it is written, Be you holy, even as I am holy.

17 And if you call on the Father, He who is impartial and who judges every man according to his works, conduct yourselves reverently during the time of your sojourning here,

18 Knowing that you have not been redeemed from your empty works which you have received from your fathers, by corruptible silver and gold,

19 But with the precious blood of the Lamb (Yahshua the Christ) without blemish and without spot which is Yahshua the Christ,

20 Who verily was foreordained for this very purpose before the foundation of the world, and was manifest in these last times for your sakes,

21 Who by him you believe in Lord Yahweh, who raised him up from the dead and gave him glory, that your faith and hope may rest on Lord Yahweh.

22 Let you souls be sanctified by obedience to the truth, and be filled with sincere love so that you may love one another with pure and perfect hearts,

23 Being born again, not of corruptible seed but of incorruptible, by the word of Lord Yahweh, the word which lives and abides forever.

24 For all flesh is as grass, and all its glory is as the flower of the field. The grass withers and the flower fades away,

25 But the word of our God endures forever. And this is the very word which has been preached to you.

CHAPTER 2

Therefore lay aside all malice and all guile, hypocrisies, envies, and evil accusations,

2 And become like newborn babes, and long for the word as for pure and spiritual milk, that you may grow to salvation by it,

3 If you have tasted and found out that the Lord is good.

4 The one to whom you are coming is the living "stone," whom men have rejected, and yet he (Yahshua the Christ) is chosen and precious with Lord Yahweh;

5 You also, as living "stones," build up yourselves and become spiritual temples and holy priests to offer up spiritual sacrifices which are acceptable to Lord Yahweh by Yahshua the Christ.

6 For as it is said in the scriptures, Behold, I lay in Zion, a chief "cornerstone," approved, precious; and he who believes on him shall not be ashamed.

7 It is to you who believe, therefore, that this honor is given; but to those who are disobedient, he is a stumbling "stone" and a "stone" of trouble.

8 And they stumble over "it" (he, Yahshua the Christ) because they are disobedient to the word for which they were appointed.

9 But you are a chosen people, ministers to the kingdom, a holy people, a congregation redeemed to proclaim the glories of Him who has called you out of darkness to his marvelous light;

10 You, who in the past were not considered a people, but who are now the people of Lord Yahweh, the people who had not obtained mercy, but now you are the people who have mercy poured out upon you.

11 Dearly beloved, I beseech you as strangers and pilgrims, abstain from carnal desires which wage war against the soul;

12 And let your conduct be good before all men, so that those who speak evil words against you may see your good works and glorify Lord Yahweh at the day of trial.

13 Submit yourselves to all human authority for the sake of Lord Yahweh, whether it be to kings because of their power,

14 Or to judges because from them, officers are sent to punish offenders and to bestow honor on those who do good.

15 For such is the will of Lord Yahweh that by your good works, you may silence the mouths of foolish men who know not Lord Yahweh.

16 Act as free men; not as men who use their liberty as a cloak for their maliciousness, but as the servants of Lord Yahweh.

17 Honor all men. Love your brethren. Fear Lord Yahweh. Honor the king.

18 And as for the servants among you, let them be submissive to their masters with due respect, not only to those who are good and gentle, but also to those who are severe and difficult.

19 For such men have favor before Lord Yahweh; because of a good conscience, they endure sorrows which come upon them unjustly.

20 What praise have they who endure suffering because of their faults? But when you do good and are made to suffer and you take it patiently, then your glory is greater with Lord Yahweh.

21 For to this purpose you were called, because Yahshua the Christ also died for us, leaving us an example, that we should follow in his steps.

22 Yahshua the Christ did no sin, neither was guile found in his mouth;

23 When he was reviled, he did not revile again; he did not threaten when he suffered, but committed his cause to him who judges righteously;

24 And Yahshua the Christ bore all our sins and lifted them with his body on the cross so that we, being dead to sin, should live through his righteousness; and by his wounds, you were healed.

25 For you had gone astray like sheep, but you have now returned to the Shepherd and Guardian of you souls.

CHAPTER 3

Likewise, you wives, be submissive to your own husbands so that those who obey not the word may be won without difficulty through your good example,

2 When they see that you conduct yourselves with respect and modesty.

3 And do not adorn yourselves with outward adornments such as the plaiting of your hair or the wearing of ornaments of gold or costly apparel;

4 But adorn yourselves by the spiritual man of your heart, with a meek and quiet spirit which is incorruptible and is an ornament which is rich in the sight of Lord Yahweh.

5 For so also in the past did the holy women who trusted in Lord Yahweh adorn their lives and were submissive to their own husbands,

6 Even as Sara was submissive to Avraham, and called him "my lord;" her daughters you are, as long as you do good and are not confused by any kind of false value.

7 Likewise, you husbands, live with your wives with understanding, and hold them with tenderness like delicate vessels because they also will inherit with you the gift of everlasting life; do this so that you may not be hindered in your prayers.

8 Finally, live in harmony, share the suffering of those who suffer, be affectionate one to another, and be kind and gentle;

9 Not rendering evil for evil nor railing for railing, but instead, render blessing; for to this end, you have been called so that you may inherit a blessing.

10 Now, therefore, he who desires eternal life and wants to see good days, let him refrain his tongue from evil, and his lips so that they speak no guile:

11 Let him refrain from evil, and let him do good; let him seek and pursue peace.

12 For the eyes of the Lord are on the righteous, and his ears are open to their prayers, but the countenance of the Lord is against the wicked.

13 And who is he that can harm you if you are zealous followers of that which is Good?

14 But if you suffer for righteousness' sake, you are blessed; and be not afraid of those who terrify you, neither be troubled.

15 But sanctify the Lord Yahshua the Christ in your hearts; and be ready to give an answer in meekness and reverence to everyone who seeks from you a reason concerning the hope of your faith,

16 Having a good conscience so that they who speak evil of you, as evildoers, may be ashamed as men who belittle your good works in Yahshua the Christ.

17 For it is better, if it is the will of Lord Yahweh, that you suffer for good deeds rather than for evil deeds.

18 For Yahshua the Christ also once suffered for our sins, a divine person for sinners, that the divine person who is Yahshua the Christ may bring you to Lord Yahweh, wherefore while Yahshua died in the flesh, he lives in the spirit.

19 And Yahshua the Christ preached to the souls who were imprisoned in Sheol (Hades),

20 Those, who in the past, were disobedient; and in the days of Noach, when the Spirit of Lord Yahweh had patience, He commanded an ark to be made in the hope of their repentance, but only eight souls entered into it, and were saved by its floating upon the water.

21 You also are saved in that very manner by baptism, not merely by washing the filth from the body, but by confessing Lord Yahweh with a clean conscience and by the resurrection of Yahshua the Christ,

22 Who is taken up to heaven and is at the right hand of Lord Yahweh, angels and authorities and powers being made subject to him.

CHAPTER 4

Forasmuch then as Yahshua the Christ has suffered for you in the flesh, arm yourselves also with this very thought: he who subdues his body ceases from all sin,

2 That he should no longer live the rest of his time in the flesh to the lusts of men, but to the will of Lord Yahweh.

3 For the time past sufficed to have wrought the will of the pagans when you lived in lasciviousness, drunkenness, reveling, indecent singing, and worship of idols.

4 And behold, they think it strange that you do not indulge with them in the past excesses, and they blaspheme against you.

5 And they shall answer to Lord Yahweh who is to judge the quick and the dead.

6 For this cause, the gospel was preached also to those who are dead, that they may be judged according to men in the flesh, and live according to Lord Yahweh in spirit.

7 But the end of all things is at hand; be devout therefore, and be mindful of prayer.

8 And above all things, have fervent love toward one another because love covers a multitude of sins.

9 Be hospitable to strangers without grudging.

10 So let every one of you according to the gift he has received from Lord Yahweh, minister the same to your fellowmen like good stewards of the manifold grace of Lord Yahweh.

11 If any man preach, let him preach the word of Lord Yahweh; and if any man minister, let him do it according to the ability which Lord Yahweh has given him so that in everything you do, Lord Yahweh may be glorified through Yahshua the Christ. The glory and the honor are his forever and ever. Amen.

12 My beloved, do not think it strange at the trials which are to try you, that some strange thing has happened to you, because that thing is to prove you.

13 But rejoice, for you are partakers of Yahshua's sufferings; and when his glory shall be revealed, you may be glad also with exceeding joy.

14 If you are reproached for the name of Yahshua, blessed are you, for the glorious Spirit of Lord Yahweh rests upon you.

15 But let none of you suffer the fate of a murderer, a thief, or a malefactor.

16 If any man suffers as a Christian, let him not be ashamed, but let him glorify Lord Yahweh while bearing his name.

17 For the time is come that judgment must begin with the "house" of Lord Yahweh; and if it first begins with us, what shall be the end of those who do not obey the gospel of Lord Yahweh?

18 And if the righteous scarcely be saved, how shall the wicked and the sinner stand judgment?

19 Therefore let those, who suffer according to the will of Lord Yahweh, commit themselves to the faithful Creator while they are doing good.

CHAPTER 5

I exhort the ministers who are among you, for I also am a minister and a witness of the sufferings of Yahshua the Christ and a partaker of the glory that shall be revealed.

2 Feed the flock, of Lord Yahweh, which is entrusted to your care, and shepherd them spiritually, not by constraint, but willingly; not for filthy lucre, but with all your heart.

3 Live not as overlords over the flock, but live as good examples to them.

4 And when the chief Shepherd shall appear, you shall receive a crown of glory which will not fade away.

5 And you too, young people, submit yourselves to your elders; and clothe yourselves with humility toward one another, for Lord Yahweh resists the proud and gives grace to the humble.

6 Therefore, humble yourselves under the mighty hand of Lord Yahweh, so that He may exalt you in due time,

7 Casting all your cares upon Lord Yahweh, for He cares about you.

8 Be vigilant and be cautious, because your adversary, the devil, like a roaring lion, walks about, seeking whom he may devour.

9 Therefore, rise up against him, as you are steadfast in the faith, knowing that your brethren who are in the world also suffered these same afflictions.

10 But the God of all grace, who has called us to his eternal glory by Yahshua the Christ, whom Lord Yahweh has given to us, will strengthen us to endure these little afflictions so that we may be made steadfast and remain in Him forever.

11 To Him be glory and dominion and honor forever and ever. Amen.

12 By Silvanus, a faithful brother, I have written you these things briefly according to my opinion, exhorting and testifying that this is the true grace of Lord Yahweh wherein you stand.

13 The chosen church which is at Babylon, and Mark my son, salute you.

14 Greet one another with a holy kiss. Peace be with you all who are in Yahshua the Christ. Amen.

The Second Epistle of Kefa (Peter)

CHAPTER 1

Shim'on Kefa, a servant and apostle of Yahshua the Christ; to those who, through the righteousness of our Lord and Savior Yahshua the Christ, have been made equal with us in the precious faith:

2 Grace and peace be multiplied to you through the knowledge of our Lord Yahshua the Christ,

3 Who has given us all things that pertain to the power of Lord Yahweh, for life and worship of Lord Yahweh, through the knowledge of Him who has called us by his glory and excellence,

4 Whereby are given to us exceeding great and precious promises, so that by these you may be partakers of the divine nature, having escaped the corruption that is in the world through lust.

5 And besides this, giving all diligence, add to your faith, virtue; and to virtue, knowledge;

6 And to knowledge, self-control; and to self-control, patience; and to patience, godliness;

7 And to godliness, brotherly kindness; and to brotherly kindness, love.

8 For when these things are found among you and abound, you are not empty nor unfruitful in the knowledge of our Lord Yahshua the Christ.

9 But he who lacks these things is "blind" and cannot see afar off, and has forgotten that he was cleansed from his former sins.

10 For this very reason, my brethren, be diligent; for through your good deeds, you make your calling and your election sure; and when you do these things, you shall never fall,

11 For by doing these things, an entrance shall be given freely to you into the everlasting kingdom of our Lord and Savior Yahshua the Christ.

12 Wherefore I will not be negligent to put you always in remembrance of these things, though you know them well and you rely on this very truth.

13 Therefore I think that it is right, as long as I am in this body, to stir you up by putting you in remembrance,

14 Knowing that shortly I must depart this life, even as our Lord Yahshua the Christ has shown me.

15 Be diligent always, that you may be able to keep these things in remembrance even after my departure.

16 For we have not followed cunningly devised fables when we made known to you the power and coming of our Lord Yahshua the Christ, for we were eye-witnesses of his majesty.

17 For Yahshua received from Lord Yahweh, the Father, honor and glory when there came such a voice to him from the excellent and majestic glory which said: This is my beloved Son, in whom I am well pleased.

18 And this very voice, which came from heaven, we also heard when we were with him on the holy mountain.

19 We have also a true word of prophecy; you do well when you look to it for guidance, as you look to the lamp that shines in a dark place until the dawn of day, the light will shine in your hearts,

20 Knowing this first, that no prophecy of scripture comes from any private interpretation.

21 For the prophecy did not come by the will of man, but holy men of Lord Yahweh spoke when they were inspired by the Holy Spirit.

CHAPTER 2

But there were false prophets also among the people, even as there will be false teachers among you, teachers who shall bring in damnable heresies, even denying the Lord who has redeemed them, and thus bringing upon themselves swift destruction.

2 Many will follow their very destructive ways, by reason of whom evil will be spoken of the way of truth.

3 And through covetousness they will exploit you with feigned words, whose judgment from the very beginning has not ceased and their damnation is always active.

4 Lord Yahweh did not spare the angels who sinned, but cast them down to hell (not yet having fire?) and delivered them into chains of darkness to be reserved for tormenting judgment;

5 And Lord Yahweh did not spare the old world, but He saved Noach the preacher of righteousness, and his family, eight in all, when He brought the flood upon the wicked people,

6 And He set afire the cities of Sodom and Gomorrah, and He condemned them with an upheaval, making them an example to those who hereafter should live ungodly lives;

7 And delivered righteous Lot who was mortified by the filthy conduct of the lawless;

8 For while that pious man dwelt among them, in seeing and hearing their unlawful deeds, Lot the righteous soul was vexed from day to day.

9 The Lord knows how to deliver from distress those who revere Him, and He will reserve the wicked to be punished at the judgment day.

10 And especially will He punish those who follow after filthy lusts of the flesh and have no respect for authority. Bold and self-willed are they who do not tremble when they blaspheme against the glory;

11 Whereas angels, who are greater in power and might, do not bring upon themselves the condemnation of blasphemy.

12 But these men, as natural brute beasts, made for slaughter and destruction, speak evil of the things which they do not understand; and shall utterly perish in their own corruption,

13 And shall receive the reward of iniquity as they consider it a delightful thing to revel in the daytime. Spots and blemishes they have, and they sport themselves with their own pleasures as they feast in idleness,

14 And have eyes full of adultery and of sin that does not cease; beguiling, unstable souls are they, whose hearts are well versed in covetousness; accursed sons are they,

15 Who have forsaken the right path and are gone astray, following the way of Balaam, the son of Beor, who loved the wages of unrighteousness;

16 But who was rebuked for his iniquity; a "dumb ass," speaking with man's voice, halted the folly of the prophet.

17 These men are springs without water, clouds that are carried with a tempest; the mist of darkness is reserved for them forever.

18 For when they speak great swelling words of vanity, they allure through the sensual lusts of the flesh; but there are those who flee at a word of warning from them who live in error.

19 They, while they promise liberty, themselves are the slaves of corruption; for a man is overcome by whatever it is that enslaves him.

20 For if after they have escaped the pollutions of the world through knowledge of our Lord and savior Yahshua the Christ, they are again entangled by these very things and overcome, the latter end is worse with them than the beginning.

21 Verily it would have been better for them not to have known the way of righteousness than, after they have known it, to turn away from the holy commandment that was delivered to them.

22 It will come to pass with them according to the true proverb: The dog returns to his own vomit, and the sow that was washed returns to her wallowing in the mire.

CHAPTER 3

It has been a long time since I have written to you, my beloved, but now I write this second epistle; in both of them I have endeavored to stir up your pure minds by way of remembrance,

2 That you may be mindful of the words which were spoken before by the holy prophets, and of the commandment given through us, the apostles of our Lord and Savior:

3 Knowing this first, that there shall come in the last days mockers who scoff, following after their own lusts,

4 And saying, Where is the promise of his coming? For since our fathers died, all things continue as they were from the beginning of creation.

5 Of this they are willingly ignorant, that by the word of Lord Yahweh the heavens were of old, and the earth standing out of water and in the water;

6 And those men, because of whose deeds the world of that time was overflowed with water, perished;

7 But the present heavens and earth are sustained by his word, and are reserved for fire on the day of judgment which is the day of destruction of ungodly men.

8 But, my beloved, do not forget this one thing, that one day is with the Lord as a thousand years, and a thousand years as one day.

9 The Lord is not negligent concerning his promises, as some men count negligence; but is long-suffering toward you, not wishing that any should perish, but that all should come to repentance.

10 But the day of the Lord will come as a thief in the night, when the heavens shall suddenly pass away and the elements shall separate as they burn, and the earth also and the works that are in it shall not be found.

11 Now since all these things are to be dissolved, what manner of persons ought you to be in your holy conduct and godliness,

12 Looking for and longing for the coming of the day of Lord Yahweh, wherein the heavens being tested with fire shall be dissolved, and the elements shall melt with fervent heat?

13 Nevertheless we, according to his promise, look for new heavens and a new earth in which dwells righteousness.

14 Therefore, my beloved, while you look for these things, be diligent so that you may be found by Him in peace, without spot and blameless.

15 And consider that the long suffering of the Lord is salvation; even as our beloved brother Sha'ul also, according to the wisdom given to him, has written to you;

16 As also in all his epistles, he spoke concerning these matters, in which there are certain things so hard to be understood that those who are ignorant and unstable pervert their meaning, as they do also the other scriptures, to their own destruction.

17 You therefore, my beloved, seeing that you know these things beforehand, beware lest you follow the error of the lawless, and fall from your own steadfastness.

18 But grow in grace and in the knowledge of our Lord and Savior Yahshua the Christ and of Lord Yahweh the Father. To Him be glory both now and forever and through all eternity. Amen.

The First Epistle of Yochanan (John)

Chapter 1

He who was from the beginning, the one whom we have heard, and have seen with our eyes, have looked upon and have touched with our hands, we declare to you is the Word of life.

2 For the life was manifested, and we have seen it and we bear witness to it, and we preach to you eternal life which was with the Father (Lord Yahweh) and was revealed to us;

3 It is that which we have seen and heard that we declare to you, so that you also may have fellowship with us; and truly our fellowship is with the Father and with his Son Yahshua the Christ.

4 And these things we write to you, so that our joy in you may be complete.

5 This then is the good news which we have heard from him and declare to you; that Lord Yahweh is light, and in Him is no darkness at all.

6 If we say that we have fellowship with Him and yet live in darkness, we lie and do not follow the truth;

7 But if we live in the light as He is in the light, we have fellowship with one another, and the blood of Yahshua his Son cleanses us from all sin.

8 If we say that we have no sin, we deceive ourselves and the truth is not in us.

9 If we confess our sins, Yahshua the Christ is faithful and just to forgive us our sins and to cleanse us from all our unrighteousness.

10 If we say that we have not sinned, we make him a liar and his word is not in us.

CHAPTER 2

My little children, these things I write to you so that you do not sin. And if any man sin, we have an advocate with the Father, Yahshua the Christ who is the righteous;

2 And he is the appeasement for our sins; and not just for our sins only, but also for the sins of every one of the whole world.

3 And hereby we know that we know him, if we keep his commandments.

4 He who says "I know him" but does not keep his commandments is a liar, and the truth is not in him.

5 But whoever keeps his word in him verily is the love of Lord Yahweh perfected; hereby we know that we are in Him.

6 He who says that he abides in Him, ought himself also to so walk even as he walked.

7 My beloved, I do not write a new commandment to you, but an old commandment which you had from the beginning. The old commandment is the word which you have already heard.

8 Again, a new commandment I do write to you, which thing is true in him and in you, because the darkness is past and the true light now shines.

9 He who says that he is in the light, but hates his brother, is therefore in darkness even until now.

10 He who loves his brother abides in the light, and there is no cause for displeasure in him.

11 But he who hates his brother is in darkness and he walks in darkness, and he does not know where he is going, because that darkness has blinded his eyes.

12 I write to you, little children, because your sins are forgiven you for his name's sake.

13 I write to you, fathers, because you have known Lord Yahweh from our beginning. I write to you, young men, because you have overcome the evil one. I write to you, little children, because you have known the Father who is Lord Yahweh.

14 I have written to you, fathers, because you have known Lord Yahweh from the beginning. I have written to you, young men, because you are strong and the word of Lord Yahweh abides in you, and you have overcome the evil one.

15 Love not the world, neither the things that are in the world. He who loves the world, the love of the Father is not in him.

16 For all that is in the world is the lust of the body, the lust of the eyes, and the pride of material things; these things (lusts and pride) do not come from the Father, but from the world.

17 And the world passes away, and the lust thereof; but he who does the will of Lord Yahweh, abides forever.

18 My children, it is the last time; and as you have heard that a false christ shall come, even now there are many false christs, and from this we know that it is the last time.

19 They went out from among us, but they were not of us; for if they had been of us, they would have continued with us; but they left us so that it may be known that they did not belong to us.

20 But you have been anointed by the Holy One, and you are enabled to distinguish between men.

21 I have written to you; not because you do not know the truth, but because you do know the truth, and you are aware that no lie comes out of the truth.

22 Who is a liar but he who denies that Yahshua is the Christ? He is a false christ; and whoever denies the Father, denies the Son also.

23 Whoever denies the Son, the same does not believe in the Father; but whoever acknowledges the Son (Yahshua), acknowledges the Father (Lord Yahweh) also.

24 As for you, let that, therefore, abide in you which you have heard from the very beginning. For if that which you have heard from the beginning shall remain in you, you also shall continue in the Father and in the Son.

25 And this is the promise that He has promised us, even eternal life.

26 These things I have written to you concerning those who seduce you.

27 And you also, if the anointing which you have received from Him abides among you, need no one to teach you; that same anointing which is of Lord Yahweh will teach you all things; it is the truth, and there is no lie in it; and even as I have taught you, abide in it.

28 And now, my children, abide in Him, so that when He shall appear, we may not be ashamed before Him, but have confidence at his coming.

29 If you know that he is righteous, you know also that every one who does righteousness is of Him.

CHAPTER 3

See how abundant the love of the Father is toward us, for He has called us "sons" and made us; therefore the world does not know us because it does not know Him.

2 My beloved, now we are the sons of Lord Yahweh, and as yet it has not been revealed what we shall be; but we know that when Yahshua the Christ shall appear, we shall be in his likeness; for we shall see him as he is.

3 Let every man who has this hope in him purify himself, even as Yahshua is pure.

4 Whoever commits sin, commits evil; for all sin is evil.

5 And you know that Yahshua the Christ was manifested to take away our sins; and in him there is no sin.

6 Whoever abides in him does not sin; and whoever sins has not seen him, neither has he or she known him.

7 My children, let no man deceive you; he who does righteousness is righteous, just as Yahshua the Christ is righteous.

8 He who commits sin is of the devil, because the devil has been a sinner from the beginning. For this purpose, the Son of Lord Yahweh appeared so that he may destroy the works of the devil.

9 Whoever is born of Lord Yahweh does not commit sin because Lord Yahweh's seed is in him, and he cannot sin because he is born of Lord Yahweh.

10 In this, the children of Lord Yahweh can be distinguished from the children of the devil; whoever does not practice righteousness, and does not love his brother, does not belong to Lord Yahweh.

11 For this is the commandment that you have heard from the beginning, that you must love one another,

12 Do not do as Kayin did, who slew his own brother and belonged to the wicked one. And why did he kill his brother? Because his own works were evil, and those of his brother were righteous.

13 So be not surprised, my brethren, if the world hates you.

14 We know that we have passed from death to life, because we love our brethren. He who does not love his brother abides in death.

15 Whosoever hates his brother is a murderer; and you know that no murderer has eternal life abiding in him.

16 By this we know Yahshua's love for us, because he laid down his life for us; and we ought to lay down our lives for our brethren.

17 Whoever has worldly goods and sees his brother in need and shuts his mercy from his brother, how can the love of Lord Yahweh dwell in he who shuts his mercy?

18 My children, let us not love one another only in word and in tongue, but love one another in deed and in truth.

19 And by this we shall know that we are of the truth, and shall assure our hearts before he comes.

20 For if our hearts condemn us, how much more, then, will Lord Yahweh who is greater than our hearts and knows all things, condemn us?

21 My beloved, if our hearts do not condemn us, then we have confidence before Lord Yahweh.

22 And whatever we ask, we receive from Him, because we keep his commandments and do those things that are pleasing to Him.

23 And this is the commandment: That we should believe in the name of his Son Yashua the Christ and love one another as He commanded us.

24 Whosoever keeps his commandments will be guarded by Him, and Lord Yahweh will dwell in whosoever keeps his commandments. And by this we know that He abides in us, by the Spirit which He has given us.

CHAPTER 4

My beloved, do not believe every prophecy, but examine the prophecies to find out if they are of Lord Yahweh because many false prophets have appeared in the world.

2 The Spirit of Lord Yahweh is known by this: Every prophecy, which declares that Yahshua the Christ is come in the flesh, is from Lord Yahweh.

3 And every spirit which does not declare that Yahshua the Christ has come in the flesh, is not from Lord Yahweh, but they are the spirits of the antichrist, of whose coming you have heard and who is even now already in the world.

4 But you are of Lord Yahweh, my children, and have overcome the spirits of antichrist, because He who is among you is greater than he who is in the world.

5 They are of the world; therefore they speak of the world, and the world hears them.

6 But we are of Lord Yahweh; he who knows Lord Yahweh, hears us; he who is not of Lord Yahweh, does not hear us. By this we know both the spirit of truth and the spirit of error.

7 My beloved, let us love one another; for love is from Lord Yahweh; and every one who loves, is born of Lord Yahweh and knows Lord Yahweh.

8 He who does not love, does not know Lord Yahweh; for Lord Yahweh is love.

9 By this was the love of Lord Yahweh which is toward us, made known; for Lord Yahweh sent his only begotten Son into the world, that we may live through him.

10 Herein is love, not that we loved Lord Yahweh, but that Lord Yahweh loved us and sent his Son to be the appeasement for our sins.

11 My beloved, If Lord Yahweh so loved us, we ought also to love one another.

12 No man has seen Lord Yahweh at any time. If we love one another, Lord Yahweh abides in us, and his love is perfected in us;

13 Hereby we know that we abide in Him, and we also know that He abides in us because He has given us of his spirit.

14 And we have seen and do testify that the Father sent his Son to be the Savior of us.

15 Whoever shall confess that Yahshua the Christ is the Son of Lord Yahweh, Lord Yahweh abides in whoever so confesses; and whoever so confesses, abides in Lord Yahweh.

16 And we have believed and have known the love which Lord Yahweh has for us. Lord Yahweh is love; and whoever dwells in love, abides in Lord Yahweh.

17 Herein is his love made perfect in us, so that we may have boldness in the day of judgment; because as He is, so are we in this world.

18 There is no fear in love; but perfect love casts out fear, because fear restrains us. He who fears is not made perfect in love.

19 We love Lord Yahweh because He first loved us.

20 If a man says: I love Lord Yahweh, and yet hates his brother, he is a liar; for he who does not love his brother whom he has seen, how can he love Lord Yahweh whom he has not seen?

21 And this commandment we have received from Lord Yahweh, that he who loves Lord Yahweh ought to love his brother also.

CHAPTER 5

Whoever believes that Yahshua is the Christ, is born of Lord Yahweh; and everyone who loves Him who begot, also loves him who is begotten of Lord Yahweh.

2 And by this we know that we love the children of Lord Yahweh, when we love Lord Yahweh and keep his commandments.

3 For this is the love of Lord Yahweh, that we keep his commandments; and his commandments are not difficult.

4 For whoever is born of Lord Yahweh, triumphs over the world; and this is the victory which overcomes the world, even our faith.

5 Who is he who triumphs over the world? It is he who believes that Yahshua is the Son of Lord Yahweh.

6 This is he who came by water and blood, even Yahshua the Christ, not by water only, but by water and blood. And it is the Spirit which bears witness, because that very Spirit is the truth.

7 For there are three that bear record in heaven, the Father, the Word, and the Holy Spirit; and these three agree in one.

8 And there are three that bear witness in earth, the Spirit, the water, and the blood; and these three agree in one.

9 If we accept the testimony of men, how much greater is the testimony of Lord Yahweh; for this is the testimony of Lord Yahweh which He has testified of his Son, Yahshua the Christ.

10 He who believes in the Son of Lord Yahweh, has the testimony in himself; he who does not believe Lord Yahweh, has made Him a "liar;" because he does not believe the testimony that Lord Yahweh gave of his Son.

11 And this is the testimony: That Lord Yahweh has given to us eternal life, and this life is in his Son.

12 He who believes in the Son has life; he who does not believe in the Son of Lord Yahweh does not have life.

13 These things I have written to you who believe on the name (Yahshua) of The Son of Lord Yahweh, that you may know that you have eternal life.

14 And this is the confidence which we have in Yahshua the Christ, that if we ask anything according to his will, he hears us;

15 For if we beseech him to hear us concerning the things that we ask of him, we are assured that we have already received from him, those things which we desire.

16 If any man sees his brother commit a sin which is not worthy of death, let him ask and life will be granted him. There is a sin worthy of death; I do not say that anyone shall pray for it.

17 All unrighteousness is sin; but there is a sin which is not worthy of death.

18 We know that everyone who is born of Lord Yahweh does not sin; for he who is born of Lord Yahweh, guards himself, and the evil one does not come near him.

19 And we know that we are of Lord Yahweh, and the entire world lies in wickedness.

20 And we know that the Son of Lord Yahweh has come and has given us an understanding, that we may know Him who is true; and we are in Him who is true, even in his Son Yahshua the Christ. This is the true God and eternal life.

21 My children, keep yourselves from idols.

The Second Epistle of Yochanan (John)

CHAPTER 1

The minister to the mother church and "her" children, those whom I love in the truth, and not I only, but also those who have known the truth,

2 For the sake of the truth which dwells in us, and is with us forever.

3 Grace be with us, mercy, and peace from Lord Yahweh the Father, and from the Lord Yahshua the Christ who is the Son of the Father, in truth and love.

4 I rejoiced greatly that I found some of your children living in the truth, as we have received a commandment from the Father.

5 And now I beseech you, O mother church, not as though I wrote a new commandment to you, but that which we had from the beginning, that we love one another.

6 And this is love, that we walk according to his commandments. This is the commandment, that as you have heard from the beginning, you should follow it.

7 For many deceivers have appeared in the world, who do not acknowledge that Yahshua the Christ has come in the flesh. Such a person is a deceiver and an antichrist.

8 Look to yourselves, that you lose not those things which you have accomplished, but that you receive a full reward.

9 Whoever transgresses and does not abide in the teaching of Yahshua the Christ, does not have Lord Yahweh. He who does abide in his doctrine, has both the Father and the Son.

10 If anyone comes to you and does not bring this doctrine, do not welcome him to your house, neither bid him to eat;

11 For he who bids him to eat is partaker of his evil works.

12 I have many things to say to you which I do not want to write with paper and ink; but I trust to come to you and speak face to face, that our joy may be full.

13 The children of your elect sister church greet you. Grace be with you. Amen.

The Third Epistle of Yochanan (John)

CHAPTER 1

The elder to the well beloved Gaius, whom I love in the truth.

2 Our beloved, I pray above all things that you may prosper and be in good health, even as you, as a soul, prosper.

3 For I rejoiced greatly when the brethren came and testified concerning the truth that is in you, even as you live a true life.

4 I have no greater joy than to hear that my children follow the truth.

5 Our beloved, you do faithfully that which you do to the brethren, especially to those who are strangers.

6 Who have borne witness concerning your love before the whole church for the good things which you have done for them by supplying their needs, as is pleasing to Lord Yahweh,

7 Because they have gone forth for his name's sake, taking nothing from the Gentiles.

8 We, therefore, ought to welcome such, so that we may be fellow helpers to the truth.

9 I wrote to the church that Diotrephes, who loves to have the preeminence among them, would not receive us.

10 Therefore, if I come, I will mention the things which he did, gossiping against us with malicious words; and not content with this, he not

only did not receive the brethren, but he also forbade those who would like to receive them, and he cast them out of the church.

11 Our beloved, do not follow that which is evil, but follow that which is good. He who does good is of Lord Yahweh; but he who does evil has not seen Lord Yahweh.

12 Demetrius has been given a good report by all men and of the church, and of the truth itself; yea, we also testify for him, and we know that our testimony is true.

13 I had many things to write, but I do not want to write them to you with ink and pen;

14 However I trust that I shall shortly see you, and we shall speak face to face.

15 Peace be to you. Our friends salute you. Salute the friends every one by his name.

The General Epistle of
Y'hudah (Jude)

JUDE 1

Y'hudah, the servant of Yahshua the Christ, and brother to Ya'akov, to the Gentiles who have been called and are loved by Lord Yahweh the Father, and are protected by Yahshua the Christ;

2 Mercy and peace, with love, be multiplied to you.

3 My beloved, I write to you with all diligence concerning our common salvation, and it is needful that I should write and warn you earnestly to contend hard for the faith which was once for all time delivered to the saints.

4 For certain men have falsely entered among you, and these were preordained from the very beginning to this condemnation; they are ungodly men, turning the grace of Lord Yahweh into lasciviousness, and denying the only God, and denying our Lord Yahshua the Christ.

5 I will therefore, remind you, though you once knew this; that Lord Yahweh, having redeemed and saved the people out of the land of Egypt, afterward destroyed those who did not believe.

6 And the angels which did not keep their first estate but left their own habitation, Lord Yahweh has reserved in everlasting chains under darkness until the judgment of the great day,

7 Even as Sodom and Gomorrah, and the neighboring cities which in like manner, gave themselves over to fornication, they also followed after other carnal lusts so that they are condemned to judgment and placed under everlasting fire;

8 Likewise also, these filthy dreamers defile the flesh, despise authority, and blaspheme against the glory.

9 Yet Michael the archangel, when contending with the devil about the body of Moshe, did not dare to bring angry accusation against him, but said, The Lord rebuke you.

10 But these men blaspheme against those things about which they do not know; and they also blaspheme against what they know naturally as dumb beasts, in those things they corrupt themselves.

11 Woe to them! For they have gone in the way of Kayin, and have run greedily after the error of Balaam for reward and have perished in the rebellion of Korah.

12 These people are those who lead a wasteful, feasting life and are blemished; they do not conduct themselves in reverence; they are clouds without rain and driven by winds; trees whose blossoms have withered without fruit, having died a second time, being pulled up by the roots;

13 Raging waves of the sea, foaming out their own shame; wandering stars, to whom is reserved the blackness of darkness for ever.

14 And Hanokh also, the seventh from Adam, prophesied of these, saying, Behold, the Lord comes with ten thousands of his saints,

15 To execute judgment upon all, and to punish all who are ungodly for all their ungodly deeds which they have committed in an ungodly manner, and for all the harsh words which the ungodly sinners have spoken.

16 These are the ones who murmur and complain, following after their own lusts, and their mouths speak idle flattering words, praising people for the sake of gain.

17 But you, my beloved, remember the words which were spoken before by the apostles of our Lord Yahshua the Christ,

18 How they told you there will be mockers until the end of time, and they will always follow their own ungodly lusts.

19 These are those who prefer to associate with selfish people because they do not have the Spirit in them.

20 But you, my beloved, build up yourselves anew in the holy faith through the Holy Spirit, by means of prayer.

21 Let us keep ourselves in the love of Lord Yahweh, looking for the mercy of our Lord Yahshua the Christ, and for the life which is ours forever.

22 And on some of them, whoever they may be, heap coals of fire;

23 And when they repent, have mercy on them with compassion; despise even a garment which is spotted with the things of the flesh.

24 Now to him who is able to keep you from falling, and to present you faultless before the presence of his glory with exceeding joy,

25 To the only God our Savior, through our Lord Yahshua the Christ, be glory and majesty, dominion and power, both now and for ever. Amen.

The Revelation of Saint Yochanan (John) The Divine

CHAPTER 1

The Revelation of Yahshua the Christ, which Lord Yahweh gave to Yahshua to show to his servants those things which must soon come to pass; Yahshua signified and sent it by his angel to his servant Yochanan,

2 Yochanan bore record of the word of Lord Yahweh, and of the testimony of Yahshua the Christ, and of all the things that he saw.

3 Blessed is he who reads, and blessed are they who listen to the words of this prophecy and keep those things which are written in this prophecy; for the time is at hand.

4 Yochanan said to the seven churches which are in Asia: Grace be to you, and peace from Lord Yahweh who is, who was, and who is to come; and from the seven Spirits which are before his throne;

5 And from Yahshua the Christ who is the faithful witness, the first to rise from the dead, and the Prince of the kings of the earth. To Yahshua who loved us, and washed us from our sins in his own blood,

6 And he made us a spiritual kingdom to Lord Yahweh his Father, to Lord Yahweh be glory and dominion forever and ever. Amen.

7 Behold! Yahshua the Christ will come with the clouds; and every eye shall see him, even the men who pierced him; and all the kindreds of the earth shall wail over him. Even so. Amen.

8 I am Alpha and Omega, the beginning and the ending, says Lord Yahweh; who is, who was, and who is to come, the Almighty.

9 I, Yochanan, your brother and companion in suffering and in the hope of Yahshua the Christ, was on the island which is called Patmos because of the word of Lord Yahweh and because of the testimony of Yahshua the Christ.

10 I was in the Spirit on the Lord's day, and I heard behind me a great voice, as of a trumpet, saying,

11 What you see, write in a book and send it to the seven churches, to Ephesus, to Smyrna, to Pergamos, to Thyatira, to Sardis, to Philadelphia, and to Laodicea.

12 And I turned to see the voice that spoke to me. And as I turned, I saw seven golden candlesticks,

13 And in the midst of the seven candlesticks was one resembling the Son of man, wearing a long vestment, and was girded round his breast with a golden girdle.

14 His head and his hair were white as wool, as white as snow; and his eyes were as a flame of fire;

15 And his feet were like the fine brass of Lebanon, as though they were burned in a furnace; and his voice was as the sound of many waters.

16 And he had in his right hand seven stars; and out of his mouth came a sharp two-edged sword; and his countenance was like the sun shining in its strength.

17 And when I saw him, I fell at his feet as dead. And he laid his right hand upon me, saying, Fear not; I am the first and the last;

18 I am he who lives, and was dead; and, behold, I am alive for evermore. Amen. And I have the keys of death and of hell.

19 Write, therefore, the things which you have seen, and the things which are, and the things which shall be hereafter,

20 The mystery of the seven stars which you saw in my right hand, and the seven golden candlesticks. The seven stars are the angels of the seven churches, and the seven candlesticks are the seven churches.

CHAPTER 2

To the appointed head of the church of Ephesus write: These things, says the Omnipotent One who holds the seven stars in his right hand and who walks in the midst of the seven golden candlesticks,

2 I know your works, your labor, your patience, and how you cannot endure those who are ungodly; you have tried those who say that they are apostles but are not, and you have found them to be liars;

3 And you have patience, and have borne burdens for my name's sake, and have not wearied.

4 Nevertheless I have something against you, because you have left your first love.

5 Remember therefore from whence you have fallen, repent and do the first works; or else I will come to you very soon, and I will remove your candlestick from its place unless you repent.

6 But this you have in your favor, you hate the works of the Nicolaitanes, which I also hate.

7 He who has ears, let him hear what the Spirit says to the churches: To him who overcomes, I will give to eat of the tree of life which is in the midst of the paradise of my God.

8 And to the appointed head of the church in Smyrna write: These things says the first and the last, which was dead and is alive:

9 I know your works, your suffering, and your poverty, but you are rich, and I know the blasphemy of those who say that they are Jews and are not, but those are of the synagogue of Satan.

10 For none of those things which you shall suffer; behold, the devil will cast some of you into prison, that you be tried; and you will be oppressed for ten days. Be faithful even to death, and I will give you a crown of life.

11 He who has ears, let him hear what the Spirit says to the churches: He who overcomes shall not be hurt by the second death.

12 And to the appointed head of the church in Pergamos write: These things says he who has the sharp two-edged sword:

13 I know your works and where you dwell, even where Satan's seat is; and you uphold my name, and you do not deny my faith, even in those days when that witness of mine appeared, that faithful one of mine who was slain among you, where Satan dwells.

14 But I have a few things against you because you have there, those who hold teaching of Balaam, who taught Balak to cast a stumbling block before the children of Israel, to eat things sacrificed to idols, and to commit adultery.

15 And also you have those among you who hold to the teaching of the Nicolaitanes.

16 Repent; or else I will come to you very soon and will fight against them with the sword of my mouth.

17 He who has ears, let him hear what the Spirit says to the churches: To him who overcomes, I will give to eat of the hidden manna, and I will give him a white stone, and on the stone a new name written which no man knows except he who receives it.

18 And to the appointed head of the church in Thyatira write: These things says the Son of Lord Yahweh, who has eyes like a flame of fire, and whose feet are like fine brass from Lebanon;

19 I know your works, your love, your faith, your service, and your patience; and your last works are to be more abundant than the first.

20 Notwithstanding I have a few things against you because you allowed that woman of yours, Jezebel, who calls herself a prophetess, to teach and to seduce my servants to commit fornication, and to eat things sacrificed to idols.

21 And I gave her time to repent, but she did not repent from her fornication.

22 Behold I will cast her into a sick-bed; and those who commit adultery with her will be cast into great tribulation, unless they repent of their deeds.

23 And I will smite her children with death (children raised by Jezebel would perhaps die in their sins); and all the churches shall know that I am he who searches the minds and hearts; and I will give to every one of you according to your works.

24 But I (Yahshua the Christ) say to you, the rest of you in Thyatira, those who do not have this doctrine, and those who have not known, as they say, the depths of Satan; that I will not put upon you another burden.

25 But hold fast to that which you already have till I come.

26 And he who overcomes and keeps my works until the end, to him I will give authority over the nations;

27 And he shall shepherd them with a rod of iron; like the vessels of the potter, they shall be shattered, even as I was disciplined by my Father.

28 And I will give him the morning star.

29 He who has ears, let him hear what the Spirit says to the churches.

Chapter 3

And to the appointed head of the church in Sardis write: These things says he who has the seven Spirits of Lord Yahweh and the seven stars: I know your works; you have a name that you are alive and yet you are dead.

2 Awake, and hold fast to the things which remain but are ready to die; for I have not found your works perfect before my God.

3 Remember, therefore, just as you have received and heard, so hold fast and repent. And if, therefore, you do not awake, I will come against you as a thief, and you shall not know at what hour I will come upon you.

4 But you have a few members at Sardis who have not defiled their names; and they shall walk with me in white, for they are worthy.

5 He who overcomes, the same shall be clothed in white robes; and I will not blot his name out of the book of life, but I will confess his name before my Father and before his angels.

6 He who has ears, let him hear what the Spirit says to the churches.

7 And to the appointed head of the church in Philadelphia write: These things says he who is the holy one, he who is true, he who has the key of David, he who opens and no man shuts, and shuts and no man opens;

8 I know your works and behold, I have set before you an open door which no man can lock, for you have but little strength and yet you have obeyed my word and you have not denied my name.

9 Behold, I turn over those of the synagogue of Satan, who say that they are Jews and are not, but do lie; behold, I will make them to come and worship before your feet, and to know that I have loved you.

10 Because you have kept the word of my patience, I also will keep you from the hour of temptation which shall come upon all the world to try those who dwell upon earth.

11 Behold, I come quickly. Hold fast that which you have, so that no man take your crown.

12 He who overcomes I will make a pillar in the temple of my God, and he shall not go out again; and I will write upon him the name of my God and the name of the new Jerusalem which comes down out of heaven from my God; and I will write upon him my new name.

13 He who has ears, let him hear what the Spirit says to the churches.

14 And to the appointed head of the church in Laodicea write: These things says the Amen, the faithful and true witness, the beginning of the creation by Lord Yahweh;

15 I know your works, that you are neither cold nor hot; it is better to be either cold or hot.

16 So then because you are lukewarm, and neither cold nor hot, I will spew you out of my mouth.

17 You say, I am rich and my wealth has increased and I need nothing; and you do not know that you are miserable, a wanderer, poor, blind, and naked.

18 I advise you to buy of me, gold refined in the fire so that you may become rich; and white raiment, that you may be clothed so that the shame of your nakedness may not be seen; and anoint your eyes with salve, that you may see.

19 I rebuke and chastise all those whom I love; be zealous, therefore, and repent.

20 Behold, I (Yahshua the Christ) stand at the door and knock; if any man hear my voice and open the door, I will come in to him and will sup with him, and he with me.

21 To him who overcomes, I will grant to sit with me on my throne, even as I also overcame and have sat down with my Father on his throne.

22 He who has ears, let him hear what the Spirit says to the churches.

CHAPTER 4

After these things I looked and behold, a door was open in heaven; and the first voice which I heard was like a trumpet talking with me, which said, Come up here and I will show you things which must come to pass.

2 And immediately I was in the spirit; and behold, a throne was set in heaven, and One sat on the throne.

3 And Lord Yahweh who sat on the throne, resembled a stone of jasper and sardonyx; and round about the throne was a rainbow resembling emeralds.

4 Round about the throne were four and twenty seats; and upon the seats I saw four and twenty elders sitting, clothed in white robes; and they had on their heads crowns of gold.

5 And out of the throne preceeded, lightnings, and thunderings and noises; and there were seven lamps of fire burning before the throne, which are the seven Spirits of Lord Yahweh.

6 And the throne was a sea of glass resembling crystal; and in the midst of the throne, and round about and in front of the throne were were four "animals," full of eyes before and behind.

7 And the first "animal" was like a lion, the second "animal" was like a calf, the third "animal" had a face like a man, and the fourth "animal" was like a flying eagle.

8 And the four "animals" each had six wings; and they were full of eyes within; and they had no rest day and night saying, Holy, holy, holy, the almightly God, Lord Yahweh who was, is, and will be. ("was, is, and will be" is the definition of the name: "Yahweh")

9 And when those "animals" give glory, honor, and thanks to Lord Yahweh who sits on the throne, and worship Him who lives forever and ever, and cast their crowns before the throne, saying,

10 Thou art wothy, O our Holy Lord and God, to reveive glory, honor, and and power, for Thou hast created all things, and by Thee they are, and by thy will they are and were created.

CHAPTER 5

And I saw on the right hand of Lord Yahweh who sat on the throne, a book written within and on the back and sealed with seven seals.

2 Then I saw a mighty angel proclaiming with a loud voice, Who is worthy to open the book and to loose the seals thereof?

3 And no man in heaven above nor on earth neither under the earth was able to open the book, neither to look upon it.

4 And I wept exceedingly because no man was found worthy to open the book, neither to look upon it.

5 And one of the elders said to me, Weep not; behold the lion of the tribe of Judah, the scion of David, has prevailed and he will open the book and the seven seals thereof.

6 And I beheld, and lo, in the midst of the elders, stood a "Lamb" (Yahshua the Christ) as he had been slain, having seven horns and seven eyes, which are the seven Spirits of Lord Yahweh sent forth into all the earth.

7 And he came and took the book from the right hand of Lord Yahweh who sat upon the throne.

8 And as he took the book, the four "animals" and the four and twenty elders fell down before the "Lamb," and everyone of them had a harp and a cup of gold full of incense, and these were the prayers of the saints.

9 And they sang new praise saying, Thou art worthy to take the book and to open the seals thereof; for thou was slain and has redeemed us to Lord Yahweh by the blood out of every tribe, tongue, people, and nation;

10 And has made them for our God, kings, and priests; and they shall reign on the earth.

11 And I looked, and I heard as it were the voice of many angels round about the throne, the "animals," and the elders; and their number was ten thousand times ten thousand, and thousands of thousands,

12 Saying with a loud voice, Worthy is the "Lamb" that was slain to receive power, riches, wisdom, might, honor, glory, and blessing.

13 And every creature which is in heaven, on the earth, under the earth, all that are in the sea, and all that are in them, I heard saying, To Lord Yahweh who sits on the throne and to the "Lamb" be blessing, honor, glory, and dominion forever and ever.

14 And the four "animals" said, Amen. And the four and twenty elders fell down and worshipped Him who lives forever and ever.

CHAPTER 6

I saw when the "Lamb" opened one of the seven seals, and I heard one of the four "animals" saying in a voice as of thunder, Come and see.

2 And I looked and beheld a white horse, and he who sat on him had a bow, and a crown was given to him; and went forth conquering, and to conquer.

3 And when he opened the second seal , I heard the second "animal" say, Come and see.

4 And there went out another horse, and it was red, and to him who sat on it was given power to take away peace from the earth, that people should kill one another; and there was given to him a great sword.

5 A when he had opened the third seal, I heard the third "animal" say, Come and see. And behold, I saw a black horse; and he who sat on him had a pair of balances in his hand.

6 And I heard a voice in the midst of the four "animals" say, A measure of wheat for a penny, and three measures of barley for a penny; and see that you do not damage the oil and the wine

7 And when he had opened the fourth seal, I heard the fourth "animal" saying, Come and see.

8 And I looked and beheld a green horse; and the name of him who sat on the green horse was Death, and Sheol followed after him. And power was given to him over the fourth part of the earth, to kill with sword, famine, death, and with the wild beasts of the earth.

9 And when he had opened the fifth seal; I saw under the altar, the souls of those who had been slain for the sake of the word of Lord Yahweh, and for the testimony of the "Lamb" which they had;

10 And they cried with a loud voice saying: How long, O Lord, holy and true, dost thou not judge and avenge our blood on those who dwell on the earth?

11 And a white robe was given to every one of them; and it was said to them that they should rest yet for a little while, until the time should be fulfilled when their fellow servants and their brethren should be killed also as they had been.

12 And I looked when he had opened the sixth seal, and behold, there was a great earthquake; and the sun became black as sackcloth of hair, and the moon became as blood;

13 And the stars of heaven fell to the earth, even as a fig tree casts its green figs when it is shaken by a mighty wind.

14 And the heavens separated, as a scroll when it is rolled separately; and every mountain and island shifted from its resting place.

15 And the kings of the earth, the great men, the commanders of thousands, the rich, the mighty men, every bondman, and every freeman hid themselves in caves and in clefts of the mountain,

16 And they said to the mountains and rocks: Fall on us, and hide us from the face of Him who sits on the throne, and from the wrath of the "Lamb;"

17 For the great day of his wrath is come, and who shall be able to stand?

CHAPTER 7

And after these things, I saw four angels standing on the four corners of the earth, holding the four winds of the earth, that the wind should not blow on the earth nor on the sea nor on any tree.

2 And I saw another angel, and he ascended from the direction of the rising sun, having the seal of the living God; and he cried with a loud voice to the four angels to whom it was given to hurt the earth and the sea, saying,

3 Do not hurt the earth, neither the sea nor the trees, till we have sealed the servants of our God upon their brows.

4 And I heard the number of those who were sealed; and it was a hundred forty and four thousand, of all the tribes of the children of Israel.

(verses 5 through 8 simply indicate the tribes of the special 144,000 servants)

9 After these things, I beheld, and lo, a great multitude which no man could number (more than **144,000**), of every nation, people, kindred, and tongue stood before the throne and in the presence of the "Lamb," clothed with white robes and with palms in their hands,

10 And cried with a loud voice, saying, Salvation to our God who sits upon the throne, and to the "Lamb" (Yahshua the Christ),

11 And all the angels stood round about the throne and about the elders and the four "animals," and fell before his throne on their faces, and worshipped Lord Yahweh,

12 Saying, Amen! Blessing, glory, wisdom, thanksgiving, honor, power, and might to our God forever and ever. Amen.

13 And one of the elders aswered, saying to me, Who are these who are arrayed and white robes? And from whence did they come?

14 And I said to him, My lord, you know. And he said to me, These are those who came out of the great tribulation, and have washed their robes and

made them white in the blood of the "Lamb" (Yahshua the Christ). (these saved are in addition to of the **144,000**)

15 Therefore they are before the throne of Lord Yahweh, and serve Him day and night in his temple; and He who sits on the throne shall shelter them.

16 They shall hunger no more, neither thirst anymore; neither shall they be stricken by the sun nor by the heat.

17 For the "Lamb" who is in the midst of the throne shall shepherd them, and he shall lead them to fountains of living water. And Lord Yahweh shall wipe away all tears from their eyes.

CHAPTER 8

And when he opened the seventh seal, there was silence in heaven for about the space of half an hour.

2 Then I saw the seven angels who stood before Lord Yahweh, and seven trumpets were given to them.

3 And another angel came and stood at the altar, and he had a golden censer; and abundant incense was given to him, that he may offer it with the prayers of all saints upon the golden altar which was before the throne.

4 And the smoke of the incense, which came with the prayers of the saints, ascended up out of the angel's hand before Lord Yahweh.

5 And the angel took the censer and filled it with fire of the altar, and he cast it upon the earth; and there were voices, thunderings, lightnings, and an earthquake.

6 And the seven angels who had the seven trumpets prepared themselves to sound.

7 The first angel sounded, and there followed hail and fire mingled with water, and they were poured upon the earth; and a third part of the earth was

burnt up, and a third part of the trees was burnt up, and all green grass was burnt up.

8 Then the second angel sounded, and somrthing as a great mountain burning with fire was cast into the sea; and the third part of the sea became blood;

9 And the third part of the creatures which were in the sea, and had life, died; and the third part of the ships were destroyed.

10 And the third angel sounded, and there fell a star from heaven, burning as though it were a lamp, and it fell upon the third part of the rivers and upon the fountains of waters;

11 And the name of the star is called: Wormwood; and the third part of the waters became wormwood; and many men died of the waters, because the waters were made bitter.

12 And the fourth angel sounded, and the third part of the sun was eclipsed, and the third part of the moon and the third part of the stars were darkened; and the day was darkened for a third part of it, and the night likewise.

13 And I beheld, and heard an eagle, having a tail red as it were blood, flying through the midst of heaven, saying with a loud voice, Woe, woe, woe to those who dwell on the earth, by reason of the other sounds of the trumpets of the three angels which are yet to sound!

CHAPTER 9

And the fifth angel sounded, and I saw a star fall from heaven upon the earth; and to him was given the key of the bottomless pit.

2 And he opened the bottomless pit; and there arose a smoke out of the pit like smoke belching from a great furnace; and the sun and the air were darkened by reason of the smoke of the pit.

3 And there came out of the smoke, locusts upon the earth; and to them was given power as the scorpions of the earth have power.

4 And it was commanded them that they should not hurt the grass of the earth, neither any green thing, neither any tree; but only those men who do not have the seal of Lord Yahweh on their brows.

5 And they were commanded that they should not kill them, but that they should torment them for five months; and the torment was as the torment of a scorpion when it strikes a man.

6 So in those days, men shall seek death but shall not find it; and shall desire to die, and death shall flee from them.

7 And the shapes of the locusts were like horses prepared for battle; and on their heads were, as it were, crowns like gold, and their faces were like faces of men.

8 And they had hair like the hair of women, and their teeth were like the teeth of lions.

9 And they had breastplates as though they were breastplates of iron; and the sound of their wings was like the sound of chariots of many horses running to battle.

10 And they had tails like scorpions, and there were stings in their tails; and they had power to hurt men five months.

11 And they had a king over them, who was the angel of the bottomless pit, whose name in Hebrew is Abaddo but in Greek his name is Apollyon.

12 The first woe is passed; and behold, two more woes follow after.

13 And the sixth angel sounded, and I heard a voice from the horn of the golden altar which is before Lord Yahweh,

14 Saying to the sixth angel which had the trumpet, Loose the four angels which are bound by the great river Euphrates.

15 And the four angels were loosed, those which were prepared for that hour, for that day, for that month, and for that year, so that they may slay the third part of men.

16 And the number of the army of the horsemen was two hundred thousand thousand, otherwise known as two hundred million; I heard the number of them.

17 And thus I saw the horses in the vision and those who sat on them, and they had breastplates of fire and of jacinth, and of brimstone; and the heads of the horses were like the heads of lions, and out of their mouths issued fire, smoke, and brimstone.

18 And by there three plagues was the third part of men slain, by the fire, smoke, and brimstone which issued out of their mouths.

19 For the power of the horses was in their mouths and in their tails; for their tails were like serpents and had heads, and with them they do harm.

20 And the rest of the men who were not killed by these plagues neither repented of the works of their hands, that is to say, the worship of devils and idols of gold, of silver, of brass, of stone, and of wood, which can neither see nor hear,

21 Nor repented of their murders, their witchcraft, their fornication, nor of their thefts.

CHAPTER 10

And I saw another mighty angel coming down from heaven, clothed with a cloud; and the rainbow of the cloud was upon his head, and his face was as though it were the sun, and his legs were as pillars of fire;

2 And he had in his hand, a little book open; and he set his right foot upon the sea, and his left foot on the land,

3 And cried with a loud voice as when a lion roars, and when he had cried, seven thunders sounded their voices.

4 And when the seven thunders had spoken, I was about to write; but I heard a voice from heaven, saying, Seal up those things which the seven thunders uttered, and do not write them.

5 And the angel which I saw standing upon the sea and on the land raised his right hand to heaven,

6 And swore by Lord Yahweh who lives forever and ever, who created heaven and the things which are therein, and the sea and the things which are therein, that there should be no more reckoning of time;

7 But in the days of the voice of the seventh angel, when he shall begin to sound, the mystery of Lord Yahweh will be fulfilled, as He has proclaimed to his servants, the prophets.

8 And the same voice which I had heard from heaven spoke to me again, saying, Go and take the little book which is open in the hand of the angel which stands on the sea and on the land.

9 And I went to the angel, and as I was about to say to him, Give me the little book, he said to me, Take it and eat it; and it shall make your belly bitter, but it shall be sweet as honey in your mouth.

10 So I took the little book out of the hand of the angel, and ate it; and it was as sweet as honey in my mouth; but as soon as I had eaten it, my belly was bitter.

11 Then he said to me, You must prophesy again about many peoples and nations and the heads of nations and kings.

CHAPTER 11

And there was given to me a reed like a rod; and the angel stood, saying, Arise and anoint the temple of Lord Yahweh, and anoint the altar and those who worship therein.

2 But leave out the outer court of the temple, and do not anoint it; for it has been given to the Gentiles; and they shall tread the holy city under foot for forty and two months.

3 Then I will give power to my two witnesses, and they shall prophesy a thousand and two hundred and threescore (**1,260**) days, clothed in sackcloth.

4 These are the two olive trees and the two candlesticks standing before the Lord of the earth.

5 And if any man desires to harm them, fire will come out of their mouths and will consume their enemies; and if any man desires to harm them, he must in this manner be killed.

6 These have power to control the sky, so that it will not rain in those days; and have power over waters to turn the waters into blood, and to smite the earth with all plagues, as often as they will.

7 And when they have finished their testimony, the wild beast which ascends out of the bottomless pit shall make war against them, and shall overcome them.

8 And their dead bodies shall be upon the street of the great city, which spiritually is called Sodom and Egypt, where also their Lord was crucified.

9 And their dead bodies will be seen by the peoples, kindred, nations, and tongues for three and a half days, and it will not be permitted to bury their dead bodies in graves.

10 And those who dwell upon the earth shall rejoice over them and make merry, and shall send gifts one to another, because these two prophets tormented those who dwelt on the earth.

11 And after these three and a half days, the Spirit of life from Lord Yahweh entered into the two witnesses, and they stood upon their feet; and great fear fell on those who saw them.

12 And they heard a great voice from heaven saying to them, Come up here. and the two witnesses went up to heaven in a cloud; and their enemies saw them.

13 And at the same hour there was a great earthquake, and the tenth part of the city fell, and the number of men killed in the earthquake was seven thousand; and the survivors were frightened, and they gave glory to Lord Yahweh.

14 The second woe is passed; and behold, the third woe comes quickly.

15 And the seventh angel sounded and there were great rumblings of thunders, saying, The kingdoms of this world have become the kingdom of our Lord Yahweh and of his Christ; and He shall reign forever and ever.

16 And the four and twenty elders who sat on their seats before the throne of Lord Yahweh, fell upon their faces and worshipped Lord Yahweh,

17 Saying, We give thanks to Thee, O Lord Yahweh Almighty, who is, was, and will be, because Thou has taken to thyself thy great power and has reigned.

18 And the nations were angry, and thy wrath has come, and the time of the dead, that they should be judged, and to reward thy servants, prophets, saints, and those who revere thy name, small and great; and to destroy those who corrupt the earth.

19 And the temple of Lord Yahweh was opened in heaven, and there was seen in his temple the ark of his covenant; and there were lightnings, thunderings, voices, an earthquake, and a great hailstorm.

Chapter 12

And a great sign was seen in heaven; a woman (the virgin Miryam) clothed with the sun, with the moon under her feet, and upon her head a crown of twelve stars;

2 And she being with child (Yahshua the Christ) cried, travailing in birth, and pained to deliver.

3 And there appeared another sign in heaven; and behold, there was a great fiery dragon (Lucifer, renamed: Satan), having seven heads and ten horns, and seven crowns upon his heads.

4 And his tail cut off a third of the stars (one third of the angels) of heaven and cast them to the earth; and the dragon stood before the woman who was ready to deliver, so as to devour her child as soon as he was born.

5 And she brought forth a male child (Yahshua the Christ), who was to shepherd all the nations with a rod of iron; and her child was caught up to Lord Yahweh, and to his throne.

6 And the woman fled into the wilderness where she had a place prepared by Lord Yahweh, that they should feed her there a thousand and two hundred and threescore (1,260) days.

7 And there was war in heaven. Michael and his angels fought against the dragon; and the dragon and his angels fought,

8 But they did not prevail, neither was their place found anymore in heaven.

9 Thus the great dragon was cast out, that old serpent called: the Devil and Satan who deceives the whole world; and he was cast out into the earth, and his angels were cast out with him.

10 And I heard a loud voice in heaven saying, Now the deliverance, the power, the kingdom of our God, and the power of his Christ have been

accomplished; for the accuser of our brethren, who accused them before Lord Yahweh day and night, is cast down.

11 And they have conquered him (Satan) by the blood of the "Lamb" (the Christ) and by the word of their testimony; and they did not spare themselves even to death.

12 Therefore rejoice, O heavens and you who dwell in them. Woe to the inhabitants of the earth and of the sea! For the devil has come down to you; and his wrath is great because he knows that his time is short.

13 And when the dragon saw that he was cast down to the earth, he pursued the woman who had given birth to a son.

14 And to the woman were given two wings of a great eagle, so that she may fly from the presence of the serpent to the wilderness, into her place, where she would be nourished for years, months, and days.

15 Then the serpent sent a flood of water out of his mouth after the women, so that he may cause her to be swept away by the flood.

16 But the earth helped the woman, and the earth opened its mouth and swallowed up the water which the dragon had spouted out of his mouth.

17 And the dragon was enraged at the woman, and he went to make war with the rest of her children, who keep the commandments of Lord Yahweh and have the testimony of Yahshua the Christ.

CHAPTER 13

And as I stood on the sand of the shore, I saw a beast rise up out of the sea, having ten horns and seven heads, and upon his horns were ten crowns, and upon his heads were blasphemous words.

2 And the beast which I saw was like a leopard, and his feet were like the feet of a bear, and his mouth was like the mouth of a lion; and the dragon gave him his power, his throne, and great authority.

3 And one of his heads was as though mortally wounded; but his deadly wound was healed; and all the world wondered about the beast.

4 And they worshipped the dragon because he had given power to the beast, saying, Who can prevail against him, to fight him?

5 And there was given to him a mouth, that he may utter boastful things and blasphemies; and power was given to him to make war for forty and two months.

6 And he opened his mouth in blasphemy against Lord Yahweh, to blaspheme his name, his dwelling place, and those who dwell in heaven.

7 And power was given to him over every tribe, kindred, tongue, and nation; and it was given to him to make war with the saints, and to overcome the saints.

8 And all who dwell upon the earth shall worship him, even those whose names are not written in the book of life of the "Lamb" (Yahshua the Christ) slain from the foundation of the world.

9 If any man has ears, let him hear.

10 He who leads into captivity, shall go into captivity; he who kills with the sword, must be killed with the sword. Here is the patience and the faith of the saints.

11 And I beheld another beast coming up out of the earth; and he had two horns like a lamb, and he spoke as a dragon.

12 And all the power of the first beast before him was exercised by him, and he caused the earth and those who dwell therein to worship the first beast, whose deadly wound was healed.

13 And he performed great wonders, to such an extent that he could even make fire come down from heaven on the earth in the sight of men,

14 Beguiling those who dwell on the earth to make an image to the beast who was wounded by the sword and yet lived.

15 And he had power to give life to the image of the beast, and to cause all those who would not worship the image of the beast to be killed.

16 And he compelled all, both small and great, rich and poor, freeman and servant, to receive a mark on their right hands or on their foreheads,

17 So that no man may buy or sell unless he had the mark of the name of the beast or the number of his name.

18 Here is wisdom; Let him who has understanding, count the number of the beast; for it is the number of a man; and his number is six hundred and sixty six.

CHAPTER 14

And I looked, and lo, the "Lamb" stood on Mount Zion, and with him were a hundred and forty-four thousand in number, having the name of his Father written on their foreheads.

2 Then I heard a voice from heaven, like the sound of many waters and like the sound of a great thunder; and the voice I heard was like the music of many harpists playing on their harps;

3 And they sang a new song before the throne, before the four animals, and before the elders; and no man was able to learn that song except the hundred and forty-four thousand who were redeemed from the earth.

4 These are those who were not defiled with women, for they are pure. These are those who follow the "Lamb" (Yahshua the Christ) wherever he goes. These were redeemed by Yahshua the Christ from among men to be the first fruits to Lord Yahweh and to the Lamb.

5 And in their mouths were found no deceit; for they are without fault.

6 And I saw another angel fly in the midst of heaven, having the everlasting gospel to preach to those who dwell on the earth, and to every nation, every kindred, every tongue, and every people,

7 Saying with a loud voice: Serve Lord Yahweh and give glory to Him; for the hour of his judgment has come; and worship Him who made heaven and earth, and the sea, and the fountains of waters.

8 And another angel, a second, followed the flying angel who had the gospel, saying: "Babylon" has fallen, that great city which made all nations drink of the wine of the passion of her whoredom.

9 Then another angel, the third, followed the flying angel and the second angel, saying with a loud voice: If any man worships the beast and the beast's image, and receives the beast's mark on his forehead or on his hand,

10 He also shall drink of the wine of the wrath of Lord Yahweh, which is mixed with bitterness in the cup of his anger; and he shall be tormented with fire and brimstone in the presence of the holy angels and before the throne;

11 And the smoke of their torment will rise forever and ever; and those who worship the beast and his image, will have no rest day or night.

12 Here is the patience of the saints; here are they who keep the commandments of Lord Yahweh and keep the faith of Yahshua the Christ.

13 And I heard a voice from heaven saying, Write: Blessed are the dead who die in the Lord from henceforth. Yes, says the Spirit, that they may rest from their labors, for their works will follow them.

14 And I looked, and lo, I saw a white cloud, and upon the cloud sat one resembling the Son of man, having on his head a crown of gold, and in his hand a sharp sickle.

15 And another angel came out of the temple, and after he cried with a loud voice to him who sat on the cloud,

16 He thrust his sickle upon the earth, and the earth was harvested.

17 And another angel came out of the temple which is in heaven; and he also had a sharp sickle.

18 Then out from the altar came another angel, who had power over fire, and he cried with a loud voice to him who had the sharp sickle, saying, Thrust in your sharp sickle and gather the clusters of the "vineyards" of the earth, for her "grapes" are fully ripe.

19 And the angel thrust his sickle into the earth and gathered the "vineyards" of the earth, and he cast the "grapes" into the "winepress" of the wrath of the great Lord Yahweh.

20 And the "winepress" was trodden until the "juice" (blood) which came out reached even up to the horse bridles, and the circumference of the "winepress" was a thousand and six hundred furlongs. (one furlong equals **220** yards)

CHAPTER 15

And I saw another sign in heaven, great and marvelous, seven angels having the seven last plagues; for in them is fulfilled the wrath of Lord Yahweh.

2 And I saw what looked like a sea of glass mingled with fire; and those who were victorious over the beast, over his image, and over the number of his name were standing on the sea of glass and had the harps of Lord Yahweh.

3 And they were singing the song of Moshe, the servant of Lord Yahweh, and the song of the "Lamb," saying, Great and marvelous are thy works, Lord Yahweh Almighty; just and true are thy ways, O King of ages.

4 Who shall not revere Thee, O Lord Yahweh, and glorify thy name? For Thou only are holy. All nations shall come and worship before Thee; for thy righteousness has been revealed.

5 And after these things, I looked and behold, the temple of the tabernacle of the testimony in heaven was opened;

6 And the seven angels having the seven plagues came out of the temple, clothed in pure and fine linen and having their breasts girded with golden girdles.

7 And one of the four animals gave to the seven angels, seven golden bowls full of the wrath of Lord Yahweh who lives forever and ever.

8 And the temple was filled with smoke from the glory of Lord Yahweh and from his power; and no man was able to enter into the temple, until the seven plagues of the seven angels were fulfilled.

CHAPTER 16

And I heard a great voice saying to the seven angels, Go your ways and pour out the seven bowls of the wrath of Lord Yahweh upon the earth.

2 And the first angel went and poured out his bowl upon the earth; and there came a severe and malignant sore upon the men who had the mark of the beast and upon those who worshipped his image.

3 Then the second angel poured out his bowl upon the sea; and it became as the blood of a dead man, and every living (material /animal) soul died in the sea.

4 And the third angel poured out his bowl upon the rivers and fountains of waters; and they became blood.

5 Then I heard the angel who has charge over the waters say, Thou are righteous, O Holy One who was, is, and will be, because Thou has condemned them.

6 For they have shed the blood of saints and prophets, and Thou has given them blood to drink; for they deserve it.

7 And I heard another out of the altar say, Yes, O Lord Yahweh Almighty, true and righteous are thy judgments.

8 And the fourth angel poured out his bowl upon the sun; and power was given to the sun to scorch men with fire.

9 And men were scorched by intense heat, and they blasphemed the name of Lord Yahweh who has power over these plagues; and they did not repent to give Him glory.

10 And the fifth angel poured out his bowl on the throne of the beast; and his kingdom was darkened; and men gnawed their tongues from pain,

11 And they blasphemed the God of heaven because of their wounds and sores, and they did not repent of their deeds.

12 Then the sixth angel poured out his bowl upon the great river: Euphrates; and its waters dried up, so that the king of the East may be prepared.

13 And I saw three unclean spirits like frogs coming out of the mouth of the dragon, and out of the mouth of the beast and out of the false prophet.

14 For they are the spirits of devils, who work miracles which go forth to the kings of the whole world, to gather them to the battle of that great day of Lord Yahweh Almighty.

15 And behold, I come as a thief. Blessed is he who watches and keeps his "garments," lest he walk "naked" and they see his shame.

16 And he gathered them together in a place which, in the Hebrew tongue, is called Armageddon.

17 Then the seventh angel poured out his bowl into the air; and there came a great voice out of the temple from the throne, saying, It is done.

18 And there were voices, and thunders and lightnings; and there was a great earthquake, the like of which had never happened since man was upon the earth, so mighty an earthquake, and so great.

19 And the great city was divided into three parts, and the cities of the nations fell; and great Babylon came in remembrance before Lord Yahweh, to give to her the cup of wine of the fierceness of his wrath.

20 And every island fled away, and the mountains could not be found.

21 And great hail, about the size of a talent, fell out of heaven upon men; and men blasphemed Lord Yahweh because of the plague of the hail; for the destructive force of the hail was exceedingly great.

CHAPTER 17

Then came one of the seven angels which had the seven bowls and talked to me, saying, Come, I will show you the condemnation of the great harlot who sits upon many waters,

2 With whom the kings of the earth have committed fornication, and the inhabitants of the earth have been made drunk with the wine of her fornication.

3 So he carried me away in the spirit into the wilderness; and I saw a woman sitting on a scarlet beast inscribed with many words of blasphemy and having seven heads and ten horns.

4 And the woman was arrayed in purple and scarlet, and adorned with gold and precious stones and pearls; and she had a golden cup in her hand full of abominations and filthiness of her fornication on earth.

5 And upon her forehead was a name written that not all could understand: BABYLON THE GREAT, THE MOTHER OF HARLOTS AND ABOMINATIONS OF THE EARTH.

6 And I saw that the woman was drunk with the blood of the saints and with the blood of the martyrs of Yahshua the Christ; and when I saw her, I wondered with great amazement.

7 And the angel said to me, Why do you wonder? I will tell you the mystery of the woman and of the beast that carries her, which has the seven heads and the ten horns.

8 The beast that you saw was, and is not, and is ready to come up from the bottomless pit and go to be destroyed; and those who dwell on earth whose names were not written in the book of life from the foundation of the world, shall wonder when they behold the beast that was, and is not, and now whose end has come.

9 Here is understanding for him who has wisdom: The seven heads are seven hills (Rome is the city of seven hills) on which the "woman" sits.

10 And there are seven kings; of whom five have fallen, one is, and the other has not yet come; and when he comes he shall continue only for a short time.

11 And the beast that was, and no more is, even he is the eighth and is one of the seven destined to be destroyed.

12 And the ten horns which you saw, are ten kings who have received no kingdom as yet, but receive authority as kings for one hour with the beast.

13 These are of one accord, and they shall give their strength and authority to the beast.

14 They will make war with the "Lamb," and the "Lamb" will conquer them, for the "Lamb" (Yahshua the Christ) is Lord of lords and King of kings; and those who are with him are called and chosen, and faithful.

15 Then he said to me, The waters which you saw, where the harlot sits, are peoples, multitudes, nations, and tongues.

16 And the ten horns and the beast which you saw shall hate the harlot, and shall make her desolate and "naked," and shall "eat her flesh" and burn her with fire.

17 For Lord Yahweh has put into their hearts to do his will and to be of one accord, and to give their kingdom to the beast until the words of Lord Yahweh shall be fulfilled.

18 And the "woman" whom you saw is that great city (Rome, see Rev. **17:9**) which has dominion over the kings of the earth.

CHAPTER 18

After these things, I saw another angel come down from heaven, having great power; and the earth was lighted by his glory.

2 And he cried with a mighty voice, saying, "Babylon" the great is fallen and has become a habitation of those possessed with devils, and has become the shelter of every foul spirit and the shelter of every unclean and loathsome beast.

3 Because all nations have drunk of the wine of the wrath of her fornication, and the kings of the earth have committed fornication with her, and the merchants of the earth have become rich through the power of her trade.

4 And I heard another voice from heaven, saying, Come out of her, O my people, so that you may not become partakers of her sins and lest you be smitten by her plagues.

5 For her sins have reached up to heaven, and Lord Yahweh has remembered her iniquities.

6 Reward her even as she has rewarded you, and return to her a double portion according to her works; in the cup which she has mixed, mix double for her.

7 For as much as she has "glorified" herself and lived deliciously, give her so much torment and sorrow; for she says in her heart: I sit a queen, and am no widow and shall see no sorrow.

8 Therefore, her plagues shall come in one day, death, mourning, and famine, and she shall be burned with fire; for mighty is Lord Yahweh who judges her.

9 And the kings of the earth who committed fornication and lived deliciously with her, will weep, mourn, and wail over her when they see the smoke of her burning.

10 Standing afar off for the fear of her torment, saying, Woe, woe, that great city "Babylon," that mighty city! For in one hour you have been condemned.

11 And the merchants of the earth shall weep and mourn over her; for no man buys their merchandise anymore.

12 Never again will there be cargoes of gold, silver, precious stones, pearls, and fine linen of purple....(only more "cargoes" are listed until Rev. **18**:14)

14 And the fruits which you the soul lusted after, are departed from you; and all things which were luxurious and goodly are lost to you, and you shall never find them anymore at all.

15 The merchants of these things, who were made rich by her, shall stand afar off for the fear of her torment, and they shall weep and wail,

16 Saying, Woe, woe, that great city, which was clothed with fine linen and purple and scarlet, inlaid with gold, and precious stones and pearls! For in one hour these great riches are destroyed.

17 And every shipmaster and all the travelers in ships, sailors, and all those who labor at sea, stood afar off,

18 And they cried when they saw the smoke of her burning, saying, What city is like to this great city!

19 And they threw dust on their heads and cried, weeping and wailing, saying, Woe, woe that great city, where all who had ships on the sea were made rich by reason of her preciousness! For in one hour she is destroyed.

20 Rejoice over her, O heaven and angels, apostles and prophets, for Lord Yahweh has avenged you on her.

21 And a mighty angel took up a stone like a great millstone and he cast it into the sea, saying, So shall that great city "Babylon" be overthrown with violence and shall be found no more at all.

22 And the sound of harpers, musicians, singers, and trumpeters shall not be heard in you again; and no craftsman of whatever craft he be, shall be found anymore in you;

23 And the light of a lamp shall shine no more at all in you; and the voice of the bridegroom and of the bride shall be heard no more at all in you; for your merchants were the great men of the earth; for by your sorceries, were all peoples deceived.

24 And in her was found the blood of prophets, of saints, and of all who were slain upon the earth.

CHAPTER 19

And after these things, I heard a great voice of a great multitude in heaven, saying, Halleluia! Salvation, power, glory, and honor to our God,

2 For his judgments are true and righteous; for He has condemned the great harlot who has corrupted the earth with her fornication, and He has avenged the blood of his servants at her hand.

3 And a second time, they said, Halleluia! And her smoke rose up forever and ever.

4 And the four and twenty elders, and the four animals, fell down and worshipped Lord Yahweh who sat on the throne, saying, Amen, Halleluia!

5 And a voice came out from the throne, saying, Praise our God, all you his servants and you, both small and great, who worship Lord Yahweh.

6 And I heard as it were the voice of a great multitude, like the voice of many waters and like the sound of mighty thunderings, saying, Halleluia! For Lord Yahweh, omnipotent, reigns.

7 Let us be glad and rejoice and give glory to Lord Yahweh, for the time of the marriage feast of the "Lamb" has come, and his "bride" has made "herself" ready.

8 And it was given to "her" that "she" should be arrayed in fine pure linen, clean and white; for the fine linen is the righteousness of saints.

9 And the angel said to me, Write, Blessed are those who are invited to the wedding feast of the "lamb." Then the angel said to me, These words of mine are the true sayings of Lord Yahweh.

10 And I fell at his feet to worship him. And the angel said to me: Do not do that; I am your fellow servant, and of your brethren who have the testimony of Yahshua the Christ; worship Lord Yahweh, for the testimony of Yahshua the Christ is the spirit of prophecy.

11 And I saw heaven opened, and behold, I saw a white horse; and he who sat upon him was called Faithful and True, and in righteousness he judges and makes war.

12 His eyes were like a flame of fire, and on his head were many crowns; and he had names written thereon, and one of the names written, no man knew but he himself.

13 And he (Yahshua the Christ) was clothed with a vesture dipped in blood; and he called his name, The Word of Lord Yahweh.

14 And the armies which were in heaven followed him on white horses clothed in fine linen, pure and white.

15 And out of his mouth came a sharp two-edged sword, that with it he should smite the nations; and he will rule them with a rod of iron; and he will tread the "winepress" of the fierceness and wrath of Almighty Lord Yahweh.

16 And he had a name written on his vesture and on his thigh: KING OF KINGS AND LORD OF LORDS.

17 And I saw an angel standing in the sun; and he cried with a loud voice, saying to all the fowls that fly in the midst of heaven, Come and gather yourselves together for the great supper of Lord Yahweh,

18 That you may eat the flesh of kings, of captains, of thousands, of mighty men, of horses, of those who sit on them, and of all men both free and servant, both small and great.

19 Then I saw the beast and the kings of the earth; and their armies gathered together to fight against Yahshua the Christ who sat on the horse, and against his armies.

20 And the beast was taken, and with him the false prophet who wrought miracles before him with which he deceived those who had received the mark of the beast and those who worshipped his image. These both were cast alive into a lake of fire burning with brimstone.

21 And the others were slain by the sword that came out from the mouth of him who sat upon the horse; and all the fowls were filled with their flesh.

Chapter 20

And I saw an angel come down from heaven, having the key of the bottomless pit and a great chain in his hand.

2 And the angel seized the dragon, that old serpent, which is the Tempter and Satan, who deceived the whole world, and the angel bound him for a thousand years,

3 And cast him into the bottomless pit and shut him up, and set a seal over him so that he should no more deceive the nations until the thousand years should be past; after that, he will be loosed for a short time.

4 And I saw thrones and those who sat upon them, and judgment was given to them; and the souls who were beheaded for the witness of Yahshua the Christ, and for the word of Lord Yahweh, and who had not worshipped the beast nor his image, and who had not received his mark upon their foreheads or their right hand; lived and reigned with Lord Yahshua the Son for these thousand years.

5 This is the first resurrection.

6 Blessed and holy is he who has part in the first resurrection; over such, the second death has no power, but they shall be the priests of Lord Yahweh and of his Son Yahshua, and they shall reign with him for a thousand years.

7 And when the thousand years come to an end, Satan shall be loosed out of his prison,

8 And he shall go out to deceive the nations which are in the four corners of the earth, even to China and Mongolia, to gather them together for war; the number of them is as the sand of the sea.

9 And they went up on a broad plain, and surrounded the camp of the saints and the beloved city; and fire came down from Lord Yahweh out of heaven and consumed them.

10 And the devil who deceived them, was cast into the lake of fire and brimstone where also are the beast and the false prophet; and shall be tormented day and night forever and ever.

11 And I saw a great white throne and Him who sat on it, from whose presence the earth and the heavens fled away; and there was no place found for them.

12 Then I saw the dead, small and great, stand before the throne; and the books were opened; and another book was opened, which is the book of life; and the dead were judged by those things which were written in the books, according to their works.

13 And the sea gave up the dead which were in it; and death and sheol (hades) gave up the dead which were in them; and they were judged every man according to his works.

14 And death and sheol (hades, or the second heaven which is the demon realm) were cast into the lake of fire. This is the second death, which is the lake of fire which is known as hell.

15 And whoever was not found written in the book of life was cast into the lake of fire.

CHAPTER 21

And I saw a new heaven and a new earth; for the first heaven and the first earth had passed away; and the sea was no more.

2 And I saw the holy, new Jerusalem, coming down from Lord Yahweh, prepared as a bride adorned for her husband.

3 And I heard a great voice from heaven saying: Behold, the tabernacle of Lord Yahweh is with men, and He will dwell with them, and they shall be his people, and Lord Yahweh Himself shall be with them and be their God;

4 And Lord Yahweh shall wipe away all tears from their eyes; and there shall be no more death, neither sorrow nor wailing, neither shall there be any more pain; for the former things have passed away.

5 And He who sat upon the throne said, Behold, I make all things new. Then He said to me, Write; for these are the trustworthy and true words of Lord Yahweh.

6 And Lord Yahweh said to me: I am Alpha and Omega; the beginning and the end, the first and the last. I will freely give of the fountain of living water to him who is thirsty.

7 He who overcomes shall inherit these things; and I will be his God, and he shall be my son.

8 But as for the fearful, the unbelieving, the sinful, the abominable, murderers, whoremongers, sorcerers, idolaters, and all liars; their portion shall be in the lake that burns with fire and brimstone, which is the second death.

9 And there came to me one of the seven angels who had the seven bowls full of the seven last plagues, and he talked with me, saying: Come, I will show you the "bride," the "wife" of the "Lamb."

10 And he carried me away in the spirit to a great and high mountain, and showed me that great city, the holy Jerusalem, descending out of heaven from Lord Yahweh,

11 Having the glory of Lord Yahweh, radiant as a brilliant light, resembling a very precious gem like a jasper stone, clear as crystal.

12 It had a wall great and high, and it had twelve gates with names inscribed thereon, which are the names of the twelve tribes of the children of Israel.

13 On the east were three gates, on the north three gates, on the south three gates, and on the west three gates.

14 And the wall of the city had twelve foundations, and on them the twelve names of the twelve apostles of the "Lamb" (Yahshua the Son).

15 And he who talked with me had a measuring rod of golden reed to measure the city and the gates and the wall.

16 And the city laid foursquare, and the length is as large as the breadth; and he measured the city with the reed, twelve thousand furlongs. The length and the breadth and the height of it are equal.

17 And he measured the wall thereof, a hundred and forty and four cubits, according to the measure of a man, that is, of the angel.

18 And the wall was of jasper; and the city was pure gold, like unto clear glass.

19 And the foundations of the wall of the city were adorned with all kinds of precious stones. The first foundation was jasper; the second, sapphire; the third, a chalcedony; the fourth, emerald;

20 The fifth, sardonyx; the sixth, sardius; the seventh, chrysolyte; the eighth, beryl; the ninth, topaz; the tenth, a chrysoprasus; the eleventh, jacinth; the twelfth, amethyst.

21 And the twelve gates were twelve pearls; every gate was made of one giant pearl; and the street of the city was pure gold, as it were transparent glass.

22 But I saw no temple therein, for the Almighty Lord Yahweh and Yahshua the Son are the temple of it.

23 The city has no need of the sun, neither of the moon, to shine in it because the glory of Lord Yahweh brightens the city, and Lord Yahshua is the lamp of it.

24 And the people who have been saved shall walk by that very light; and the kings of the earth shall bring their own glory and the honor of the peoples into it.

25 And the gates of the city shall not be barred by day, and there is no night there.

26 And they shall bring the glory and the honor of the peoples into it.

27 And there, shall not enter into it anything which defiles nor anyone who works abominations and lies; only those whose names are in the book of life shall enter.

Chapter 22

And the angel showed me a pure river of water of life, clear as crystal, gushing out of the throne of Lord Yahweh and of Lord Yahshua.

2 In the midst of the great street of the city, and on either side of the river, was the tree of life which bore twelve kinds of fruits, and each month it yielded one of its fruits; and the leaves of the tree were for the healing of the peoples.

3 And that which withers shall be no more, but the throne of Lord Yahweh and of Lord Yahshua shall be in it; and his servants shall serve Him;

4 And they shall see his face, and his name shall be on their foreheads.

5 And there shall be no night there; and they shall neither need a candle nor the light of the sun; for Lord Yahweh shines on them, and they shall reign forever and ever.

6 And he angel said to me, These sayings are faithful and true; and Lord Yahweh who is the spirit of the prophets sent his angel to show to his servants, the things which soon must come to pass.

7 Behold, I am coming soon; blessed is he who keeps the sayings of the prophecy of this book.

8 And I, Yochanan, saw and heard these things, and when I had seen and heard them, I fell down to worship before the feet of the angel who showed these things to me.

9 And the angel said to me: Do not do that; I am your fellow servant and of your brethren, of the prophets, and of those who keep the words of this book (the entire Bible). Worship Lord Yahweh.

10 Then he said to me, Do not seal the words of the prophecy of this book, for the time is at hand.

11 He who is unjust will continue to be unjust, and he who is filthy will continue to be filthy, and he who is righteous will continue to be righteous and do righteousness, and he who is holy will continue to be holy.

12 Behold, I am coming soon and my reward is with Me, to give every man according as his work shall be.

13 I am Alpha and Omega, the beginning and the end, the first and the last.

14 Blessed are those who do the Lord's commandments, that they may have the right to the tree of life, and may enter in through the gates into the holy city.

15 For without the vicious, the sorcerers, the immoral, the murderers, the idolaters, and whoever loves to tell lies.

16 I, Lord Yahshua the Christ, have sent my angel to testify to you these things in the churches. I am the root and the offspring of David, the bright morning star.

17 And the Spirit and the "bride" say, Come. And let him who hears, say, Come. And he who is thirsty, let him come. And whosoever will, let him take of the living water freely.

18 I testify to every man who hears the words of the prophecy of this book, If any man shall add to (the Bible, not a mere "Bible textbook") these things, Lord Yahweh shall add to him the plagues that are written in this book (the Bible);

19 And if any man shall take away from (the Bible, not a mere "Bible textbook") the words of the book of this prophecy, Lord Yahweh shall take away his portion from the tree of life, from the holy city, and from the things which are written in this book (the Bible).

20 He who testifies these things, says, Surely I am coming soon. Amen. Come, Lord Yahshua the Christ.

21 The grace of our Lord Yahshua the Christ be with you all, all you holy ones. Amen.

THE BIBLICAL TEXTBOOK OF SALVATION

www.ingramcontent.com/pod-product-compliance
Lightning Source LLC
Chambersburg PA
CBHW051358070526
44584CB00023B/3203